POETS' POETS
A RENAISSANCE OF WORDS

Edited by Dennis Barone

SPUYTEN DUYVIL
New York City

Cover Image: Zbigniew Grzyb, *Circle Series #1*, ink on paper.
Courtesy of the artist and the Cooley Gallery.

Charles Bernstein's essay was first presented at the Leslie Scalapino Memorial, Poetry Project at Saint Mark's Church, New York, June 21, 2010.Reprinted, with the permission of the author, from *Pitch of Poetry* (University of Chicago Press 2016).

ISBN 978-1-963908-76-3

Library of Congress Control Number: 2025941433

Contents

INTRODUCTION

Soon you will have forgotten all things:
soon all things will have forgotten you.
Marcus Aurelius

In high school my favorite poet was Richard Brautigan. My writerly friends—there were two or three—imitated Hemingway's *In Our Time* while I modeled my musings after *In Watermelon Sugar*. By college I had broadened my horizons to include William Carlos Williams as well as the contemporary poets Michael Lally and Terry Stokes.

As Lyn Hejinian told me, "Literary history includes so many overlooked or wrongly disregarded poets." This anthology of essays represents a modest endeavor to recover and reconsider some of America's poets worthy of wider recognition and larger readership. Three dozen contemporary American poets have selected a poet to discuss in a short essay. In each essay-entry, an example of the selected lesser-known poet's work appears. I had no list of under-recognized authors, and each contemporary poet made his or her own selection. I offered a few suggestions for the essays: what significance does the chosen poet's writing have for your own work, describe the poet's overall work and career as well as the poet's biography and poetics, consider the reason why the poet's work is not well-known and perhaps include something particular to be remembered. What does this poet mean to you as a poet? I asked.

I solicited contributions from many more writers than included herein. Some did not reply, some complimented the project idea but said they had too many other commitments, and a few, alas, noted that ill health precluded their participation.

The final list of contributors to some extent emerged from a mixture of intent and chance. And the list of poets discussed has a richness of aesthetic diversity. Once a contemporary poet chose a poet to write about then that voice would be claimed: it was a first come, first selected method of choice. The anthology has a chronological organization beginning with the poet selected from the earliest date and ending with the most recent. Many of the essays conclude with a poem by the poet under discussion while some essays work an entire poem into the text of the essay near its end. There are divergent methods of documentation in these essays, but not too diverse. This book has its flexible rigor, but it rejects the formality of a textbook.

The idea of reconsideration of authors abandoned by tradition has long been one that most poets have contemplated. The subtitle here echoes the title of Jerome Rothenberg's 1974 anthology *Revolution of the Word: A New Gathering of American Avant Garde Poetry 1914-1945*. Renaissance means rediscovery. The poets herein when polished by essay and example will not yet be enshrined but will be back in readers' hands where they might shine a little more brightly.

What do I mean by an abandoned poet: Marcia Nardi, for example. Nardi, discussed by Julie R. Enszer in the pages that follow, was the mid-twentieth-century poet who William Carlos Williams quoted at length in *Paterson*. She published one brief book during her life, but never a full-length volume. She published scores of poems and reviews and knew-well many of her literary contemporaries. Most of those who recognize her name today still know her only as the lady with the long letters in *Paterson*—if they know her name at all.

Barry Schwabsky told me, "I remember many years ago, like when I was in college, *Esquire* polled a lot of writers, mostly novelists, about which writers they considered underrated. The response of Tennessee Williams made a permanent impression on me: 'All writers are underrated.' All the more so, poets."

And I wonder if this situation has worsened in America during the past decades. Late in the prior century some poets took solace in the expansion (later curtailed) of federal support for the arts. Others saw and sought the university as a sanctuary for literature and arts in an otherwise indifferent land.

Here's a brief simple poem I wrote in response to changing times:

ADMINISTRATION

They needed the poetry fund
to purchase new football helmets.
They needed the poetry fund to pave
additional parking spaces.
They needed the poetry fund to buy
more advertising.
They needed the poetry fund
to bribe someone at
US News & World Report.
They needed the poetry fund for a
cover-up to hide how and
why and when they depleted
the fund.

Or consider the following less didactic and more imagistic poem by Timothy Liu entitled "American Poetry":

No voices for miles around.
A glint caught my eye nonetheless.
A pair of child's sandals,
Left at the foot of an abandoned well.
A cape thrown down.
Any tug at all comes as a surprise.

Do these two poems mean any poem at all must find its limited space on the field of play and that all we are left with for this ancient art is "any tug at all"? As Andrew Mossin told me while working on this book: "I'm intrigued by this project's emphasis on 'lesser known' poets, since these days pretty much all of us living or dead remain unknown. Your list thus far includes some folks that one would think had wider purchase on the reading public, e.g. Leslie Scalapino, Barbara Guest, but as we are now living in a culture where reading of any kind is endangered, perhaps these names would seem as obscure as everyone else's."

Against this diminishing pulse many are working to enliven poetry. Amiel Alcalay has hosted his Lost and Found project at the Graduate Center of the City University of New York. Joy Katz and Kevin Prufer have edited anthologies such as *Dark Horses*, an earlier book of lesser-known poets than this one (2006). The *Chicago Review* in 1990 published its Neglected Poets issue. Many well-known and lesser-known poets can be heard at the PennSound archive, a huge collection of recorded poetry material—readings, interviews, etc. (https://writing.upenn.edu/pennsound). At present the series *Minor Notes* publishes under-recognized Black poets from America's past. I found my model for this book in the 2022 volume edited by Charles C. Eldridge *The Unforgettables: Expanding American Art*. Instead of an essay and an image, this volume presents an essay and a poem.

For a poetry anthology a concern must be permission fees. In the present this makes no sense. Ada Calhoun notes in her recent book *Also a Poet* (page 173) that "for permission to share these six lines [Auden] I had to sign two contracts and pay $285.37." She adds, "So for the rest, please look up the poem for free on the Internet." A publisher who requires a substantial fee from an author or editor for print publication has no power over online publication where a poem let's say by William Carlos Williams that New Directions charges so many dollars per line to reprint will be available on scores of sites. *Poets' Poets* is an essay anthology.

As the number of college students in the United States majoring in English continues to decline, one welcomed countertrend is the effort to bring back forgotten or under-appreciated poets from the past. Examples abound: a new selection of works by and about Bert Meyers (1928-1979) has recently been published in the Unsung Masters series from Pleiades

Press; Sublunary Editions released a two-volume *Collected Works* by Emanuel Carnevali (1897-1942); New York Review Books reissues many wonderful out-of-print titles in attractive and inexpensive editions. And these are just the tip of the iceberg of the wonderful archival work being conducted.

The philosopher Pierre Nora once said, "We speak of memory because there is so little of it left." Do we devotees of literature seek so many forgotten voices and works of the past, I wonder, because we fear there may be so few in the future?

I remember while in graduate school the joy of stumbling across lesser-known voices from the early American past. In the venerable Historical Society of Pennsylvania, while viewing a commonplace book from the Peters family papers, I realized this wasn't just a commonplace book, there were poems: a manuscript collection by Henry Brooke (1676-1736), highly regarded in his day. This find increased Brooke's extant works from a single poem to more than thirty complete poems, and the scholar David S. Shields went on to make good use of this material.

Later, in the University of Pennsylvania Archives, I read Provost William Smith's (1727-1803) "Lectures on Rhetoric." This manuscript of 1760 may be better considered as Smith's poetics. Smith used illustrative examples from Milton, Shakespeare, and Pope, as well as from the foremost Scots poet of the time, James Thomson. Smith also mentored a generation of Philadelphia poets: Nathaniel Evans, Frances Hopkinson, and Thomas Godfrey. With an introduction and notes, I published Smith's treatise in the *Proceedings of the American Philosophical Society* in 1990.

Central to Smith's thinking on language had been Longinus's *On the Sublime*, a work of influence for future Penn student and poet William Carlos Williams. As a first-year professor in 1986-1987, I taught a seminar on Williams, though I was in over my head; fortunately, some extraordinary students rescued me and saved the seminar. One, Elizabeth Murrie O'Neil, became fascinated by Marcia Nardi (1901-1990), the author whose letters Williams incorporated into *Paterson*. Beth eventually met and befriended

Nardi and published an award-winning scholarly edition of the Nardi-Williams correspondence. Beth and I also tried to get a press to publish Nardi's complete poems, but alas, we had no success and eventually gave up.

More than a decade ago, I edited a historical anthology of Connecticut poetry for Wesleyan University Press. In doing so, I included all the poets one would expect, from Timothy Dwight (1752-1817) to the contemporary master Marilyn Nelson. I offered one discovery, however: Anna Hempstead Branch (1875-1937), a wonderful poet well-regarded in her day but completely forgotten today. If Wallace Stevens's "The River of Rivers in Connecticut" is not my favorite poem about the state, then it surely must be "Connecticut Road Song" by Anna Hempstead Branch. There are 169 towns in Connecticut and many of these towns have multiple municipal libraries. Yet, to my amazement, not very many of these libraries have this "official" state anthology of poetry in their collection.

As the new century continued, literature from my own Italian heritage became of increased interest. I especially liked the poetic works of the aforementioned Emanuel Carnevali and also the writings of Pascal D'Angelo (1894-1932); I put together a little Carnevali book in 2006, published several essays on D'Angelo, and in 2024 Sublunary Editions published a D'Angelo poetry book for which I wrote the introduction and notes. Both Carnevali and D'Angelo mixed prose and poetry together in their writings in interesting ways—a bit like Dante in *La Vita Nuova*.

Maybe the circulation of these lesser-known voices and lost poems from the past can promote *vita nuova*, new life, in our time—a time when though it can feel like interest in literature is on its wobbling last legs, those who stand behind the cry *long live literature* are doing all they can to preserve and promote it.

In this spirit remember for a moment my friend the poet Peter Ganick. He died just as the pandemic began and perhaps because of that harsh fact his passing went -- to a large extent -- unnoticed. Born in 1947, he devoted his life to art, music, philosophy, poetry, and math. His long ongoing poem *Remove a Concept* might just be the longest one in the English language. His press—Potes & Poets—published more than sixty perfect bound books and one hundred and fifty issues of the poetry newsletter *A.bacus*.

Once we travelled together to San Francisco for two readings by west coast contributors to the anthology *The Art of Practice* that we co-edited in 1994. After the reading north of the city Peter went to the piano at the urging of David Bromige and pounded the keys in a crazy festive jazz rhythm.

Peter had strong opinions, but he often revised and expanded his thinking. Practice mattered most to his work whether painting or poetry. Peter practiced meditation and his artwork was a form of that meditative practice. I am sure that on more than one occasion I righteously suggested he slow down and revise something rather than constantly move on to the next thing—projective verse gone wild!

Potes & Poets published Leslie Scalapino and Jean Day; Ron Silliman and Cid Corman. I remember once when we met for coffee, Peter handed me a manuscript and asked my opinion regarding whether Potes & Poets should publish it. To my surprise, the manuscript came from Hayden Carruth. I don't recall if it had been *The Collected Longer Poems* or *The Collected Shorter Poems*, but one of those, both of which were published by Copper Canyon Press.

The archives for Peter's press are at the Dodd Research Center, University of Connecticut. The collection includes manuscripts, correspondence, financial records, personal papers, and publications. Other collections at UCONN include Donald Allen's Frank O'Hara Letters, Bill Berkson Papers, Curbstone Press Records, Diane Di Prima Papers, Marilyn Nelson Papers, Charles Olson Research Collection, and John Wieners Papers.

The Potes & Poets Press archive comes to 95.2 linear feet. Slightly larger is the Joel Oppenheimer collection. It holds 100 linear feet of correspondence, poetry, prose, and ephemera. Oppenheimer (1930-1988), Black Mountain poet, *Village Voice* columnist, and first director of the Saint Mark's Poetry Project, did not use capital letters in the text of his poems. Ganick for many years did not include the letter "e" in the word "the". In his poem "The Teacher," Oppenheimer said, "despite its simplicity / the poem is a difficult thing" whereas for Ganick that would be, I think, reversed: "despite its difficulty / the poem is a simple thing." And yet ... neither archive, according to a Dodd Research Center archivist, ever gets a visitor. Here's wishing that won't be so for this volume. May it be loud enough to be heard above the silence.

Dennis Barone

A RENAISSANCE OF WORDS

ERIC HOFFMAN

JAMES GATES PERCIVAL (1797-1856)

It is an odd trick of fate that James Gates Percival numbers among "lesser known" poets, given that, during his lifetime in the early decades of the nineteenth century in the post-Revolutionary United States, he commanded as large an audience as any poet could ever hope to attain. His poetry was published in all the best-known and most well-respected journals and magazines, and reprinted in newspapers—attributed, mis-attributed, and non-attributed, yet published nevertheless—and in several major anthologies. Contemporaries given to memorization or quotation of poetry often recited or referenced his work.

Then a curious thing happened. Midway through his life, Percival's star, which had quickly risen among the literati, abruptly fell. So precipitous was his decline that, when musicologists subsequently discovered among Edward Elgar's papers the attribution "Words by Percival" on the sheet music for his "The Landscape of Flowers" (1872), Elgar's earliest extant composition, composed when he was just fourteen years old, they were surprised to find the lyrics credited to Percival; he had reached such obscurity that most had assumed that Elgar himself had written the lyrics.

In fact, Percival's entry into lesser-known poet status began during his own lifetime, and his gradual regression into obscurity was obvious even to his contemporaries. If anything, his career follows a diametrically opposite trajectory from many artists who achieve similar consequence: ignored or perhaps only somewhat known during their lifetime, they gradually receive greater recognition, as happened with certain of Percival's successors (Whitman, Dickinson, and Poe most famously). Percival is also notable for the severity and rapidity of this decline: not long out of college—he attended Yale, and early on had designs on a career in law and, like his father, medicine, though he was too much of an eccentric to

19

be successful at either—Percival's poetry was already competent enough to attract the attention and admiration of editors, publishers, and audiences. Then, after a brief period of frenetic publication—he published three volumes in 1822 alone, followed by a major collection in 1823—Percival gradually withdrew from the public eye. Just over a decade later, perhaps troubled by the frequency with which his poems were published without a subsequent financial windfall, he almost entirely abandoned publication of his work in favor of the pursuit of his other passion, that of geology, and in 1835, he was commissioned to survey Connecticut to locate raw materials for a nascent railroad industry. Unsurprisingly, these exploits proved to be far more remunerative than poetry.

Despite his literary successes, Percival had his detractors, who did their part to diminish his chances at literary immortality. James Russell Lowell wrote disparagingly of Percival in an influential essay published in 1867, roughly one decade after Percival's death, describing him as "pertinaciously and unappeasably dull." A reader of Percival's blank verse, observes Lowell, "feels as if a mob of well-draperied clothes-lines were rioting about him in all the unwilling ecstasy of a thunder-gust." While Percival's poetry did not shy away from themes that would in their day seem controversial— as in suicide, or spousal neglect in the proto-Jarrell dramatic monologue "The Deserted Wife"—his idiom is resolutely (one might say recklessly) neoclassical and the generation of poets that followed him, Lowell among them, were eager to shed the stylistic restrictions in which Percival's poetry is inescapably bound. After all, the majority of Percival's poems were written decades before Herbert Spencer in his influential *Philosophy of Style* (1852) came to prize "minor images" over abstractions, arguing that simplicity, efficiency, economy, and precision in language resulted in "more vivid impressions," values that helped to inaugurate post-classical, modernist poetry. There is no dispute that Percival was, by nineteenth century standards, a perfectly competent lyricist, yet competence and excellence are often not synonymous; incompetent artists are capable of masterpieces, just as competent artists are fully capable of producing dreck.

This handicap is in large part the result of Percival's stubborn refusal to revise his work. Associating poetry with inspiration, Percival insisted that the initial composition was the best composition, and that, contrary to his position as a translator (he is said to have been fluent in more than twenty languages and translated numerous works of both poetry and prose, and in many different subjects, both literary and scientific), proofreader (he assisted Noah Webster with the first two editions of Webster's *Dictionary* [1828, 1841]), and science writer (his in-depth, comprehensive geological reports are still referenced today by geologists and minerologists), in poetry he viewed careful and judicious refinement unnecessary impingements on the creative impulse. By comparison, one observer notes how for Percival, at work on Webster's dictionary, "Nothing could be passed over until thoroughly finished; and the consequence was that he would sometimes spend days upon some single insignificant word, whose history, if attainable, was of no importance." Percival himself writes in his introduction to *Poems* (1823),

> I consider Poetry in a twofold view, as a spirit and a manifestation. Perhaps the poetic spirit has never been more justly defined, than by Byron in his Prophecy of Dante,—a creation "From overfeeling good or ill, an aim at an external life beyond our fate." This spirit may be manifested by language, metrical or prose, by declamation, by musical sounds, by expression, by gesture, by motion, and by imitating forms, colors, and shades; so that literature, oratory, music, physiognomy, acting, and the arts of painting and sculpture, may all have their poetry; but that peculiar spirit, which alone gives the great life and charm to all the efforts of genius, is as distinct from the measure and rhyme of poetical composition, as from the scientific principles of drawing and perspective.

To Percival, the creative impulse *is* itself the point, above and beyond what individual poems might accomplish, and any attempts at refinement of this is, in a sense, a needless muddying of inspirational waters. His aesthetic ethos had the unfortunate and predictable result of reams of bad poetry, and in a timeless sense; there are reams of similar verse composed before and after the nineteenth century that excels much of Percival's.

Nevertheless, not infrequent bright spots remain. His precise and penetrative meditations on nature, "The Coral Grove" and "Seneca Lake," two of his best-known poems, for example, have managed to resist the weathering effects of time:

> How sweet, at set of sun, to view
> Thy golden mirror spreading wide,
> And see the mist of mantling blue
> Float round the distant mountain's side.
>
> At midnight hour, as shines the moon,
> A sheet of silver spreads below,
> And swift she cuts, at highest noon,
> Light clouds, like wreaths of purest snow. ("Seneca Lake")

Critic John Hay points to a similar "power" found in other passages of Percival, as in "Lines on Viewing, One Summer Evening, the House of My Birth, in a State of Desertion":

> To see a spot so sweet, so dear,
> Now laid on desolation's bier,
> And view a scene of loveliness
> In ruin's wildest, roughest dress.

In his "Paraphrase of Isaiah 34," a lesser-known poem, the spectacularly bloody prophecy of God laying waste all earthly enemies—an Old

Testament depiction of Armageddon—is rendered by Percival in rhymed iambic pentameter with an assured, R-rated gusto:

> The purple of their crime has filled the sky,
> And stained it with a deep, a guilty die;
> And there Jehovah bathes his burning sword:
> High o'er Chaldea's land that falchion waves,
> A people doomed and destined to their graves;
> It falls,—urged onward by the avenging Lord.
>
> It falls,—and every soul a victim dies;
> In mangled heaps their weltering corpses rise,
> The king, the prince, the servant, all are gone:
> That sword, with slaughter wearied, drips in gore;
> With clots and hair and brains bespattered o'er,
> It rests,—the work of vengeance now is done.

Percival eventually published just one final collection, *The Dream of a Day*, in 1843, sixteen years after the previous volume, and one year after the publication of his geological survey of Connecticut; he'd attempted publication of a collection twelve years before yet was unable to solicit enough subscribers to pay his printers. This curious volume features translations from the Norwegian, Russian, Polish, Slovakian, Gaelic, as well as "several varieties of ancient measures," including, among others, heroic hexameter, iambic tetrameter catalectic, and other choriambic polyschematist verse. One is hard pressed to think of a more pedantic late career move pre-Louis Zukofsky.

After Percival relocated to the small western outpost of Hazel Green, Wisconsin in 1854 to undertake a second geological survey, he wrote less frequently. There were occasional contributions to a local newspaper, and, having taken up the accordion, Percival would also publish a number of his songs, which he would perform in public while he sang in a near-whisper;

a bout of typhoid at an early age had left him with permanently impaired speech. To the worldly people of the small village of Hazel Green, Percival was nothing less than a genius, yet to those who knew him he remained aloof, nearly a stranger. He cared more for matters of the intellect than in the flesh, such as appearance or financial success; he wore shabby clothes and was always on the brink of financial ruin. He spent nearly every penny he earned on his enormous library of books, which numbered in the tens of thousands. His eventual late-in-life complete withdrawal from society into the comfortable silence of the printed word—he never married and died childless—resulted in his occupancy of the third floor of a converted New Haven hospital that consisted of three rooms: one for his living space, another for his collection of rocks, and the third for his library of books. He died in 1856, after he became ill on a journey from New Haven back to Hazel Green, and lies buried in a cemetery there.

To review Percival's collected works seems at first to be an exercise in superfluous antiquery, like trying to salvage obsolete machinery that serves no ostensible functional or even an aesthetic purpose. His poetry exists in an orbit outside the boundaries of mere nostalgia; it's likely that few alive today have read his work. Mention his name even to someone familiar with nineteenth century poetry, American or otherwise, or even to a current resident of his hometown of Kensington, Connecticut, where the house into which he was born still stands on Percival Street, and chances are they won't know who he is or what his many accomplishments are. It's more likely that a geologist familiar with the history of this science would have some idea of the continued merit of his scientific studies, which include some of the earliest speculations about plate tectonics and whose maps of the features and mineral resources of Connecticut and Wisconsin, as mentioned above, are still of practical use today. His poetry serves no comparable function, certainly not pragmatic and oftentimes not even aesthetic. So why bother?

In truth, much of Percival rightfully deserves the fate it has been accorded. For every gem to be discovered, there are hundreds of unremarkable stones to toss aside; the stripping ratio of his oeuvre remains frustratingly small. This has not prevented contemporary critics from making the occasional attempt, often without much success, to resituate Percival's literary work within a modernist and postmodernist idiom, and yet his decidedly abstract and archaic poetry is frustratingly allergic to such efforts of recovery. Percival remains obstinately affixed within his place and time, and only with rare exception do any of his lines manage to transcend these inherent limitations and, even then, almost by accident rather than design. Given these factors, it is a decidedly uphill task for literary historians or those who hope to remove Percival from the tailings of literary history. Because of the inherent limitations of his work by modernist standards, those who attempt generally lean on fairly creative interpretations. Critic William Crisman (1998), for example, in his brief overview of Percival speculates that Percival's fascination with language—both his philology and poetry—and his concomitant "insistence on being heard," are the result of his speech impairment. Percival's reticence to speak, Crisman theorizes, soon evolved into a reticence to publish. Furthermore, his embarkation into science, Crisman notes, quoting geology historian George Merrill, in a sense replaced the philological role poetry previously held, as his report was more interested in lithology—the categorization of rock types—than in the intended study of the rock's formation. On this point Crisman and Merrill stretch their credulity.

While a dual existence as poet and professional is not unusual for artists of any period (e.g. Doctor Williams or Stevens the insurance executive), yet with Percival it possesses a special fascination among literary revivalists, as if his scientific interests might provide modern audiences contextual or thematic interest that the lyrics themselves generally do not invite. As with Crisman, critic John Hay (2020), for example, searched in vain for a "hidden link" between Percival the poet and Percival the geologist yet, unlike Crisman and Merrill, who struggle to make the case that specific mineralogical concerns color Percival's poetic landscape, Hay concluded that there is about as much hard science in Percival's poetry as there is poetry in his hard science. Which is to say, practically speaking, none at all.

Another potential window that might be opened in order to resuscitate Percival's moribund literary state and rescue him from cultural indifference is that of the poet's somewhat disturbed psychological condition. Similar considerations have led to posthumous reevaluations of Clare, Smart, and Very. Other opportunities can be gleaned from Percival's biography; for example, he long possessed a nervous disposition that, in contemporary terms, would likely be diagnosed as manic depressive. He apparently inherited this condition from his mother, who suffered from what was described at the time as an "excessive mental development." As a young man, Percival attempted suicide by running headlong into a rock and an overdose of opium, he contemplated a self-inflicted gunshot in the head or to drown himself in the ocean. An early poem, "The Suicide," can be viewed as a semiautobiographical meditation on his melancholic state:

What's earth, what's life, to space, eternity?
'Tis but a flash, a glance—from birth to death;
And he, who ruled the world, would only be
Lord of a point—a creature of a breath;

And what is it to gain a hero's name,
Or build one's greatness on the rabble's roar?
'Tis but to light a feeble, flickering flame,
That shines a moment, and is seen no more.

Yet there exists a far more evocative and powerful autobiographical poem, and one that perfectly symbolizes Percival's fate as poet, namely its meteoric rise and descent. Early in Percival's life, he was haunted by the vision of a star, fallen from the heavens. This vision later became the subject of "A Vision," a remarkable example of the romantic lyricism that has dominated American poetry since its inception. The poem is among his best-known and most Byronic and apocalyptic, a meditation on cosmic doom and the inevitability of individual fate. It is included here below.

In a purist sense, Percival was correct to view inspiration as the foundation for any great art, yet, as his work frequently evidences, inspiration is often insufficient and not an end in itself; most poems like most stones require polish for their brilliance to be revealed. It is a testament to his literary talents that Percival managed the infrequent excellent poem despite his apparent apathy toward excellence. And it is those poems, apart from the infrequently brilliant images or lyrics stumbled upon among copious reams of the coma-inducing archaic rhetoric, by which the Percival should be judged, particularly if there is any hope for recovery from his ongoing critical and readerly neglect.

Sources

Crisman, William. "James Gates Percival," in *Encyclopedia of American Poetry: The Nineteenth Century*, ed. Eric L. Haralson, Chicago: Fitzroy Dearborn Publishers, 1998: 325-327.

Hay, John. "The Limits of Recovery: The Failure of James Gates Percival," *Early American Literature*, Volume 55, Number 1, 2020: 114-144.

Housley, Karen L. *Stone Breaker: The Poet James Gates Percival and the Beginning of Geology in New England*. Middletown, CT: Wesleyan University Press, 2023.

Lowell, James Russell. "The Life and Letters of James Gates Percival." 1867.

Percival, James Gates. *The Poetical Works of James Gates Percival*. Boston: Ticknor and Fields, 1859.

_____. "*A Vision.*" *Clio* 3 (1827): 108-110.

Spencer, Herbert. *The Philosophy of Style*. New York: Appleton and Co., 1872.

Wachuta, Joshua. "Remembering James Gates Percival," *A Tree Left Standing* (website), posted September 23, 2010. https://atreeleftstanding.com/2010/09/23/remembering-james-gates-percival/

Ward, Julius. *The Life and Letters of James Gates Percival*. Boston: Ticknor and Fields, 1866.

James Gates Percival

A Vision

I have been haunted by an awful dream,—
A vision of my childhood,—one that grew
From an o'erheated fancy, nursed to fear
In a dark, visionary creed. A star,
Of a malign aspect, had been to me,
For a few weeks of dread uncertainty,
The prophet of evil; and I saw in it
The minister of judgments, such as oft
Had been denounced before me, and had grown
To an undoubting faith.
　Methought that star,
As in a vision of the night I lay,
Stood with its train directed to the earth;
And every moment it did spread itself,
And grew a deeper crimson. Where I was,
I could not tell; but I stood gazing on it
With unaverted eye, and I could watch it
Taking ten thousand fiery shapes, and changing
To every terrible hue and form, and still
Widening and widening out its burning orb,
Till a whole quarter of the heavens was red
And glowing like a furnace. Then, methought,
A form stood visible within it, vast
And indistinct, as a far mountain seen
Through a dense vapor, when the morning strikes it,
And makes it such a thing as the mind frames,
When it goes wandering through the infinite,
And builds on dreams. I gazed upon it, charmed

And fascinated by its terrible glory,
And with it such a sense of fear, the drops
Stood thick upon my forehead, and my heart
Was near to bursting. 'T was an agony
Of wonder and of death; for I beheld
Already come the day of doom, and earth
Seemed parched and burnt by the intensity
Of that approaching flame. The sky above
Was like a vaulted furnace, and it quivered
And sparkled in the heat, and at the centre,
Transparent in the fierceness of its fire,
Still that illimitable form did frown
Blacker than tenfold night. His quick approach
Left me no time to scan him, but he seemed
To gather in himself all I had heard
Or dreamed of horrible. A muttering sound,
Like that of far-off winds, or smothered flame
Roaring in caves,—a sound that fell like fate
On my stunned ear,—came as a warning voice,
That earth was now within the wasting sphere
Of that consuming plague. At once the wind
Seemed to blow over me, with hot, thick breath,
Wafting such clouds of smoke and sheets of fire,
That all around me seemed one conflagration;
And even the firm foundations of the hills
Cracked and fell inward, and one long, long peal
Gave warning, that this ponderous globe was rent
And shivered. Suddenly a burst of flame,
So clear and strong no thought can image it,
Filled the whole visible space; and still it flashed,
And flashed, till in an instant utter darkness
Closed heavily around me, and I woke:

I woke, and yet the horrors of that dream
Would visit me at times, even when I grew
To know its causes, and could reason of it;
And though the mind moved in its own pure light,
And stood aloof from fear, yet there were moments,
When the dark memory of this dream would quell me
Well-nigh to trembling.

David Cappella

Jones Very (1813-1880): An Idiot of God

If ever there was an individual one could apply the phrase 'a riddle wrapped in a mystery inside an enigma,' it was the poet Jones Very, the off-the-grid, offbeat poet of the Transcendentalist Movement, if it in fact was a movement. Considered crazy, sent to an asylum, this Christian mystic who found himself smack-dab in the center of one of the most important intellectual times in the development of New England thought flew under the radar for decades. This friend of Emerson, Very's poetry was admired by the likes of Thoreau and many others, including Bronson Alcott, Richard H. Dana and William Cullen Bryant.

Very has been characterized as a Vatic poet, a Visionary, a Mystic, a Saint, a Romantic, a Messianic prophet, a Quietist, and a Buddhist. In 1838, he apparently went insane, according to some, mostly conservative Unitarian clergy. According to others, he had a mystical experience. That he had a true mystical experience seems more than likely.

For a period of eighteen months, he proclaimed to students, friends, important clergymen, and his Harvard Administrators that he was alternately, John the Baptist, Jesus, and God, and sometimes all three. Given the intellectual, religious, and social milieu of nineteenth century New England, such behavior didn't sit well. Harvard University administrators along with several influential Protestant ministers in Cambridge and Salem found his behavior and words extremely irrational. Thus, he was admitted to McLean Asylum for the Insane on September 17, 1838, for a month. However, in an eighteen month period from 1838 until some point in 1840, Very composed "under the direct influence of a recent overwhelming mystical experience" (Deese 35), ecstatic poems which make up his contribution to American Literature.

Several clergy and intellectuals of the day, including Emerson, disagreed about his madness. James Freeman Clarke defended him, noting, "The charge of Insanity is almost always brought against any man who endeavors to introduce to the common mind any very original ideas" … and he found "no evidence even of…partial derangement" (qtd in Deese 25).

Very was an unassuming man, a quiet and lonely individual, with a staunch innocence. Bronson Alcott, sympathetic to Very when he was connected to the Transcendentalists, caught Very's quiet, alienated nature when he wrote being in the room with him "was like having 'a corpse in the apartment.'" Even Hawthorne sketched a glimpse of Very in his story, *The Hall of Fantasy*, where he imagined "that in that same part of the hall [with Emerson] Jones Very stood alone, within a circle of which no other of mortal race could enter, nor could he himself escape" (qtd in Deese 27). Even so Very captured the attention of many New England writers. Though Richard H. Dana thought Very was insane, and though he blamed it on his connection to the Transcendentalists, he reviewed his poetry and essays favorably some twenty years later. Bryant included some of his poems in *Poets and Poetry in America* where the *New York Evening Post* noted that Very's poems were "some of the very finest sonnets in the English language" (xxvii).

***

There is little doubt of Very's mystical experience because Very himself described this experience in a December 1838 letter to a former classmate, Henry W. Bellows then a Unitarian minister. As Deese notes, this letter has been analyzed by Harry L. Jones, and he "sees in it three typical stages described in Jesse Underhill's study of mysticism: illumination, purgation, and union" (30). Friends and antagonists accepted that Very, indeed, had an experience of some type. Deese observes, "No evidence exists that any one of his contemporaries, friend or foe, doubted his sincerity when he

32

was at the height of his ecstasy. Those who considered him insane were manifestly convinced of his earnestness" (33).

Regarding the close to eight hundred poems that Very wrote in his lifetime, one glaring fact remains: the poems Very wrote prior to his mystical experience and those written after this experience are markedly common. Yet, from his senior year at Harvard until the end of his stay at McClean's, Very wrote some three hundred ecstatic poems of a caliber light years from poems that preceded them or from those that followed during the remaining forty years of his life.

The early poems, beginning from 1833 are "largely imitative of English neoclassical and romantic poets, notably Wordsworth" (Deese 26). His early poetry was sentimental, written in long, blank verse though sometimes in heroic couplets. It's the self-conscious work of a poet trying to find his voice. Over time, he gravitated to the sonnet form.

***

I was first introduced to Jones Very as a nineteen-year-old sophomore in college sitting in an American Literature course with Professor Barbara Chellis. Throughout her brief discussion of his work in relation to the works of Emerson, Whitman and to Transcendentalism in general, Professor Chellis mentioned that Very's noteworthy poetry was mystical in nature. That comment caught my attention. In early 1968, in my world, words like 'mystic' floated in the air, in late night conversations about music, philosophy, and all things spiritual.

The small sampling of Very's sonnets struck a chord that has lasted throughout my writing life. These sonnets were tight, tense, and abstract in ways that I didn't immediately understand. After all, Very set upon annihilating his will then tried to capture and render that experience in sonnet form, let alone proclaim his voice as alternately that of God's, John the Baptist, and Jesus (sometimes all at the same time).

Very's latest biographer, Clark Davis, labels this poetic effort "messianic ventriloquism" (155). Deese believes "it is preferable to think in terms of a double or a layered voice" (44) These sonnets initially confounded me, specifically, the now much discussed, "I am the Way":

Thy way is simple for I am the light
By which thou travelest on to meet thy God
Brighter and brighter still shall be thy sight
Till thou hast ended here the path I trod
Before thee stretches far the thorny way
Yet smoothed for thee by him who went before
Go on it leads you to the perfect day
The rest I to the patriarch Abraham swore
Go on and I will guide you safely through
For I have walked with suffering feet thy path
Confide in me the Faithful and the True
And thou shalt flee the approaching day of wrath
Whose dawn e'en now the horizon's border shows
And with its kindling fires prophetic glows.

This complex mixing of voices, whether intentional or not, certainly reveals Very's poetic voice as divine since he includes it in this poem. The hubris of the messianic.

***

It's been over eighty years since Ivor Winters declared "Jones Very as the third major rediscovery in this century of neglected nineteenth-century American writers following Emily Dickinson and Herman Melville" (qtd in Deese 38). That controversial statement started the critical ball rolling and scholars have since dug deep into both his life and these special poems written over such a brief period. One important result was the 1993 publication of *Jones Very: The Complete Poems* edited

34

by Helen Deese, which provided a catalogue of all the poems found and added textual, historical, and editorial notes to them.

I never pursued learning more about Very's poetry, but his innocent, open claim of divinity stuck with me. His journey from a sentimental Romantic poet with hints of John Clare and Wordsworth to such ecstatic, messianic heights never left me. Here was a poet who truly seemed to have been struck by God's lightning.

***

One poem, "The Torn Flower," reveals his romantic inclination, love of nature, and his passion for women (which he fought throughout his days at Harvard).

I tore thee—though who looked so sweet,
And shed thy fragrance at my feet;
I tore thee in my wrath;
Scattered thy sweetness to the wind,
Nor left one look of love behind
To smile upon my path.

I mourn too late! Ah! Ne'er again
Shall visit thee the small-dropped rain,
The gently falling dew;
Nor morn, nor noon, nor eve's still hour
Shall watch the spot, ill-fated flower!
Where once thy beauty grew.

The storms that filled the troubled sky
Have lightly passed thy shelter by,
Pleased with thy sweet perfume;
More cruel than angry blast

I madly crushed thee as I past,
And robbed thee of thy bloom.

Would that the tears I o'er thee shed
Might raise again thy dropping head
To life and joy once more;
Then would I learn me of the storm
To spare thy bright and tender form,
My heart's mad passion tore.

Another poem, "The Autumn Leaf" reveals a tone of "quiet loss and isolation" (Davis 141), written late in his early stage of his poetry, before his *"change of heart,"* and since it comes after his reading of Emerson's *Nature*, displays Very's "meditative and experiential lyric side" (Davis 141). Here are the first thirteen lines of the poem:

Thou fair yet lifeless leaf! On whom decay
Seems beautiful, red glowing as thou hangest
Beneath the earliest touch of autumn's hand;
I pluck thee fluttering from thy parent vine,
Before the rude wind tears thee from its fond
Embrace to toss thy form, in idle play,
Shrivelled and brown upon the winter air:
For thou art as a tablet to the thoughts
That now are gushing fresh, as if my soul
Had drank new life amid these lofty shades,
And felt its being moved by sympathy
With unseen power.
Brief monitor of frail humanity!

One of his first sonnets, "Beauty," hints at Very's "enormous overflow of spiritual sonnets that began a year later" (Davis 154).

I gazed upon thy face—and beating life,
Once stilled its sleepless pulses in my breast,
And every thought whose being was a strife
Each in its silent chamber sank to rest;
I was not, save it were a thought of thee,
The world was but a spot where thou hadst trod,
From every star thy glance seemed fixed on me,
Almost I loved thee better than my God.
And still I gaze—but 'tis a holier thought
Than that in which my spirit lived before,
Each star a purer ray of love has caught,
Earth wears a lovelier robe than then it wore,
And every lamp that burns around thy shrine
Is fed with fire whose fountain is Divine.

The turmoil of emotions in this poem are held in tight check. His recent biographer, Clark Davis, aptly called Very's poetics 'clenched'. Here, it's as though the threat of the speaker's desire must be circumscribed at all costs. This pivotal sonnet, written in September 1837, hints at the mystical sonnets to come.

***

This Very sonnet, "The New Birth," as Deese notes, "announces and demonstrates his new style, subject matter, and new manner of composition" (36):

'Tis a new life—thoughts move not as they did
With slow uncertain steps across my mind,
In thronging haste fast pressing on they bid

37

The portals open to the viewless wind;
That comes not, save when in the dust is laid
The crown of pride that gilds each mortal brow,
And from before man's vision melting fade
The heavens and earth—Their walls are falling now –
Fast crowding on each thought claims utterance strong,
Storm-lifted waves swift rushing to the shore
On from the sea they send their shouts along,
Back through cave-worn rocks their thunders roar,
And I a child of God by Christ made free
Start from death's slumbers to eternity.

The sense of pressing need opens the poem—"In thronging haste fast pressing on they bid." The need to break free is captured in the line "The portals open to the viewless wind." And the word 'viewless'! The strength of these fast flow of thoughts is caught on the metaphor of the "Storm-lifted waves swift rushing to the shore." The final couplet not only intrigues because the paradox of the temporal world leading to the atemporal world, but the last line breaks the iambic flow by beginning with a sudden spondee, a jumpstart to a new kind of freedom. In his attempt to capture his mystical experience in this poem, Very's poetry drastically changed register and scope.

One of the more interesting of Very's ecstatic/mystical sonnets is "The Hand and the Foot" shown here:

The hand and foot that stir not, they shall find
Sooner than all the rightful place to go;
Now in their motion free as roving wind,
Though first no snail so limited and slow;
I mark them full of labor all the day,
Each active motion made in perfect rest;

They cannot from their path mistaken stray,
Though 'tis not theirs, yet in it they are blest;
The bird has not in their hidden track found out,
Nor cunning fox though full of art he be;
It is the way unseen, the certain route,
Where ever bound, yet thou art ever free;
The path of Him, whose perfect law of love
Bids spheres and atoms in just order move.

Many scholars have commented on this poem, thematically and stylistically. That's all well and good. What strikes me about this sonnet is Very in the still point of the turning world. He has been called a 'quietist,' and this poem demonstrates that aspect of his work and state of mind. The poem is not about any conflict; it's about being beyond resolution. The halting, unsure start of the poem melts into viewing "Each active motion made in perfect rest." This is a paradoxical state; "It is the way unseen, the certain route, /Where ever bound, yet thou art ever free;". The paradox seems to be that to achieve this state no action was needed, only a passive letting go of the self.

***

It is hard for me not to think of William Blake when reading Jones Very. Very created his own prophetic amalgam of scriptural language with his own idiosyncratic syntax and vocabulary. He believed in the divinity of his words. He saw his poems as delivered messages from God. Unsurprisingly, Bronson Alcott called him "a gifted saint." This astonishingly well read and extremely intelligent young man who wanted to reinvigorate the epic nature of poetry, wrote, with a few exceptions, mundane, secular verse early in his career. After undergoing a mystical experience for a period of approximately eighteen months, he produced a unique body of extremely intense and prophetic poetry unlike anything he'd ever written or would ever write again. This ecstatic poetry earned him a distinctive place in American Literature.

***

This quiet, unassuming man, an inveterate walker, could be found walking along the streets of Peabody, or on the road to Cambridge, to Boston, or to Concord to visit Emerson. He loved his solitary walks. I love the fact that he walked. And always alone. I wonder what he thought about those ecstatic poems that spilled from his pen for such a short period of time, poems radically, startlingly different in theme, tone, and syntax from anything he had ever written. It was as though his subjection to God not only released his will but also released a part of his imagination that would have lain dormant if he hadn't experienced his *change of heart*, as he called it.

Whatever his thoughts about his poetry, his reflection about his mystical experience appears in a poem written in July 1853, nearly fifteen years after it. Interestingly, it was never published in his lifetime. It's a pensive, honest poem, tinged with sadness, maybe. In it Very captured the experience that changed not only his poetry but blackballed him from society and made him, for a time, the center of attention with the Transcendentalists.

Sources

Davis, Clark. *God's Scrivener: The Madness and Meaning of Jones Very*. Chicago: University of Chicago Press, 2023.
Very, Jones. *The Complete Poems*. Edited by Helen R. Deese. Athens, GA: University of Georgia Press, 1993.

JONES VERY

ON FINDING THE TRUTH

With sweet surprise, as when one finds a flower,
Which in some lonely spot, unheeded, grows;
Such were my feelings, in the favored hour,
When Truth to me her beauty did disclose.
Quickened I gazed anew on heaven and earth,
For a new glory beamed from earth and sky;
All things around me shared the second birth,
Restored with me, and nevermore to die.
The happy habitants of other spheres,
As in times past, from heaven to earth came down;
Swift fled in converse sweet the unnumbered years,
And angel-help did human weakness crown!
The former things, with Time, had passed away,
And Man, and Nature lived again for aye.

MICHAEL GESSNER

ALEXANDER LAWRENCE POSEY (1873-1908)

The Indian talks in poetry.
—Alex Posey

In our national literature of the nineteenth century, there was little room for indigenous writers, and what literature did emerge, particularly among Native American poets received little attention.

Into this literary culture, against this background, like a *bas-relief*, stands the figure of Alexander Posey, Muscogee (Creek). So why Posey? Perhaps his contributions are best summarized by Alexia Kosmider:

> Posey's work shows us the way out of a limited literary perspective, opening up a new and perhaps a more thorough understanding of American Indian literature. Alex Posey, silenced for almost one hundred years, helps us circle back to the roots of contemporary American Indian literature, giving critics and readers a different basis for understanding the difficulty of negotiating, and ultimately expressing, bicultural experiences. (98-99)

The facts of Posey's life are as few as they are significant: the eldest of 12 children born to a father of Scots Irish Muscogee Creek ancestry who had been abandoned as a child and raised Creek, member of the Broken Arrow tribe, and a Creek mother, Posey was raised in a bilingual home with access to a literary library. After a public education, he went on to the Indian University in Muscogee. At 23 he married Minnie Harris, a teacher, and they had three children, each named after admired literary figures: Yaholo Irving, Pachina Kipling, and Wynema Torrans. Alex Posey, at the age of 34, drowned by accident attempting to cross the flooded North Canadian River in Oklahoma.

This was the same river on which he spent his youth, in which he swam, fished, boated, and memorialized in his poem, "Song of the Oktahutchee" (Creek: Okta, sand; Hutchee, river), a paean to the river that took him.

So much for the facts of a brief life, one exceeded immeasurably by the productions of that life. Posey created the first daily newspaper published by a Native American, *The Eufaula Indian Journal* in 1902. As an activist for Native American land rights, and as secretary for the Sequoyah Constitutional Convention,he composed most of the constitution for a Native American state during a time when Oklahoma and Indian territories were being pushed to be a state of the Union; served as an administrator to tribal schools, supervised the Creek Asylum for Orphans at Okmulgee, and created a collection of stories, orations, and oral traditions published as *Chinnubbie and the Owl, Collected Journals, Collected Poems,* and *The Fus Fixico Letters.*

The Fus Fixico Letters are central to Posey's world view and to his historical importance. Most readers have noted them as the work of a humorist. There is humor in them, certainly, but they are satire and the work of a political satirist.

Fus Fixico, (Creek: "Heartless Bird,") is Posey's fictional persona. The 72 *Fus Fixico Letters* mock the political ambitions of the government and its representatives in Creek dialect among four characters. Intentional malapropisms abound: President Roosevelt becomes "Rooster Feather," and Ethan Hitchcock, Secretary of the Interior, is "Itscocked," diminishing the stature of those figures who determined the period's treatment of the Native American's survival conditions, territories, and future promise, if any. The surface dialogue of the characters is often presented as naïve, but just under the surface, the hallmarks of satire run concurrently throughout the text: irony, contempt, and ridicule. Here's a rather transparent example: Fus had learned of the death of Choela (a blacksmith who found his way to the status of a medicine man) and reports:

Well, so I was tell you bad news about my old friend Choela.
He was gone to be good Injin, like white man say when Injin

43

die. It was look like all old Injins die now and make good Injin
in that way. Maybe so pretty soon Fus Fixico was make good Injin too.
(Littlefield 167)

Although *The Fus Fixico Letters* are *sui generis* by virtue of the synthesis of Creek dialect, the perceptions of a unique historical period, and the portrayal of a people's plight in satiric form written by an indigenous author, it was poetry that Posey pursued more than any other genre.

He saw himself primarily as a poet. His wife described his daily routine which placed poetry before any other pursuit, and for which he had a central affinity, confirmed by friends and associates (Connelley "Introduction" *Poems*).

Posey's poetry carries a unique signature. Since his university days, all of his poems were written over the pseudonym of Chinnubbie Harjo. In Creek Mythology, Chinnubbie was a versatile figure, sometimes heroic warrior, and in other situations, a villain. Harjo is derived from Muscogee Creek, from his mother's side, the Wind Clan, and thus from Hadcho, meaning "crazy," or "so brave as to appear crazy." Connelley writes, "After his graduation Posey published no poem, that I have found, over any other name" (59).

A feature of Posey's poetry, if not an irresistible attraction, is the opportunity of reading the poems through the lens of Chinnubbie, the (omnipresent) mythic speaker. This device gives different shades of meaning that, without it, would be otherwise impossible to disclose. When the speaker of "On the Capture and Imprisonment of Crazy Snake,[1] January, 1900" exclaims in the ultimate line "I bow to him, exhalt his name!" it is Chinnubbie, the great hero speaking then, as if his presence in the poem lends power and compassion to his declaration, greater than Posey's voice alone.

Early poems include such titles as "Chinnubbie Scalps the Squaws," and "Chinnubie's Courtship." Creek phrases and names are woven throughout Posey's poems, a practice unique in his time. There are poems to the winds,

44

"Husse Lotka Enhotulle," and "Wahilla Enhotulle," to flowers, animals, and there are political poems of praise or condemnation. Stechupo, a Creek mythic wood-spirit, a male Dryad or Drus, appears in "Flowers of Tulledega," and should he be seen, the person fortunate enough to see him will be given gifts from the forest. There are also, often in the same poem, Greek and Roman allusions so that it would appear to some readers that a homogenous blend of mythic references was an attempt to foreshadow the ultimate—and necessary—reality of a hybrid culture, an ideal that Posey championed as shown in his letters and journals.

Any discussion of Posey's poetry must include Thoreau. It is inescapable. Even Posey admitted his adoration, certainly with the intensity of his admiration of Sequoyah, or Chitto Harjo, but for different reasons. In a letter to a friend, he wrote, "Thoreau was a man after my own heart, because, perhaps, there is so much Indian in him. I carry a pocket edition of *Walden* in my jeans constantly mainly just to have it near me" (Kosmider 33).

Thoreau's 'Indian' as a dignified, but vanishing image, was not Posey's, as may be seen in poems like "The Indian's Past Olympic," where ". . . gaping wounds by war clubs torn, / Gush torrents, streams of clotting gore," (lines 43-33). Here, the 'Indian' persists, struggles, and survives. Rather the affinity with Thoreau was a mutual sensibility with nature as a source of refuge, inspiration, and spiritual elevation. This is most clearly seen in his poems of place, "Spring in Tulwa Thlocco," or "On Piney," a stream in the Tulledega Hills, or in any of the poems that include Posey's boyhood landscapes.

Taken from the ruthless ball court of "The Indian's Past Olympic," where injured players were left to suffer on the field, often to die, when ". . . not one tear is shed, / Or words of grief or sorrows said/ . . . Where men their kindreds, fellows slay," (lines 56-57; 59) we have a kinder, gentler poetry which typifies the greater arc of Posey's poems, and strongly suggests the Thoreauvian connection.

THE DEW AND THE BIRD

There is more glory in a drop of dew,
  That shineth only for an hour,
Than there is in the pomp of earth's great Kings
  Within the noonday of their power.

There is more sweetness in a single strain
  That falleth from a wild bird's throat
At random in the lonely forest's depths,
  Than there's in all the songs that bards e'er wrote.

Yet men, for aye, rememb'ring Caesar's name,
  Forget the glory in the dew,
And praising Homer's epic, let the lark's
  Song fall unheeded from the blue.

The structural virtuosity throughout Posey's collected poems is something that should bear more than casual note. There are sonnets, epigrams, verse dramas with speaking characters, prose poems, inventive end-line rhymes and nuances of meaning as found in "The Deer," when out of "folded hills," a deer "comes to drink / From Limbo's[2] waters . . ." and leaves, as does the narrator, with their images "lying in the stream" (Posey 103). Taken together, the body of the poems, "draw[s] heavily upon Posey's Muscogee cultural traditions and cannot be measured by conventional Euro-American ideas of literary worth" (Sivils xxxix).

Although Posey's verse has been neglected in our age, one increasingly troubled by the intentional and unnecessary destruction of natural resources, the anxieties of material acquisition, a growing insensitivity to the suffering of others along with the diminution of their meaning or importance, perhaps it is time for a redivivus of the best prospects of an affinity to nature and to the promise of a multi-cultural existence.

"As a poet, prose writer, journalist, and humorist, Alex left a corpus greater in variety than that of any [Native American] Indian writer" (Littlefield 259). This too might suggest a return to a rich source of natural and cultural renewal.

Notes

[1]Chitto from the Harjo clan of the poet's mother, thus Chitto Harjo, who resisted the governmental nullification of Native American rights.

[2]Limbo serves as both an actual creek near Eufaula, and the spiritual netherworld, a nebulous place for "lying" images; human and animal—a questioning of identity—as if to suggest an Ethereum of mysterious displacement.

Sources

Kosmider, Alexia. *Tricky Tribal Discourse, The Poetry, Short Stories, and Fus Fixico Letters of Creek Writer Alex Posey*. Moscow, Idaho: University of Idaho Press, 1998.

Littlefield, Daniel F. *Alex Posey: Creek Poet, Journalist, and Humorist*. Lincoln, Nebraska: University of Nebraska Press, 1992.

Posey, Alexander. Sivils, M. W. (Ed.) *Song of the Oktahutchee, Collected Poems*. Lincoln, Nebraska: University of Nebraska Press, 2008.

Posey, Minnie, and William Elsey Connelley. *The Poems of Alexander Lawrence Posey*. Topeka, Kansas: Crane and Company, 1910.

ALEXANDER LAWRENCE POSEY

SEQUOYAH

The ages will remember thee,
Illustrious Indian, poets tell
Thy story, Thou'st a star to be;
Aye, one whose light has not yet fell
But which is shining far away
And cannot reach the world today.

ABIGAIL CHILD

LUSTY PALATE:
THE FUTURE PRESENT
OF BARONESS ELSA VON FREYTAG-LORINGHOVEN[1]
(1874-1927)

[The Baroness] is not a futurist. S H E I S the future.
—Marcel Duchamp[2]

The Baroness, perhaps— always that *perhaps* with women—is: the first female avant performer, an early sound poet, inventor of the ready-made, the Dada heroine who puts a bucket on her head or a pilot's hat, referencing war, performing war, rehearsing war. Past and future.

Born in Germany with a sensitive, cultured mother who ultimately withdraws into madness and dies in a sanitorium of uterine cancer, and a father who is a virile, "violent-tempered" bullying patriarch, Elsa heads to Berlin where eventually she is thrown out of her aunt's home and taken up by artists.[3] She performs and serves as muse, acting out her "sexlogic".[4] After many affairs within the Stefan George circle, she moves, at the turn of the century, to Munich, then a center of theatrical Dionysian modernism. Here, Elsa 'experiments' in marriage with the architect August Endell (1871-1925) who conceived of beauty as 'ecstatic pleasure', but fails as a sex partner. She has a passionate five years with the writer Felix Paul Greve, who Elsa calls her 'sex-sun.' The two write an infamous tell-all novel together, marrying in 1907. Two years later, Greve stages his own suicide and moves to the United States to escape debt. A year later, Elsa heads for the United States and ends up living and writing in Kentucky (of all places) on a farm with Greve, who ultimately abandons her. In 1913 Elsa arrives in New York City where she marries a third time to Leopold von Freytag-Loringhoven.[5] There, she befriends Djuna Barnes, Marcel Duchamp, William Carlos Williams and astonishes all.

49

A DOZEN COCKTAILS PLEASE.

NO SPINSTER LOLLYPOPP FOR ME - "YES - WE HAVE

NO BANANAS"- I GOT LUSTING PALATE - I ALWAYS

EAT THEM - - - - -

THEY HAVE DANDY CELLULOID TUBES - ALL SIZES -

TINTED DIABOLICALLY LIKE A BAMBOON'S

HIND COMPLEXION.

A MAN'S A - - -

PIFFLE! WILL 0' TH' WHISP! WHAT IS THE DREAD

MATTER WITH THE UP - TO - DATE AMERICAN

HOME COMFORTS? BUM INSUFFICIENT FOR THE

SHOULD - BE WELL GROOMED UPSY.

THERE'S THE VIBRATOR - - -

COY FLAPPERTOY! I'M ADULT CITIZEN WITH

VOTE -I DEMAND FULL SHARE IN ROOF EDEN

WITCH SABBATH OF OUR BABYLONIAN OBELISK.

WHAT'S THE RADIO FOR - IF YOU PLEASE?

"EVE'S DART PRICKS SNOOKUMS UPON WIREFENCE"

"AN APPLE A DAY - - -"

IT'LL COME

HAWHEN? I AM NO TONGUE SWALLOWING YOGI

PROGRESS IS RAVISHING.

IT DOES'NT ME! ME-

NUDGE IT -

PUSH IT -

PRODD IT-

KICK IT -

BROADCAST - - - -

THAT'S THE LIGHTNING IDEA!

S.O.S SHORTAGE OF - - -

WHAT?

HOW ARE WE GOING TO PUT IT BEFITTING
LIFTED UPSY'S?
PSH! ANY SISSY POET HAS SUFFICIENT FREEZING
CHEMICALS IN HIS FREUDIAN ICECHEST TO
SNUFF ALL COCKYNESS. WE'LL HIRE ONE.
HELL! NOT THAT! THAT'S THE TROUBLE!
COCKCROW - SILLY.
OH - FINE!
THEY 'RE IN FRANCE -AFRICA THE AIR - ON THE
LINE - THE POLES - - - - - - -
HAVE THEM SEND WAVES - LIKE CANDY - VALENTINES -
- - - - - - - -
"SAY IT WITH"- - -
BOLTS.
THUNDER!
SERPENTINE AIR CURRENTS - - - -
HHHHHHHHHPHSSSSSSSSSSSS! THE VERY WORD PENETRATES!
I FEEL WHOOZY!
I LIKE THAT. I AINT HANKERING AFTER
BILLY BOYS - BUT I AM ENTITLED TO BE
DEEPLY SHOCKED.
SO ARE WE - BUT YOU FILL THE HIATUS.
DEAR - I AINT QUEER - I NEED IT STRAIGHT -
-A DOZEN COCKTAILS - PLEASE!- - - - [6]

In a note she admits that her "sailor language" is compelling, a preference that garners attention and enables her sharp jousts at the bourgeois polite culture she both originates from and that she encounters. Her shock tactics suggest she will be ousted from polite, literary audiences in her future. They also signify that Elsa found her home with Dada, its anarchic energies releasing her to expressive force.

I was introduced in the 70s to the Baroness through Jerome Rothenberg's

51

Revolution of the World: A New Gathering of American Avant Garde Poetry 1914-1945.[7] Along with better known poets such as Eliot and Cummings, Rothenburg included two poets unknown to me: the Baroness Elsa von Freytag-Loringhoven and Abraham Lincoln Gillespie. They immediately fascinated. She, a combine of Dada, William Carlos Williams and Dos Passos with insistent attention to the present, outside of the poetic 'per se'[8] —utilizing world events, popular song, news, ads, nonsense and non-grammatical punctuation and spelling. Spilling sound song, EvFL's work is disjunct but always with voice, speaking of and intimate with a consistently gendered present, aggressive, powerful, comic. *Suckdisks clinglust*,[9] the compressed sound, the multiple meanings resulting from the improbable combination, words used as blocks to create and commingle desiring-conjunctions. Her work is endlessly modern, referencing consumer goods and slang, foregrounding female desire, puncturing male "whimseys". She is mocking and plaintive, insisting that she too is a "citizen" and deserves, in her memorable phrase, "roof eden."[10] She registers as a female Jack Smith who reached cinema and performance underground fame 50 years later.[11] Or perhaps resembling the performer Carolee Schneeman, but 60 years earlier.[12]

Elsa was not 'regular' in life or art. She was a spontaneous writer, published sporadically in our time, though in her time featured in *The Little Review* alongside chapters of James Joyce's *Ulysses*. Known for her performance and writing, the Baroness also painted and sculpted. The sculpture is particularly intriguing. The famous one entitled "God" is constructed out of a plumbing pipe (1917). Intensely personal, the sculptures are 3-dimensional messages, often created for friends. Her mother crafted with found objects from street debris, and there seems an influence in Elsa's own findings. The pipe structures are humorously elegant, machinic in ways we won't see again until the 1950s. Their titles shape image-conundrums, punchy and deep, wondrous. "XXXX"— is of feathers set in a wine glass, supposedly a portrait of Duchamp, with a rooster crown. Did her sculptures predate Duchamp's urinal? Did he

52

borrow her ideas? Indeed, she is "credited with inventing the readymade" having presented her piece *Enduring Ornament* (1913), a reused metal ring, a year before Marcel Duchamp shared his first readymade, *Bottle Rack* (1914).[13]Would he have admitted publicly that he was influenced by her wildly creative practice. Perhaps? Gammel strongly argues that Elsa brought Munich's erotic, androgynous play to the diffident Duchamp, meeting him for repeated midnight talks, influencing him as he was transitioning from painting and "searching for innovations."[14]

SPRINGSHELL
TREE
GHOST
EARTHRUBBISH.

From the poem *"Orchard Farming"*
Lyrical, nearly evanescent, and then grounded.

GLOSSGREEN
BUFF
??SULPHUR
BRICK
DAPPLED
DIMPLED
FURRED
SPIKED

SKILLPAYING
PRAISE RIPE
IS

ADORABLE

UNTIL
PLUCKED

Reminding this reader of Emily Dickinson in both women's alternate word-play, re-announcing sound and rhyme, hearing the alts... the afterglow of editing. The line of words is a spine to which Elsa hangs her words, whereas 'plucked' stops the movement, an antithetical counter to the *dimpled dappling* of previous stanzas. She blocks her rant.

In _OSTENTATIOUS:_

-

VIVID FALL
BUGLE SKY —
CASTLE CLOUD'S
LEAFY LIMBSWISH —— ——

The dashes create a sound rhythm, and simultaneously invoke an absence. They seem breath markers, as in Jackson Mac Low's markers for reading, yet also suggest the unspoken, the urge forward/desire as in the doubled dashes of the last line. The 'bugle sky' is a sky one wants to trumpet. Here clouds are castles, the two-word lines balance and the caps create depth to promote a square vista of balanced word stanzas—yet the meaning combos are blunt and unexpected, unbalanced. _Leafy limbswish_ suggests a vortex of meanings: wind and body, branch of deciduous and flesh-wise wishes, days' splendor, an opening—. The delight and entrapment of this sensual reading is met with Elsa's excessive and preposterously/ironic title: _OSTENTATIOUS._ Capturing the exuberant day and the desiring persona in four lines, the title pulls back, a meta-comment by the poet as to how she reads her own ecstasies.

Her work is noted as early sound poetry, the words/syllables sometimes dance into the abstract or symbolic, gnomic at times, but EvFL circles back or thrusts out front with her gender and sexuality. The page is to _play on_ as she lines up her words, creating sculptural fragments across the page, attentive to shape and pattern, rhythm and music. And the body's experience of the world.

ASTRIDE[15]

Saddling
Up
From

55

Fir

Nightbrimmed –

Clinkstirrupchink!

Silverbugle

Copperrimmed –

Keening –

Heathbound

Roves

Moon

Pink –

Straddling

Neighing

Stallion :

"HUEESSUEESSUEESSSOOO

HYEEEEEE PRUSH

HEE HEE HEEEEEEAAA

OCHKZPNJRPRRRR

     HÜ

    /   \

HÜÜ   HÜÜÜÜÜ

   HÜ-HÜ!"

Aflush

Brink

Through

Foggy

Bog

They

Slink –

Sink

Into

Throbb

Bated.

Hush
Falls –
Stiffling –
Shill
Crickets
Shrill –
Bullfrog
Squalls
Inflated
Bark
Riding
Moon's
Mica –
Groin –
Strident!

Hark!

Stallion
Whinny's
In
Thickets

She is both grand and light, armed and brilliant, full of terror and humor, on and off the page. Hers is a creative response to a distraught childhood, an over-bearing dad, to war, to dislocation, poverty, and her own impulses. Self-created, omnivorously sensual, humanly comic and fully emotive, a scene-stealer, a controversy, a hot mess—she is of our time. Her work and person spear into the present, outlandish, costumed, funny. She is performer and poet. Sculpting a modern world.

APHRODITE TO MARS[16]

Flashing blade –
Poniard buried –
High
Flexible tenderness web
Abdominal
Of
Systems
Equal steel
Shaped
Female

Aflirt
Mars'
Buried blade's
Keenness aggressive
Into
Keenness' receptive
Aristocratic
Fit.

Octopus charm's
Alluring
Rubberdisk tenacity –
Sucking
Soft – energetic
Into
Systems mobile
Knit
Caesar's
Digging

Point
Sharp kiss
Plenishing
Snapping thirst's
Drill gash
Rimflush
Ruby blood's desire
Equal
Of
Quality true –
Gushing –
Ejaculating silently
High
To
Stain glintedges chased
Pained tempered
Flirt
Caesar's crimson
Supreme
Cardinal
Sheath
In
Hedges
Of
Pride's beam –
Brave blade's
Flash point –
Poniard steel
Mars asleep
At
Hearth
Olympic.

Octopus love pillows
Recuperating
Capacity
Suckdisks clinglust
To
Sharp arm
Within
Ecstatic
Elasticity
Feminine

In *Hell's Wisdom,* a fragmented prose piece, Elsa explains herself poignantly.[17]

<All wisdom is profoundly trivial>
Love is gravitation

My "Derangement" dwells in absence – as—under circumstances
existing – normally – it
should be present.
It maintains in circumstance –
There I leave it.
My being in senses right is normal height.
It being uncommon – presents strange - as genius does -
uncompanioned.
Victim of circumstance I am not – as I am no dweller in
For me - to be touched - touchably - by circumstance - normal
To vacuous spectres of substance past - should so be abnormal—as to
cause revulsion
degree –

Provoking instant insanity – whence I am protected by radius of
spiritual emanation

To circumstance I am immaterial - as is circumstance to me.
Diametricaly opposed - alone we leave each other - charmed aloft
Lone I - enhanced shrouded earth – by own atmosphere mine self's
own self—out-of
circumstance cosmic star - volve revolve - evolve -I do - by starshaped
pride stygmatized
outcast from circumstanced press - presssure – I am.

Social insanity - cosmic sanity - visible flesh - I am not present.
Cosmic resident.
That means:
Responsibility sublime
Capacity to measure.
Bliss – damnation – alternating until equilibrium attainment
Sway
Balance
Scalefix....

This woman wishing to be twinned, matched as a 1+1 in her poems,
dies alone in Paris 1927, either a suicide by gas or an accident. A sad
demise in light of her history and her obsession with body and desire.[18]
Yet her work lives on, her energies unbounded by social proprieties, her
art and self a constant rebuke to the cages of women's lives, both then and
now. In her confrontational bluntness, her ironic comedy, her insistence
on lived experience, her attention to rhythm, the street and honesty,
her acknowledgement that poverty "squeezes" the "windpipe" of those
without finances, the Baroness speaks defiantly to the present.[19] She is our
radical fierce vanguard.

In *Hell's Wisdom*, the poem ends:

Life conquered – emotion solved
Measureless limitless urfigure
Assembled.
Circle
Navel
Nil.

Betwixt :
Swing –
Wheel
Scale
Until:
Shot
Middle
Spot
Hit - :
Radiance
Adash.

Notes

[1]I will on occasion refer to the poet as "the Baroness," or "Elsa" or her own initials "EvFL."

[2]Irene Gammel, *Baroness Elsa: GENDER, Dada and Everyday Modernity: A Cultural Biography*. Cambridge: MIT Press, 2002. This is a terrific, detailed biography, this first I know of, that is a joy to read with images and gossip, fact and researched devotion to its subject.

[3]Ibid. 30. The description of her father is from a quote in the Baroness's memoirs.

[4]Ibid. 54. Quoted from the Baroness's memoirs describing her entry into sex. "I

had become mensick up to my eartips—no, over the top of my head—permeating my brain, stabbing out of my eyeballs" (61).

[5]Ibid. Much of the biography I recount comes from the details of Gammel's book.

[6]Baroness Elsa van Freytag-Loringhoven, *A Dozen Cocktails Please* (original source) — See link: https:// deigital.lib.und.edu/ transition/poem%3Fpid=umd: 55430.html. Encoded documents and images are derived from manuscripts in the Papers of Elsa von Freytag-Loringhoven in Special Collections at the University of Maryland Libraries, College Park. In addition, individual pages or leaves of manuscripts are identified by the corresponding reel and frame numbers of the microfilm edition of the Freytag-Loringhoven Papers. Encoded and published by Tanya Clement.

[7]Jerome Rothenberg, *Revolution of the Word: A New Gathering of American Avant-Garde Poetry, 1914-1945* (1974).

[8]Leslie Scalapino, *The Public World / Syntactically Impermanence*. Middletown, CT: Wesleyan University Press, 1993: 3. "These temporal and causal conventions structure events and thought so that 'activity and time per se' become 'a condition of tradition.' Thus 'both time and activity are a "lost mass" at any time… '" Noted in "Reading the Minds of Events: Leslie Scalapino's Plural Time." Published in a critical feature on Leslie Scalapino in HOW2 2.2 (2004).

[9]Baroness Elsa von Freytag-Loringhoven from *Aphrodite to Mars* https:// jacket2.org/poems/poems-baroness-elsa-von-freytag-loringhoven#Hell

This is the same source for the last three poems I include (footnotes below). These are previously unpublished and were transcribed by Tanya Clement from the Baroness Archive op. cit. above.

[10]Not for nothing does Elsa ask to be considered a "citizen," as it is not until 1920 that the 19th Amendment passes, allowing women to vote in the United States.

[11]Jack Smith (definitely not the current prosecutor in the Trump case), a performer and filmmaker from the 60s who Wikipedia declares "a founding father of American performance art." Elsa is clearly in this lineage, if not a source, as her work was largely lost to history until Rothenberg's book. Smith's films involved flagrant sexuality and at the premiere of his (in)famous *Flaming Creatures*, the film was confiscated by police. His performances were another form of "affronting the audience." I attended several held at Rafik's, a sometimes screening/performance loft on lower Broadway in the 1980s, and always they would start many hours after the announced start-time, with Jack walking back and forth across the stage, moving props, muttering and sometimes cancelling the show altogether. A trail of patience: was the audience with him enough to bear the craziness?

[12]Carolee Schneemann (1939-2019), leading female performer from the 60s on who celebrated the body and sexuality while confronting masculine and

nativist heroism. Originally a painter, her performances were visual and critical commentary: she covered bodies with meat to protest war; hung from a rope nude with color stick in hand, letting gravity and weight create the resultant drawing; pulled a scroll from her vagina in a stream upstate, reading from it a feminist manifesto. "I wanted my actual body to be combined with the work as integral material." Alert, brilliant, versed in performance, writing and film, once again a lineage that would include the Baroness.

[13]For a fuller history of this sculpture please check out the link: https://www.arthistoryproject.com/artists/elsa-von-freytag-loringhoven/enduring-ornament/

[14]Op.cit Gammel 170.

[15]Baroness Elsa von Freytag-Loringhoven, *Astride*. Op. cit. *Jacket 2* and read the original manuscript in the Baroness archive at the University of Maryland Libraries.

[16]Baroness Elsa von Freytag-Loringhoven, *Aphrodite to Mars*. Op. cit. *Jacket 2* and read the original manuscript in the Baroness archive at the University of Maryland Libraries.

[17]Baroness Elsa von Freytag-Loringhoven from *Hell's Wisdom*. Op. cit. *Jacket 2* and read the original manuscript in the Baroness archive at the University of Maryland Libraries.

[18]Poetry Foundation: https://poetryfoundation.org/people/elsa-von-freytag-loringhoven

"Freytag-Loringhoven died on December 15, 1927, in Paris, France. A collection of her poems, *Body Sweats: The Uncensored Writing of Elsa von Freytag-Loringhoven*, was published posthumously in 2011. Her lover and editor Djuna Barnes preserved her papers, and the University of Maryland Libraries acquired a collection of her letters, poems, and other works. Her work was included in the Guggenheim's show *Exhibition by 31 Women* at the Art of This Century gallery in 1943."

[19]Op.cit Gammel 340.

Jed Rasula

Frederick Mortimer Clapp (1879-1969)

Frederick Mortimer Clapp, a New York native, earned advanced degrees from Yale and the Sorbonne, and had various teaching engagements before serving as an air force pilot in World War One. In 1926 he became chair of the art department at the University of Pittsburgh, and from 1931 until retirement in 1951 he was director of the Frick Collection in New York, overseeing the development of the museum from a private collection. As a scholar he was an expert on the Mannerist artist Pontormo. His wife was Italian, and the couple were lifelong friends of Robinson and Una Jeffers, who were in fact introduced to their beloved Carmel by Clapp. Clapp's early poetry is steeped in California, even as it repeatedly takes in various European locales along with his native city, where he ended up spending most of his life.

Clapp does not appear in the eclectically informative two-volume Library of America's *American Poetry, The Twentieth Century* (2000), with its zealous recovery of neglected figures (from both sides of the aesthetic aisle). Nor is he mentioned in any histories of American poetry from 1930 up to the present. He is a forgotten figure, and I've never met anyone who's even heard of him.

His collections are *On the Overland* (1916), *New York* (1918), *Joshua Trees* (1922), *New Poems* (1936), *Said Before Sunset* (1938), *Against a Background on Fire* (1943), *The Seeming Real* (1947), concluding with the book length poem *Cadenza in C Minor* (1957).

The publication gap between 1922 and 1936 reflects not only Clapp's growing professional obligations, it also marks two phases. In the latter four collections (published by Harper & Row) the poems rarely exceed a page, whereas the earlier poems are longer, with longer lines. Though by no means juvenilia, the first three collections reveal Clapp as a man of his generation, at ease with the postures of *fin de siècle* decadence (Benjamin de Casseres comes to mind, along with the delicately sour social observations of Clapp's unjustly forgotten contemporary, Donald Evans). As if a calling card, his first collection has an appendix of translations from Mallarmé. "The sand / of paths I walk with symbols quaintly teems," the young poet fancies (1916: 16); and in his fancy he imagines "a garden leprous with clots of fire" (1916: 62). "I am vibrant with serenity," he exhales (1916: 34), surveying the universe from "my jiggling dot of life" (1916: 25).

Clapp was recognized, early on, as a "vers-librist before vers-librists, imagist before the imagists"—meaning that he resisted formal verse measures, and (mostly) refrained from capitalizing the first words of lines. One reviewer recognized that, despite this seeming casualness, the poems contained "rhyme covertly distributed as bird-cries in terraces," creating an "intra-tonal" effect (Greenhood 338). Much later, the poet Ruth Lechlitner found his work "comparable to innovations in modern music," which gestures toward Schoenberg and the Vienna school, though possibly also American mavericks like Carl Ruggles and Henry Cowell (298). Clapp was keen on arranging chamber music recitals at the Frick, and makes repeated references to music in his poems, but rarely naming names. This propensity for withholding explicit references proved worrisome to some reviewers.

Clapp's later collections were respectfully reviewed, but with increasing consternation about the density of his poems. John Holmes—one of John Ciardi's mid-century clan of younger poets—tired of the "insistent hammering" in Clapp's "crackling, hurrying, angled, jabbing rhythms" (344). Another critic, while acknowledging "the astringent, severe, cacophonous shorthand of *The Seeming Real*," recognized that the poems "unfold a panorama conceived and maintained on a high level of abstraction" (Smith 361). This observation suggests that Clapp's work might be more manageably approached by readers familiar with the Objectivists, though of course Zukofsky and Oppen were barely recognized at that time. Other reviews from the Forties reveal certain assumptions about accessibility that set such work as Clapp's aside as non- or quasi-poetry—exercises in speculative thought, not affable disclosures or thematic puzzlers. Today, this may seem more like enticement than liability. In any case, he warned off the ascendant formalists of the time with his reference to "the edicts of cocksure high-hatters / that the matter's the essence of the form / and the form alone is what matters."

In going through their prescribed paces these
performing words this ink reveals,
is there something they ought to seize
known to no nose of circus-trained seals? (1947: 34)

Such artfully caustic reproach guaranteed his omission from the annals of contemporary poetry up to the present.

Clapp was the same age as Wallace Stevens, and if gathered into a single volume his poetry would be the size of Stevens's *Collected Poems*. I initially thought of him as swimming in the same current, with a gift for punctuating philosophical probing with fanciful postulations, albeit without Stevens's whimsy. Reading the poems in sequence lessens the comparison somewhat. Where Stevens tended to segregate personal views from his poems, Clapp can sound notes of aggravation and scathing social observation. In the end, both behaved somewhat decorously in their verse, even as they risked being stigmatized as modernist helots.

Both men share a fixation on "the never-resting mind" (in Stevens's "The Poems of Our Climate" [9]): mentation as touchstone but also troublesome in its submission to mechanisms of meaning. Stevens repeatedly configures it as the sun, obdurate and inhuman as rock. Clapp is more expansive, less doctrinaire (and Platonic), but more attuned to a mind's questionable authority. "I carry my mind like a falcon asleep on my wrist," he observes (1922: 39). Because "The mind can never be itself," he decides, "a man's mind is what he most must fear" (1936: 11, 28). For the seer, "The mind is a bowl of liquid light," making it possible to consider "the mind is its own lover" (1936: 70, 67). Mind is a counterweight to the "mindless atomic swarms interminable" with their "changing cycles of sameless change" (1938: 37, 41). If there is a mantra that emerges from all these deliberations, it's that "incubus of mind and succubus of things are one" (1947: 55).

The other poet comparable to Clapp is his friend Robinson Jeffers. Jeffers's penchant for narrative poems sets him apart from other modern Americans except Edwin Arlington Robinson, and there's barely a trace of storytelling in Clapp other than the occasional sharp observation that might be expanded (but rarely is). What makes the comparison compelling is Clapp's affinity for what Jeffers called "inhumanism" in his preface to *The Double Axe* (1948), "a shifting of emphasis from man to not-man." Inhumanism, Jeffers ventured, meant "the rejection of human solipsism and recognition of the transhuman magnificence," yielding nothing less than "objective truth and human value" (vii). That this outlook was in a book filled with screeds against the American involvement in both World Wars did not endear it to his publisher: Random House issued a disclaimer both in the text and on the dust jacket.

Clapp's version of inhumanism avoids the political pitfalls of Jeffers, largely because it extends far beyond earth to intergalactic realms— those "skies where time's the bobbin of a filament of space"—reflecting a sustained engagement with modern science to which Jeffers seemed indifferent.

> Unceasingly, as the neap-tide
> boundaries of time expand,
> a photon grazes milky ways
> so immense they seem to recede
> as they advance (1957: 5)

Such challenging prospects flit in and out of Clapp's verse, but he's capable of registering recognizable localities, where cosmic horizons penetrate the ordinary behavior of

those great dying swans
that, before the October rains begin,
slant out of halos of frost round a cold moon's light
and, southing, skim the mists of still warm lakes
wailing November. (1957: 33)

Clapp's observations of earthly affairs are registered with enviable precision, a testament to early appraisals of him as a proto-imagist. The coastal surf is "scratching and pawing like a trapped animal" as it "rolls long clatters of echoes / under a blotting hiss" (1943: 13). From the sky, we apprehend "the dumped thudding iron of thunder" (1938: 51).

Overall, Clapp's work charts (and marks as terrifying) the common adventure of life as a test of finitude. Ranging from the microbial to the galactic, his focal plane defies the usual parameters of modern American lyric. This can make for difficult reading, because Clapp's writing is compressed, not expansive. Nor is it very explicit about occasions, events, personal or topical prompts. One gets hints and glimpses of everyday life, but more often as if reported from the mind of a fish or a hummingbird— my analogy, not his. Rare are the occasions when a recognizable human setting comes into view, as in "Slum Dawn" (1947: 74):

Soon, beyond the patchwork of riffles and oil scum on the river,
beyond mops of smoke on factory chimneys,
dawn reaching out will erase the synchronous constellations
and with distributive indulgence bring
the dope of mechanical labor to hands and eyes
burred like magnetic filings along assembly lines

Even in this poem, though, Clapp characteristically swerves away from the concrete scene to the overarching determinate of the starry sky.

Glimpses of the gilded Park Avenue set appear as well, as when a bevy of matrons huddle enchanted around a purportedly wise man, as they "took their dust-bath of wisdom like birds" (1938: 4).

Such scenes and incidents are outliers, however. Time and again, the reader is challenged to even identify a time and place in the poems. This is not to suggest they're muddled or inefficient; rather, they lay claim to so many registers of experience and reflection all at once that they are, if anything, psycho-cosmic whirligigs—or, as he puts it in one poem's assessment of his own work, he eschews ivory and precious metals, going after "pig-iron liquid from the furnaces of living" (1936: 58). This analogy makes it clear that he has little interest in arranging the furniture of poems in the narrative, lyric, decorative ways prevalent during his lifetime, keen instead on capturing how "the spark-wink of your life flicks by" (1943: 61).

Clapp's final publication was a long poem in 83 numbered sections, *Cadenza in C Minor* (1957). Nearing eighty, the poem provides an indelible self portrait of "An old man, his arms looped like a lizard's tail / on the arms of his chair," while "A billion cells in him forget their tasks and sicken" (1957: 57). There's much in the poem about biological extremity, but it's also a work enlivened by the magnanimous curiosity Clapp had always brought to his work. It's a portrait of a mind alive with all its possibilities, reckoning with its past, and extending to its own termination.

We are nothing but the river.

So let such odds and ends of us ...
be pressed as the leaves of other ages have been
into an incubation of stone. (1957: 70)

70

Sources

Clapp, Frederick Mortimer, *On the Overland and Other Poems*. New Haven: Yale University Press, 1916.

———, *New York and Other Verses*. Boston: Marshall Jones, 1918.

———, *Joshua Tree*. Boston: Marshall Jones, 1922.

———, *New Poems*. New York: Harper, 1936.

———, *Said Before Sunset*. New York: Harper, 1938.

———, *Against a Background on Fire, 1948-1943*. New York: Harper, 1943.

———, *The Seeming Real*. New York: Harper, 1947.

———, *Cadenza in C Minor*. New York: Spiral Press, 1957.

Greenhead, David, "Without Devices," *Poetry: A Magazine of Verse* (September 1924), 336-339.

Holmes, John, "The Ear and the Mind," *Poetry: A Magazine of Verse* (September 1944), 343-346.

Jeffers, Robinson, *The Double Axe & Other Poems*. New York: Random House, 1948.

Lechlitner, Ruth, "An Intellectual Poet," *Poetry: A Magazine of Verse* (August 1938), 297-299.

Smith, Ray, "Seducing Contemplation," *Poetry: A Magazine of Verse* (March 1949), 360-362.

Stevens, Wallace, *Parts of a World*. New York: Knopf, 1942.

Frederick Mortimer Clapp

World as Fantasy

Roofs under trees a ground mist thins and flattens
come sharp an instant then blur out again
like consciousness that holds an argument
with the mood-hidden foliage of the mind:
inner and outer traceries outlined
on a counterpoint of forces that rack and twist the
  geometry of seeming.
    Nothing is made or meant
beyond the feigned coherence of the brain.
Today is but a yesterday refined
by an unlived tomorrow that flickers up to flee.
Yet something gropes within to make withoutness plain,
itself the mist, itself the mist-blurred roofs under these misty trees,
itself the sense of life's long senseless liturgies
for what will be become what was again.

(*Against a Background on Fire* p. 20)

Joel Lewis

Walter Lowenfels (1897-1976)

Walter Lowenfels's life had a Zelig-like aura. The scion of a butter-making family, he began his poetry career under the heavy shadow of T.S. Eliot, then left America to join the lively expat arts community in post-WW1 Paris. Once there, he worked as an apartment broker selling flats to clients like Tristan Tzara, hanging out with Henry Miller and starting the short-lived Anonymous Movement. He caught the Marxist bug as 20s prosperity gave way to the world Depression of the 30s and he and his family returned home to join the CPUSA (Communist Party USA). Within a few years, he stopped writing poetry, turning his energies towards journalism, eventually becoming the Pennsylvania editor of the CPUSA's *Daily Worker*. His political activities got him arrested at his home in Mays Landing, New Jersey in 1953, for violating the Smith Act. He was acquitted and slowly returned to poetry. By the 60s he was a well-known figure in the non-Academic, left-leaning poetry scene, primarily because of his many anthologies and his selected poems, issued by the prestigious Jargon imprint. The working title of his never-published autobiography seems to sum up his journey: "My Many Lives."

I discovered Lowenfels in 1978 while perusing a half-price bin at Strand Books through purchasing a selected volume called "The Portable Walter." Emerging from a left-political college world into the militantly apolitical scene at The Poetry Project in New York City, I found Lowenfels's soft-shoe left politics resonating with my own take on things. I soon acquired a small collection of Lowenfels's out-of-print work from the Gotham Book Mart and found his many anthologies in various used book bins. All of this interest finally culminated in my editing *Reality Prime: Selected Poems* for Talisman House in 1998, which remains the only in-print edition of Lowenfels's poetry.

Lowenfels was born in 1897 to a wealthy German Jewish family who owned Hotel Bar Butter—a well-known New York City brand that still exists today. An indifferent student with grades too underwhelming for college, he joined the family business until WW1 intervened and he enlisted in the Army. After the Armistice, he returned to the world of butterfat as well as beginning a poetry practice. His first published poem was a ballade to Edna St. Vincent Millay—the Taylor Swift of the 1920s—published in the popular "Conning Tower" column in the *Daily Mail*, an important venue for writers of light verse. His first book *Episodes and Epistles* (1925) reflects the proto-Modernism of popular poets like Sandburg and Masters, though the technical and industrial derived vocabulary of the poem "From an Exposition of Power and Industrial Machinery" anticipates Objectivist practices.

All this non-dairy based activity so worried Lowenfels's father that he paid for European passage so his dreamy son could be analyzed by Sigmund Freud in Vienna. Lowenfels took him up on the offer, but he skipped the visit to Vienna for the Modernist incubator that was Paris.

Lowenfels seemed to know everybody worth knowing in bohemian Paris and their influences moved the poet into the mature phase of his writing career. His major achievement as an expat poet was the *Some Deaths* trilogy which consists of: *Apollinaire an Elegy* (1930), *Elegy in the Manner of a Requiem in Memory of D.H. Lawrence* (1932), and *The Suicide* (1932). The background of these "philosophical elegies" was the poet's association with Henry Miller, Anais Nin, and Michael Frankael in the so-called "death school of writing." No doubt reflecting the world Depression that sent so many expats back home as their funding from the United States ran out, Lowenfels recalled this nihilist scrum towards the end of his life: "We had the idea the world was dead and that the only thing you could do was to write poems about it."

Lowenfels's turn to Marxism seems to have steered him away from his Woody Allenesque *mis-en-abime*. He began a serious study of Hegel and Marx and attended PCF (French Communist Party) rallies. By November

1934, he returned to the United States and to the family business. Lowenfels finally left the family enterprise in 1938 and moved his family to Philadelphia. He began working as a reporter for the *Daily Worker* and published his first volume of left-leaning poetry, *Steel 1937* (1938). This chapbook represents a fusion of advanced Modernist technique to a committed left-wing outlook. However, this is the last poetry that Lowenfels wrote until the early 50s.

Lowenfels eventually became the Pennsylvania editor of the *Daily Worker* and became immersed in the active Philadelphia CPUSA. In a page I found in his papers in the Beinecke Library at Yale, Lowenfels wrote about his 50th birthday—guests including Paul Robeson, Earl Robinson, Pete Seeger and members of the Weavers. He wondered what the guests would make of his years in Paris as a poet and literary provocateur—something none of his birthday guests knew about.

Lowenfels life was upended on July 23, 1953, when eight FBI men raided his Mays Landing, New Jersey home at 2 a.m. He was charged with violating the Smith Act, which made membership in the CPUSA illegal. Allowed to take one book with him to jail, he brought an unabridged *Leaves of Grass*. He was convicted after a six-month trial and given a two-year sentence, which was overturned on appeal in 1957. His wife, Lilian, at the same time, had been fired from her job as a Philadelphia schoolteacher as part of a purge of Communists in the city's school system.

His first two books post-arrest reflect both a return to traditional forms and the politics of the Party during the McCarthy era. The beginnings of his late style can be found in *American Voices* (1953). The French PCF poet Louis Aragon praised Lowenfels's composition: "The lines of the author alternate with a sort of prose counterpoint made up of letters from readers printed in newspapers all over the country."

Lowenfels, unlike many CPUSA members, stayed in the party after Khruschev's revelations of Stalin's crimes. However, he focused on literary matters, including an open letter to Nikita Khruschev in *New World Review* (a CPUSA journal) criticizing the Zhdanovist cultural policies of the USSR (policies that required art works conform to party lines). Lowenfels came into wider literary view with the anthologies *Walt Whitman's Civil War* (1960) and *Selections from Leaves of Grass* (1961). Coming out during the centennial commemoration of the War Between the States, both books sold well, with the former still in print.

These books would mark the beginning of his career as an anthologist, which accounted for his visibility in the poetry world and was his primary source of income. *The Poets of Today: A New American Anthology* (1964) was a popular volume that still turns up as a used book. It is a snapshot of non-Academic American poetry, with Lowenfels mixing Spanish Civil War veterans like Ray Durem and Alvah Bessie with Beat poets like Gregory Corso and Lawrence Ferlinghetti. Lowenfels also included little known and little published poets whose work appealed to him. The through line in the collection was the social angle. Lowenfels also edited groundbreaking anthologies of Black poetry and Native American poetry published by major publishers with the overarching goal of ending the "white poetry syndicate" of his time. Lowenfels was always insistent that these anthologies were part of his overall literary project.

The Jargon selected poems, *Some Deaths* (1964), brought Lowenfels to the attention of the poetry community that coalesced around Donald Allen's anthology *The New American Poetry*. Lowenfels was part of a rediscovery and reclamation of forgotten poets of the Modernist-era such as the Objectivists, H.D., Basil Bunting, and Weldon Kees.

Lowenfels gained additional general visibility as a poet with his anthology *Where is Vietnam?* published by Doubleday in 1967. It was a popular book for a large anti-war community whose demonstrations often featured poets at the podium. The *Portable Walter* was also issued in this period, issued with a psychedelic cover that stood out from somber tomes issued by the CPUSA's International Publishers. The anthology was a useful selection of his prose and poetry that focused on his post-arrest writings.

Two of his best late books, *To an Imaginary Daughter* (1964) and

The Revolution is To Be Human (1973), are prose works. Both are broad meditations on life, the arts and politics that collage correspondence, memoir, and essay. Yet, some of the poet's late projects did not see publication. His memoir *My Many Lives* only appeared as excerpts in chapbooks. There is no selection of his voluminous correspondence. His family told me of his disappointment that his massive prose collage of primary sources outlining the dark side of the American Dream, *Autobiography of an Empire* was unable to find a publisher after its intended publisher, Stonehill Press, went bankrupt. His last anthology, *For Neruda, For Chile* appeared a year before his death on 7 July 1976.

Lowenfels's *neglecterino* status is many-fold. His publication history was mostly with very small presses of variable distribution. His poetry does not fit into any specific school—in some ways his antecedents are surrealism, Paul Eluard, and Walt Whitman. American Modernism seems to have slipped past him—he writes of only discovering William Carlos Williams in the late 40s, despite having met the Doctor in Paris in the 20s. Unlike most left-wing poets, his poetry is of the middle voice and decidedly undidactic.

So why should a contemporary poet investigate Lowenfels? First, he is a terrific and original poet. His use of found materials, letters, documentary material, and collage anticipates current practice. Politically engaged poets might find a model of political poetry that is less confrontational and more imbedded in a tradition of Marxist Utopianism like that of philosopher Ernst Bloch. And for a male poet born in 1897, his poetry is remarkably free of the racial cant, Anti-Semitism, and misogyny of his generation. Additionally, no anthologist of his era did more to expose a reading audience to the vast multi-racial/multiethnic poetry communities that existed outside the shuttered gates of Academic poetry. Additionally, how can you not want to read a poet who declared: "The truth about socialism is that it's more fun"?

WALTER LOWENFELS

STEEL

What is it?A commodity?
an object of exchange? a process for reducing
the building of people and of things
to balances in the bank and sweat and blood?
Out of the earth bellyout of the September womb
crisis in embryo murderer of bodies
exploder of dreams we put together again.
Steel file that rasps against the bodies
gnaws us to hungry teeth
walking stomachs of the time
swollen bellies flopping against steel walls that hold us in.
And if it weren't steel what would it be?
We call it steelcell block of the world
prisoners of the age
in the prison of the age
and we measure all the freedom of our time.
But in our hands elsewhere and in our heads
it is a different thing
and we say the world shines tomorrow like steel in the sun.

GIAN LOMBARDO

LOST IN THE FUN HOUSE:
THE ART OF HARRY CROSBY (1898-1929)

There are many reasons why Harry Crosby is what may be termed a neglected poet. Some are valid; some spurious. One of the key players of the early twentieth century expatriate Modernist movement of American writers in France, he is the least known, or read, today. A glance at the index of Hugh Kenner's *The Pound Era*—a primer of sorts on that movement—shows absolutely no mention of him, which is inexplicable, on one level, since Pound wrote an Afterword to *Torchbearer*, a posthumous collection of Crosby's prose poems.

Harry Crosby was born at the tail end of the nineteenth century, a scion of the Boston Brahmin and a nephew of J. P. Morgan Jr. When the Great War broke out, he volunteered for the American Ambulance Service. For his service, he was awarded the Croix de Guerre. He returned home a hero in his eyes and finished off a degree from Harvard. But he grew very weary of prim Bostonian ways and fell for a married woman. He finally convinced Polly Peabody to divorce her husband and marry him. Together they fled Boston for the heart of Paris. Crosby situated himself among the American expatriate writers there, where he and Polly, now renamed Caresse, led an increasingly dissolute life of sex and drugs. They had an open marriage and held orgies at their residence.

Harry quit a job at a French bank associated with his uncle J. P. and lived off advances on his inheritance. Those monies funded his extravagant lifestyle and, also, his publishing ventures. The Crosbys started Éditions Narcisse in 1927, which morphed into their Black Sun Press the following year. Their list was a who's-who of expatriates: James Joyce, Hart Crane, Kay Boyle, Ernest Hemingway, D. H. Lawrence, and Ezra Pound, among many others. They were also involved with Eugene Jolas's avant-garde journal *transition*. At this point in his career, Crosby was at the center of literature. Not only of the English-speaking expatriates but also of the current French writers—mainly exponents of Dadaism and Surrealism. He was very much the French aesthete. And very much the purveyor (or pervert?) of hedonism. Pleasure—whether sexual, aesthetic, sensual or intellectual—was the hallmark of a Crosbian lifestyle. This hedonism also runs counter to the grand American tradition of stoicism, Puritanism (and Calvinism) and the ethic of hard work.

Both Harry and Caresse took on many lovers. Around this time Crosby met Josephine Rotch and embarked on what can best be called a cliched torrid affair that was supposed to end with her marriage to Albert Bigelow back in the States. Months later, in November 1929, Crosby returned to the States with Caresse and revived his affair with Josephine. Their passion culminated in mutually voiced desires to die with one another. Crosby fed that desire by murdering Josephine with a gunshot to the head, and then turned the gun on himself and took his life as well on December 10, 1929.

Given Crosby's social station, this murder-suicide made sensational news at a time when the Roaring 20s were coming to an inelegant close signaled by the collapse of the stock market. Crosby became notorious. American literature is littered with suicides. If anything, taking one's own life is not seen as an impediment to establishing a lasting mark, or reputation, in American letters. However, with American writers, or writers of any sort, there are few, if any, intentional murderers. On one level, that is one of the first strikes against Crosby. After all, who wants to exalt murder for any reason? The act is repugnant. Of that, there is no dispute. How does one then reconcile the perpetrator of an evil act, however misguided in its desire to prove one's love, with the perpretator's writings? It's an uncomfortable ethical situation. By acknowledging the work's value does one then exonerate any nefarious deed by the writer? That generation, and those writers, are rife with problematic writers, most notably Ezra Pound, but anti-Semitism, misogyny and homophobia were rampant among many Modernist (and expatriate) writers of the period. How does one handle the toxicity of their personalities with the output of their personalities? Murder tends to be more cut-and-dry.

But there are also other reasons Crosby's work has been shunted into ignobility and oblivion. These considerations move more in the area of literary and aesthetic considerations. Crosby immersed himself in the culture and letters of his time and place, which as noted put him squarely among the Dadaists and Surrealists. He not only read those French writers in the original, he also moved among them socially. He became part of their movement. And Crosby was not unaware of the pollination both ways across the American/French divide. One of his first publishing projects was to produce a limited illustrated edition of Poe's *The Fall of the House of Usher*. Poe had some influence on Baudelaire, and Lautréamont. Baudelaire then influenced a slew of later 19th- and early 20th-century French writers, including Mallarmé's Symbolism, which in turn influenced the American Modernists, chief among them Eliot. There has always been a dominant strain of Anglophilia in American letters. It has been, more often than not, far more preferable to have British antecedents, referents and influence than other languages or cultures. The States might have won political and economic independence, but we have this long streak of cultural dependence on the British Empire. This Anglophilia has also been compounded by the long-standing political enmity between Britain and France. There's a long-standing view that showing signs of French influence is suspect and a weakness of American writers.

One problem area for Crosby is that he really eschewed the formalities of American verse. The vast bulk of his poetry consisted of prose poetry (again, a suspect French form), and found poetry (telephone directories, racing forms, etc.). He shunned formal verse forms, and even shied away from syllabic, free verse and blank verse. If anything, Crosby can be seen, historically, as the first American prose poet. Yes, there were other noted works of prose poetry by Americans during that period—Stern's *Tender Buttons* and Williams's *Kora in Hell*—but Crosby was unique in that greater majority of his work was prose poetry. While that "form" of poetry had a tradition of nigh a hundred years by the time Crosby began writing,

81

in English there was no critical apparatus established to accommodate and evaluate prose poetry in American or British letters. It was not an accepted form to work in, mainly because there was no Anglo tradition (however short) with prose poetry. The usual refrain: It was outside the American/British tradition.

Another constraint on Crosby's work is his religiosity. Normally, if working within the Anglo-Christian tradition, this would be seen as a positive characteristic. However, the religious strain that Crosby milks is a distinctly pagan one: He worships the Sun. Following the tradition of the Egyptian sun god, Ra, many of Crosby's poems and prose poems— especially in his earlier works—are paeans to the Sun. They are eminently liturgical and proclaim their intent to proselytize unabashedly. Just another instance of Crosby working against the grain of the prevailing culture.

One thing also not working in Crosby's favor in rehabilitating his reputation is that lately he has become the poster boy of a small but vocal portion of the extremist right-wing political (and cultural) movement in the States. Crosby's disdain for the poor and the common person and the weak, has been appropriated by white supremacist groups such as the Poor Boys. They have glommed onto one aspect of Crosby's reputational persona. Where one goes online looking for environments that provide an honest discussion of Crosby's work, one must be very judicious in examining the membership of that environment.

The last criterion working against greater recognition of Crosby's work is the weight of the critic on Crosby's work itself. But in this domain, not enough is said of the critical biases working against Crosby through the 20th century. These biases are reflected in the attitudes mentioned above: Crosby's a murderer, profligate, licentious, privileged son-of-a-bitch, French *arriviste*, prose poet. Getting an objective analysis of his work can be a difficult proposition given all the baggage his name and personality carry. It must be noted that Ezra Pound never gave Crosby the advice he gave James Laughlin—namely, to forsake the writing of poetry for the publishing of poetry. (As noted, Pound did pen the Afterword to the posthumous *Torchbearer*.) Overall, critical analyses of his work has been unkind. At best, considered a minor poet with occasional sparks of ingenuity. At worst, a poetaster of the highest order. In this instance, Crosby might voice a familiar French saying, *"chacun à son goût,"* and toast his detractors with champagne. Granted, some of the criticisms hold water. Crosby was well read of his contemporaries—British, American, and French—and he learned his poetic craft by imitation.

From his readings, and his social associations, Crosby learned a number of techniques that he put to good use in his (mainly) prose poems that he gleaned from the French Surrealists. The first stepping-stone, as it were, was the concept of "automatic writing"—that the words should flow from the psyche to paper without editorial intervention of what the burgeoning psychologists of the day would call the ego and superego. To tap the realm of the subconscious. A lot of his early work shows him learning how to turn off the censorship of the self. His versions of his "Sun-Testament" are good examples of him sharpening that technique.

Yet automatic writing led him to an additional important Surrealistic technique of dream writing. Espoused mainly by Robert Desnos, two of Crosby's most complete (aesthetically) books—*Sleeping Together* and *Torchbearer*—are fairly masterful explorations into dream-writing. *Sleeping Together* exists in a prototype form as *Dreams 1928-1929*, published in the journal *transition*. This draft is closest to automatic dream writing without any editorial intervention. In *Sleeping Together*, Crosby did place some editorial framework on top of the dreamwork, but ultimately the dreamscape predominates. In a "Game of Tag" the dream narrative, and its attendant cascade of images, becomes overlaid with a more editorial afterthought about French painting:

GAME OF TAG

     I am astonished at the remarkable erudition of the art
     critic who is seated upon a high mountain of catalogues
     from which he is haranguing a regiment of spectacled

students on the superiority of contemporary French painters over the masters of the past. He is bold and daring in his assertions. He is eloquence at its zenith. But I prefer to go on with a game of tag which I am playing with you on the hot sands of a beach feeling the electric touch of your fingers on my naked shoulders, hearing the hilarity of mockery in your laughter, pursuing the mad impulsiveness of your body as you dodge back and forth like white strokes from the brush of an artist.

Crosby also, following the French writers of the time, plays with attaching imagery with narrative (or possibly appending narrative to imagery) to create quasi-logical constructions that challenge logic:

ANIMAL MAGNETISM

All the sailors are laughing. It is contagious. All the whores are yawning. It is contagious. And all night long we wear ourselves out trying to laugh and yawn at one and the same time.

In *Sleeping Together*, Crosby elevates what was originally more simple —the just automatic dream writing to a more complex frame of a varying perspective. While the dream is the core of the book, how it matters most directly is how the dream impinges on "real" life and vice versa. The reader sees a narrator appear, though thoroughly welded into the dream:

CAT

I am a lean Siamese cat who insists upon sleeping under our bed in order to watch the mouse-holes so I am not as astonished as you are when I wake up next morning to find myself under our bed.

In other prose poems, the "real" world of the awakened person makes a more direct intrusion on the dream, much like a deep-sea diver emerging on the surface of the water:

I BREAK WITH THE PAST

In a hot office building a man is dictating a letter to a bright-eyed stenographer who has just graduated from the College of Progress. Dear Madam I regret to inform you that your swans have sleeping-sickness, but I am far away in the country wandering across the golf links your bright-colored scarf around my neck. I cannot seem to find you. I look into every bunker. I ask the caddy with the gluttonous face. I call out loud to the birds. I keep remembering how good-looking you are with your bedroom eyes and your new-moon ears. I begin to run. It is growing late for the red wolf of the sun has almost disappeared into his cavern of night. I run over the wooden bridge. I break with the past and race into the future over the far end of the links feeling myself fly through the air towards two sensations of light which turn out to be your eyes. When I wake up I am as tired as a marathon runner.

The other key Surrealist technique Crosby learned (some would say appropriated) is the collision of images, starting with at least the conjoining of two disparate images to initiate a spark. Crosby is instructive, historically, to see both the development and use of the prose poem over a career (even though admittedly an abbreviated one), but also historically to see how he established a vein of American poetry founded in French Surrealist precepts that get evinced in Michael Benedikt, Phillip Lamantia, and George Kalamaras, among others. While the language of the posthumous *Torchbearer* is still entrenched in the dream world, the interplay of image takes precedence over the interplay of narrative. In addition, Crosby becomes more forthcoming on what he is attempting:

UNLEASH THE HOUNDS

They play at their game of croquet but there is no
queen to shout "get to your places" no hedgehogs for balls
no live flamingos for mallets no soldiers to stand upon
their hands and feet to make the arches—so is the game
of life a very ordinary game unless we unleash the hounds
of imagination.

And Crosby expresses more directly what he expects from the reader:

COLLISION

The accidental collision of motes in the sun is symbolic
of the accidental collision of thoughts in the brain—there
is perhaps an orchestral magnificence in these collisions—
he who has ears to hear let him hear.

One can only speculate on where Crosby could have gone, and
accomplished, as a poet and a publisher. Furthermore, with his deep
and fundamental understanding of French why he did not attempt to
translate French literature. He ended his life and another before either
had really begun to flower. From the detritus of the wide array of images
and possibilities Crosby left us, one can judge and, also, one can dream,
"What if…":

THE END OF EUROPE

The shattered hull of a rowboat stuck in the sand a fire
of driftwood a bottle of black wine black beetles the weird
cry of sea-gulls lost in the heavy fog the sound of the tide
creeping in over the wet sands the tombstone in the eel-
grass behind the dunes.

ROSANNA WARREN

THE ENDURING GIFT:
LAURA RIDING (1901-1991) AND THE TRUTH OF POEMS

"Forgive me, giver, if I destroy the gift!
It is so nearly what would please me,
I cannot but perfect it."
　　　Laura Riding, "Echoes"

Laura Riding's life can be read as a series of destructions, and her poetry is a miracle smelted out of destruction. As she suggests in her poem "Echoes," she did "destroy the gift," or at least abandoned it, but in doing so she created some of the most radical and original poetry of the 20th century. She created it almost in spite of herself and yet out of her own central necessity. She was an absolutist, a purist, authoritarian and dogmatic. She "renounced" poetry halfway through her life and then spent decades composing a hermetic, wildly arbitrary study of language that was published only after her death. She is remembered and, in some quarters, revered as a poet, and was honored by the Bollingen Prize in 1991 at the age of ninety.

The destructions begin with her names. She was born Laura Reichenthal in 1901 to poor, Jewish, immigrant parents in the garment district in New York City. In 1920, as an undergraduate student at Cornell, she married a young instructor in history and became Laura Reichenthal Gottschalk. When she began publishing poems in journals three years later, she changed "Reichenthal" to the distinctly less Jewish "Riding," signing her work Laura Riding Gottschalk. But in 1925 she left Lou Gottschalk, by then an assistant professor at the University of Kentucky at Louisville, and she spent a few hectic months in Greenwich Village where her friend Hart Crane christened her "Laura Riding Roughshod"; in December she moved to England, entering a *ménage à trois* with Robert Graves and his wife Nancy Nicholson. Her first book of poems, *The Close Chaplet*, came out in England and the United States in 1926 under the name Laura Riding Gottschalk, but for the next fourteen years she produced a torrent of poetry, critical essays, and fiction signed "Laura Riding." The Graves/ Nicholson/ Riding household (dubbed "The Trinity") broke up spectacularly in 1929 with Riding flinging herself out of a third story window and barely surviving the fractures to her skull and spine; she and Graves withdrew to Mallorca, continuing their fervent literary collaboration until the Spanish Civil war drove them out.

Laura Riding kept moulting. In 1939, she and Graves took refuge in the United States from the outbreak of World War II. Almost immediately, in another extravagant rearrangement of dramatis personae, Riding fell in love with their common friend the American critic and gentleman farmer Schuyler Jackson. Graves returned to England, and when Riding and Jackson married in 1941, she became Laura Jackson. Nor was that her final name; in 1963 she adopted the authorial identity of Laura (Riding) Jackson for the prose she continued to publish and the reprints of poems she began to allow.

In 1926, when John Crowe Ransom, the eminent poet, critic, professor of English at Vanderbilt University, and an elder member of the Fugitive group, sent Robert Graves a batch of Riding's poems, he praised Riding as "a brilliant young woman," but warned that "she tries perhaps to put more into poetry than it will bear" (Friedmann, 75). The same could be said of her demands on human relations. Ransom had divined something essential in Riding's nature; his remark would prove prophetic. Riding's initiation into literary life came about through the Fugitives, that intense group of poet-critics who had gathered in Nashville around Ransom and Donald Davison and launched one of the most sophisticated literary magazines in the country, *The Fugitive*. Riding's poems began to appear in their pages in 1923. In 1924 she was ecstatic when they awarded her the "Nashville Prize," and in November she traveled from Louisville to Nashville to read her poems in their company. One of their younger members, the poet Allen Tate, had already made his way to Louisville;

he and Mrs. Gottschalk—aged twenty-three—had a brief fling whose vicissitudes she chronicled in a series of poems. Those poems are of interest not as romantic gossip but because they show how rapidly Riding absorbed and then burned through the emerging New Critical aesthetics of the Fugitives. Both pleading and attacking, in "To a Loveless Lover" she addresses Tate as a "lyric crow" who "may come and perch/ …not to sing/ But consecrate to your pedantic church/ His ultra-polite yet energetic wing/ That flaps your piety incognito" (Riding 1938/1980, 38). Laura Riding soon left Louisville, Nashville, and the Fugitives behind, and was on her way to Greenwich Village and England.

What was it that Riding tried so strenuously to "put into poetry"? The key word is "truth." Her related terms, "reality" and "whole," suggest the scale of her ambition and the reasons why, by 1940, she had given up on poetry as an adequate instrument. Her preface to her 1938 *Collected Poems* presents her vision at that juncture and hints at her messianic tendency: "A poem is an uncovering of truth of so fundamental and general a kind that no other name besides poetry is adequate except truth" (Riding 1938/1980, 484). Nor will she be satisfied with anything less than "the whole": "Truth is the result when reality as a whole is uncovered by those faculties which apprehend in terms of entirety, rather than in terms merely of parts" (Riding 1938/1980, 484). It's clear to her that "the history of poem-writing and poem-reading is in large part a history" of "corruption" (Riding 1938/1980, 485); in 1938 she sees herself as a kind of priestess, "taking upon herself voluntarily a large share of the work of the world, or of poetry" (Riding 1938/1980, 486). Riding inspired a cult-like devotion from Graves and their entourage in London and in Mallorca; without irony, she likens herself to Saint Francis of Assisi, insisting on "the Rule for His Order" "literally, literally, literally" (Riding 1938/1980, 491).

That literalism led to her discarding poetry and to her long labors with Schuyler Jackson, and after his death, alone, on a revolutionary dictionary which was to prove, she wrote in 1980, "my commitment to a universal linguistic solution" (Riding 1938/1980, xxxix). The dictionary having run aground, the Jacksons turned it into the quixotic and stunningly turgid treatise in linguistics, *Rational Meaning: A New Foundation for the Definition of Words*, their attempt to eliminate ambiguity from language and stabilize "truth" once and for all, an endeavor they undertook in blithe disregard for all modern linguistics and philosophy: Peirce, Wittgenstein, Saussure, and Austin (hardly named or referred to) all fall short.((Riding) Jackson and Schuyler Jackson, 1997). In a related text, "The Telling," which she called her "personal evangel," published in 1967, Riding swats away the whole history of thought to make room for the one revelation: "Religion, philosophy, history, poetry" and "science" tell us "nothing" ((Riding) Jackson 2005, 339.) The closest analogy to the Jacksons' project is the effort of the Royal Society in Britain in the seventeenth century, by Bishop Spratt, Hobbes, and others, to eliminate metaphor as "an abuse of speech" in favor of an ideal of "mathematical plainness" (Hequembourg, 83-112). Riding's view of her work in the 1980 Preface to her *Collected Poems* touches on megalomania: "There has been no recognition at all of the unchallengeable logic of my linguistic position" (Riding 1939/1980, xli).

Why, then, read Laura Riding? Because in her extremism, the pressure she put on words crystallized into a few extraordinary poems and a good many extraordinary lines. I set aside her argumentative prose, and I detach the poems from the melodrama of her personality and her life. I am left with an essence, an astonishment. It's no wonder that the young Auden thrilled to her strangeness, or that years later John Ashbery devoted one of his Norton Lectures at Harvard to her. Look at these lines: each one strikes a match.

"The sun is used. The men are in the book." ("The Tiger," in Riding 1938/1980, 57)

"Weather is the dead at the hard school." ("It Is Not so Sad," Riding 1938/1980, 225)

"And death became contemporary." ("Memories of Mortalities," Riding 1938/1980, 281)

But let's consider a whole, mysterious, fully-fashioned poem. "Beyond" reflects Riding's near-suicide in her leap from the window in 1929 and her painful convalescence. It also reflects the period when she was inspired by Gertrude Stein, whose "Composition as Explanation" was published by the Woolfs' Hogarth Press in 1926, the same year they brought out Riding's *The Close Chaplet*. In an essay celebrating Stein in 1927, Riding took umbrage at T.S. Eliot's dismissal of her as "of the barbarians," and rescued the word as praise: "Does no one but Miss Stein realize that to be abstract, mathematical, thematic, anti-Hellenic, anti-Renaissancist, anti-Romantic, we must be barbaric?" (Riding 2014, 78). She quoted Stein's generative repetitions from "Composition as Explanation," and imitated the method as she described Stein's style: "This is repetition and continuousness and beginning again and again and again" (Riding 2014, 83).

In the flush of this enthusiasm, Riding and Graves published Stein's *An Acquaintance with Description* in their Seizin Press early in 1929 before the window-drama of April 27. Graves cabled Stein in Paris the day of Riding's fall, and Stein replied immediately with visionary sympathy: "It will make Laura a very wonderful person, in a strange way, a destruction and recreation of her purification" (Friedmann, 142). Graves was even more exalted in his interpretation, telling his family that Laura was "seamless, like the garment of Christ" (Friedmann, 142).

As Riding came slowly back from the dead, she stripped her poetry to elemental bareness. "Beyond" speaks from the other side of life, the other side of language. It takes for its theme not physical pain, but the predicament of communication "beyond" the boundaries of normal language: a poetics of impossibility which remains, nevertheless, a poetics.

Beyond

Pain is impossible to describe
Pain is the impossibility of describing
Describing what is impossible to describe
Which must be a thing beyond description
Beyond description not to be known
Beyond knowing but not mystery
Not mystery but pain not plain but pain
But pain beyond but here beyond

Casting off metaphor, simile, phonetic play, and punctuation, "Beyond" in its violent simplicity concentrates on syntax; juggling of parts of speech; abstraction; repetition that moves the thought forward like a wheel revolving; and the mantra-like chant of the construction Not/But. It discovers a paradoxical realm ("here beyond") and an almost transcendental language.

Fortunately for lovers of poetry, Laura (Riding) Jackson didn't destroy her poems when she abandoned poetry for linguistics and an oracular philosophy. Her poems outlive her, and remain as surprising, revelatory and outlandish today as when she wrote them.

Sources

John Ashbery, *Other Traditions* (Cambridge: Harvard University Press, 2000), 95-120

Elizabeth Friedmann, *A Mannered Grace: The Life of Laura (Riding) Jackson* (New York: Persea Books, 2005)

Stephen Hequembourg, "The Dream of a Literal World: Wilkins, Hobbes, Marvell," in *ELH*, v. 81, n. 1, Spring 2014, 83-112

Laura (Riding) Jackson, *The Laura (Riding) Jackson Reader*, ed. Elizabeth Friedmann (New York: Persea Books, 2005)

Laura (Riding) Jackson and Schuyler B. Jackson, *Rational Meaning: A New Foundation for the Definition of Words*, ed. William Harmon, introduction by Charles Bernstein (Charlottesville: University Press of Virginia, 1997)

Laura Riding, *The Poems of Laura Riding, Newly Revised Edition of the 1938/1980 Collection*, ed. Mark Jacobs (New York: Persea Books, 2001)

Laura Riding, "T.E. Hulme, the New Barbarians, and Gertrude Stein," in Riding, *Contemporaries and Snobs* (London: Jonathan Cape, 1928); reprinted in 2014, ed. Laura Heffernan and Jane Malcolm (Tuscaloosa: University of Alabama Press, 2014), 78. Riding's essay first appeared in *transition* and in 1927 was expanded as the Conclusion to the critical book she wrote with Graves, *A Survey of Modern Poetry*.

Julie R. Enszer

Marcia Nardi (1901-1990)

I first encountered Marcia Nardi in a footnote. In the epic poem *Paterson*, William Carlos Williams adapts letters from Marcia Nardi to introduce a woman's voice into his polyphonic text. In the opening section, Williams includes these lines, "In regard to the poems I left with you; will you be so kind as to return them to me at my new address? And without bothering to comment upon them if you should find that embarrassing—for it was the human situation and not the literary one that motivated my phone call and visit." When *Paterson* was originally published in four parts between 1946 and 1951,[1] Williams's use of Nardi's letters was not known. Mike Weaver's 1971 biography of William Carlos Williams brought attention to Nardi's letters. I learned about Marcia Nardi through Christopher MacGowan's extensive footnotes in the New Directions edition of *Paterson*. These footnotes opened a door into Nardi's world. In *The Last Word: Letters between Marcia Nardi & William Carlos Williams,* Elizabeth Murrie O'Neil expertly pieces together Nardi's life and poetic accomplishments.

Marcia Nardi was born in Boston, MA on August 6, 1901, and given the name Lillian Massell. She attended Wellesley College from 1919 through 1921, leaving during her junior year before graduating. She moved to Greenwich Village and lived at one time in the same rooming house as Allen Tate and Hart Crane. Nardi seems to be writing regularly and publishing between 1924 and 1929. She works for the *Modern Quarterly* in Baltimore for a short time and has three poems published in the journal. She also has poems published in *Measure, Bookman*, and the *Nation*. She also wrote reviews during this period, including a review of H.D.'s *Heliodora*. Her son, Paul, is born on October 23, 1926. She never divulged the name of her son's father. Throughout the Great Depression, Nardi works a variety of jobs in New York City to support herself and her son.

As a result of a medical issue with Paul, Nardi met William Carlos

Williams in 1942 through a connection established by Nardi's neighbor, Harvey Breit. This meeting began their correspondence and friendship. Nardi and Williams corresponded sporadically from 1942 until 1956. Williams provided professional assistance for Paul, and he also corresponded with Nardi and aided her in making literary connections. At Williams's behest, seventeen of Nardi's poems were published in New Directions Number Seven anthology. Shortly after their initial meeting and Nardi granting Williams permission to use one of her earlier letters in *Paterson*, the two lost contact.

In 1949 after seeing *Paterson* I and II at a local bookstore near Woodstock, New York, where she was living with her husband, Charles John Lang, a writer and painter, Nardi wrote to Williams again. Nardi and Williams corresponded sporadically between 1949 and 1956. In her letters to Willliams, Nardi wrote extensively about both her social and literary isolation—and even beyond the excerpts of her letters included in *Paterson* wrote eloquently about her plight as a woman artist. At various times, Williams sent Nardi money and provided assistance to her in making literary connections. One of the final things he did for Nardi was serve as a reference for a Guggenheim fellowship; she received one in the spring of 1957.

Nardi lived near Woodstock with Lang until 1950 when she left him and went to New York. The publisher A. Swallow published her full-length collection, *Poems*, in 1956. For the next two decades, Nardi published her poems in a variety of places—and using different names—including *Ladies Home Journal*, *Poetry*, *American Scholar*, and *The New Yorker*.

Unlike the multiple volumes of work that Williams produced, Nardi's output was modest. Twenty-two poems in her 1956 collection, *Poems,* which does not include all her work prior to 1956 likely a dozen additional, earlier poems. Her long poem "In the Asylum" was published in *Botteghe Oscure* in 1950. She continued producing poems and publishing them well into the 1970s. Nardi often lived in abject poverty; for many years, she struggled to support herself and her son. She died on March 13, 1990,

95

in Watertown, MA.

Nardi is a forgotten poet, today nearly completely out of print. She is also, depending on perspective, a muse or a victim. Although Nardi granted Williams permission to use the letters, his use of her words as his own in *Paterson* can be understood as a usurpation of both her words and her experience. She can also be seen, with some squinting, as a muse to Williams inspiring the completion of his master work. When I first encountered Nardi, I was outraged by Williams's actions and viewed her as a victim. Now I see her life and her work as congruent with her own aspirations and assessment; she described herself to O'Neil as "a woman poet determined to experience life for herself and to find a poetic form in which to express what is uniquely a woman's experience" (234). I also see her as constrained, profoundly, by the material conditions that shaped women's lives, particularly poor and single women's lives, during the twentieth century.

While Nardi's poetic output is modest compared to other mid-century poets, both men and women, her poems deserve consideration on their artistic merits as well as for what they illuminate politically about this time. Here is a woman, a single mother, struggling to support herself and her child, giving voice to her experiences and writing with both anger and beauty and grace about the economic conditions of her life and placing her life in a broader literary and material context. For example, in "October House Guest," Nardi writes about friends preparing to travel abroad and reflects on "how small my soul has become" because of the "tiny niche" where she lives and the lack of pathways for her mind. Poverty with its small spaces and lack of mental, spiritual, and emotional stimulation constrained the poet and Nardi lays it bare. In another poem, "How the Rich Move Softly," Nardi notes how wealthy people move "through their injustices" and spread their arms "to grab and stab and kill." Then cover up their plunders and "make so beautiful the cruelty."

Nardi writing about class is congruent with other women writers working during the 1930s.[2] Her poetry is thematically in conversation

96

with novels like Tess Slesinger's *The Unpossessed*, Meridel Le Seuer's *The Girl*, Josephine Herbst's *Rope of Gold*, and Tillie Olsen's *Yonnondio* as well as the poetry of Muriel Rukeyser, Genevieve Taggard, and Margaret Walker.

In "Love I Make It Because I Write It," Nardi reflects on "love untold and denied." She says, "The thrust is the same…snatch the name." I wonder, did Nardi regard Williams as snatching her name? Or suppressing her name? While he suppressed her name in his own work, he was also an advocate and supporter, and Nardi continued their correspondence for many years.

Through the viewable fragments from Nardi—her poems and her letters to Williams—emerge two visions of Nardi. A woman deeply committed to poetry and to living the life of a poet and a woman clear-eyed and angry about the conditions of poverty and oppression that shaped her life. In the letters, Nardi is both vulnerable and self-disclosing, and she writes as a sharp and sardonic social critic. In the poems, she alchemizes her experience and anger into sublime poetic moments. It is not kind but true to note that at different times she was angry, irascible, difficult, and obnoxious.

Nardi's capacity to occupy these emotions and to transform them into poetry is part of what I love about her. Marcia Nardi exposes a vulnerable, fearful inner life that is never eclipsed by triumph in any measure. She chided Williams that when her "actual personal life crept in, stamped all over with the *very same* attitudes and sensibilities and preoccupations that you found quite admirable as *literature*—that was an entirely different matter, wasn't it?" (87) She told him that her life and its difficulties is "something to be remembered at all times, especially by writers like yourself who are so sheltered from life in the raw by the glass-walled conditions of their own safe lives."[3] Nardi insisted on speaking truth to power and that Williams see her in her messy fullness. She continued saying about her poetry, "Only my writing (when I write) is myself: only that is the real me in any essential way. Not because I bring to literature and to life two different inconsistent sets of values, as you do. No, *I* don't

97

do that; and I feel that when anyone does do it, literature is turned into just so much intellectual excrement fit for the same stinking hole as any other kind." Difficult but committed to her work as a poet and her vision for poetry, Marcia Nardi is a forgotten poetic voice waiting to be explored and restored.

WHEN WOMEN TALK

by Marcia Nardi

When women talk,
A flower is robbed of loam;
When men converse,
A fruit is basketed
The latter is fulfilment,
But the first,
A desecrance like ravaging the dead.

A plum or grape that's left upon the ground
To rot untasted
Is partly wasted
Its sweetness never being known.
But strewn upon the grass,
What beauty petals have
May, better than in vases,
Be computed.

Say silence then is loam
From which a woman's soul
Need never be uprooted.

This poem first appeared in the *Nation* on March 30, 1927, Vol. 124

Issue 3221, p 345.

Notes

[1]Williams originally conceived of *Paterson* in four parts; he wrote a fifth part which was published in 1958.

[2]The Nekola and Rabinowitz anthology, *Writing Red: An Anthology of American Women Writers, 1930-1940*, is an excellent resource on women writers of this time.

[3]This letter appeared in the conclusion of the second book of *Paterson* (87).

Sources

Mariani, Paul. *William Carlos Williams: A New World Naked*. New York: McGraw Hill, 1981.

O'Neil, Elizabeth Murrie. *The Last Word: Letters between Marcia Nardi & William Carlos Williams*. Iowa City: University of Iowa Press, 1994.

Weaver, Mike. *William Carlos Williams: The American Background*. New York: Cambridge University Press, 1971.

Williams, William Carlos. *Paterson*. New York: New Directions Books, 1992.

BARRY SCHWABSKY

EDWIN DENBY (1903-1983)

Edwin Denby's first publication was three poems in the June 1926 issue of *Poetry*. He was 23 years old. Already, more than two decades before the publication of his first book, he was a poet of the street and of the isolated consciousness that observes it, as one poem begins:

> When I walk in the street
> Nothing touches my feet,
> When I touch a wall
> There is nothing at all,
> When I look at a face
> There is only space

One might almost make out, in these lines, a rudimentary sketch for the extraordinary 90-line "Elegy—The Streets" that would be one of the highlights of Denby's first book, *In Public, In Private* (1948), which begins:

> Your streets I take to pass some time of day
> Or nighttime in the neutral open air!
> Times when the rented room for which I pay
> As if it could resent my mind's despair
> Becomes like a trained nurse's torpid stare
> Watching dead-eyed her feeble patient's malice—
> When white walls feel like that, I leave the house.

In fact, "street" might be the keyword to *In Public, In Private*, or at least what's best and most characteristic in it. A few examples:

I myself like the climate in New York
I see it in the air up between the street
...
The sky is in the streets with the trucks and us.
("The Climate")

Peering out to the street New Yorkers in saloons
Identify the smokeless moment outside
Like a subway stop where one no longer stirs.
("City Without Smoke")

The street is where people meet according to law
Organize their natures to twenty-four hours
Say what to eat, take advantage of what they saw
And continue exercising daily powers.
("A Sonnet Sequence: Dishonor," 21)

Even when the word itself does not appear, the idea of the street pervades, for as a later sonnet, "Northern Boulevard" (written to accompany a photograph by Rudy Burkhardt) has it,

People wear the city, the section they use
Like the clothes on their back and their hygiene
And they recognize property as they do news
By when to stay out and where to go in.

Later, the second collection of Denby's criticism would be called *Dancers, Buildings and People in the Streets*—one of the best book titles ever, I think. In the lecture that lends its title to that book, Denby asked his listeners (dance students in New York, we gather) to look at their city: "Do you see what a forty- or sixty-story building looks like from straight below? Do you see the bluish haze on the city as if you were in a forest? As for myself, I wouldn't have seen such things if I hadn't seen them first in the photographs of Rudolph Burkhardt." Here, Denby is talking about how photographs taught him to consider the angle from which he looked at things. Just as important to him, and just as photographic, is the way a street can be a collage of so many apparently unrelating things and doings, a festival of contingent simultaneity, as in one of the sonnets of "Five Reflections":

Meeting a freightyard head-on, the wide street
Heaves its surfaces on steel, take to the air
Handsomely ponderous, expensively neat
Crosses the property and descends with care.

*

It's a photograph that's given me my inner picture of Denby, though not one of Burkhardt's. I think of him by way of the portrait taken by Peter Hujar in 1975, when the poet was 72 years old, and published the following year in Hujar's book *Portraits in Life and Death*. Which kind of portrait is Denby's—in life or in death? In between. Not exactly like Candy Darling on her deathbed in what might be Hujar's most famous single image—not in the moment of transition. It's a different kind of in-betweenness. With his eyes closed, rumpled bedsheets and pillows behind him though he does not appear to be laying down—sitting up uncomfortably as if roused by a bad dream from which he has not yet quite awakened, just as his rough-hewn, wrinkled face seems to have just emerged from an unfocused background—he seems to inhabit an otherworldly place, a troubled hypnagogic inscape that is larger than anything we can possibly envision.

The bed where we see Denby must have been in Hujar's studio, but it reminds me of Edith Schloss's recollection that "everyone"—all New York's postwar cultural notables from John Ashbery to Kurt Weill—

eventually made their way up the stairs to Denby's loft at 145 West 21st Street, where, she says, "Edwin sometimes received in bed, a purring cat under his arm." Who or what is he receiving in Hujar's photograph? I also owe to Schloss's posthumously published memoir *The Loft Generation: From the de Koonings to Twombly—Portraits and Sketches 1942-2011* a view of his "tall, narrow bookcase with rows of works by Greek and Roman historians, playwrights, and poets" as well as "many volumes of Defoe, Proust, and Gertrude Stein; a great deal of poetry from throughout the ages; and some ballet and music reviews. Apart from a Jane Bowles novel, I don't think I saw many other novels or contemporary English writing." Oh yes—and the works of Eugène Labiche, the once immensely popular nineteenth-century farceur whose *Un Chapeau de paille d'Italie* Denby had in 1935 translated for Orson Welles as *Horse Eats Hat*.

Ron Padgett, however—speaking about a later period in Denby's life—recalls a different canon:

> Edwin kept very few books on his shelf. In fact, his personal possessions in general were few (though more than Gandhi's!). Katie Schneeman told me that among his few books were Dante's *Commedia*; Tasso's *Gerusalemme Liberata*; *Don Quixote* (in English); *The Faerie Queen*; The Poems of Emily Brontë; Apuleius's *L'Asino d'Oro*; Sei Shonagon's *Pillow Book*; Mallory's *Morte d'Arthur*; and a Greek-English dictionary. There may have been a couple of others, which he gave to Bill MacKay before he died. Edwin kept only one copy of each of his own books—in a closet!

But as Padgett records in his Introduction to the 1986 edition of Denby's *Complete Poems*, "The book he read the most in his last years was *The Divine Comedy* (*Purgatorio* and *Paradiso*—not Inferno) in Italian."

Schloss also recalls Denby's voice: "sibilant, gurgling; he spoke in a hesitant undertone because of his reserve and the need to think clearly." "His New Yorkese," she observed, "did not sound quite natural, but rather put on, and when he used slang words he had learned from the young and the people he liked to meet in diners and bars, they stood out as if in quotes." This artifice of the colloquial, the collision of tradition-drenched formality with streetwise argot, plays as large a part in Denby's poetry as it did in his conversation, providing what Cal Revely-Calder calls the "fussiness native to Denby's style."

He'd come by that formality honestly. He was born in 1903 in Tianjin, China, where his father was the American Consul—his father's father had been Ambassador, and an uncle, Secretary of the Navy. (For Denby's biography, I rely mainly on Padgett's Introduction to the 1986 edition of *The Complete Poems*.) In 1908, the father's diplomatic career took the family to Vienna. That came to an end with the war. His father went into the automobile business, and young Edwin was sent to a New England prep school, and from there went to Harvard, which he left after two years. In 1923 he returned to Vienna, and it was there that he began studying modern dance, and also underwent psychoanalysis with Paul Federn. He joined a dance company in Germany and in the June 1926 issue of *Poetry*, published three poems, as I've mentioned.

Leaving Germany in the fateful year of 1933, Denby remained in Europe for a bit; in Basel, needing a new passport photo, he called on Rudy Burkhardt and began their lifelong friendship, which for much of the time was also a love affair—until, as Schloss reports, Burckhardt "discovered that 'girls are like kittens, they are cuddlier, softer, and sweeter.' Edwin stepped back." In New York from 1935, living with Burkhardt in the 21st Street loft, he became involved in the worlds of music and theater—writing libretti and translating plays, collaborating not only with Welles but with the likes of Aaron Copland and Virgil Thompson, and (at Copland's suggestion) writing dance criticism for the renowned quarterly *Modern Music*, not to mention the poems that would make up *In Public, In Private*, which was castigated by Dudley Fitts in the *Partisan Review* for showing "neither taste, nor ear, nor control." He quickly became renowned as a dance critic; according to Lincoln Kirstein, his writing in this field could only have been achieved by someone who was both a dancer himself and a poet. His second and last book of poems, *Mediterranean Cities*, came out in 1956. Apparently it received only a single review, but that was

Frank O'Hara's gorgeous appreciation in *Poetry* the following year, which also retrospectively acknowledged Denby success in his first book in "establishing a specifically American spoken diction which has a classical firmness and clarity under his hand" and recognized in the second one an infusion of Romantic sensibility—"the pervading melancholy which overcomes the poet when he unites with the inanimate"—that finally lends the later work "a kind of Mallerméan lucidity." Years later, Denby would tell Anne Waldman that, "as a poet, some days one feels like writing severely classic things, and some days one feels like writing shapeless romantic things."

Finally, *The Complete Poems* includes some forty "late sonnets," that is, ones subsequent to *Mediterranean Cities*, but according to Padgett, Denby's last two decades were relatively unproductive. In 1983, fearing the onset of dementia, he took an overdose of sleeping pills.

*

While Denby's second book of poems was, as its title indicates, a book of cities, it is not the book of streets that the first one was. The scope of vision is wider, more expansive than that. In a poem datelined, simply, Attica—the region around Athens—the poet notices how, "Spaciously outdoors of cafes Greeks put chairs / Set way across a square or a bare road, roomy / As if huddling weren't the point of architecture"—*as if*— while in Athens itself, "we reach a flat slum / A desolate vacant lot," still, "Colonus is seen / Past factories, rising stony from the plain." Where the crowded but often closed-in character of *In Public, In Private*, evinced an Expressionist bent toward brief explosions of raw feeling, *Mediterranean Cities* is the work of poet who smooths nothing over even as he perceives things with greater equanimity; certainly he earns the astonishing final couplet of the sequence, the envoi from Ciampino, Rome's old airport: "For with regret I leave the lovely world men made / Despite their bad character, their art is mild."

I don't want to comment on Denby's dance criticism because I am not qualified to do so, but I do feel qualified to say that the prose in which that criticism is framed is of a rare excellence (earning Frank O'Hara's comparison of Denby to Lamb and Hazlitt) that convinces me that its insights into this art of which I know so little must be profound. And I think that planted within the criticism are clues to the aesthetics of the poetry. For instance, what he says about rhythm and form in classical ballet in relation to its music, "the stresses of dynamics, of melody, of harmony, of timbre, of pathos. All these stresses offer their various support to the steps. They are like a floor with various degrees of resilience to dance on. The steps step in some places and not in others. They make a choice of stresses." Frank O'Hara wrote that Denby's criticism has "a broad, general applicability, moral as well as esthetic," and this means, I think, that it is widely applicable to life or what O'Hara calls "society," and to the other arts and especially poetry. It has to do with the necessity for disequilibrium if a new equilibrium is to be found. In an essay called "Forms in Motion and in Thought," Denby observed, "In dancing one keeps taking a step and recovering one's balance. The risk is part of the rhythm. One steps out of and into balance." And in the imbalance is at least half the pleasure.

This fundamental fact about dancing is also fundamental to Denby's poetry. What can make it seem odd or difficult, and made it repugnant to a reader such as Fitts, is just how unbalanced he is willing to let the line become before another allows for a new but transitory balance that a third line will undo. It's like watching a dancer whose steps never predict which direction the following step will take. All the stranger that he typically does this in the form of the sonnet—rhymed or half-rhymed though not metrically regular. No purling pentameters here: Denby's eccentric rhythms create a festival of surprises, full of starts and stops that nonetheless keep the reader moving inexorably forward, as in the opening lines of his sonnet from Venice:

She opens with the gondola's floated gloze
Lapping along the marble, the stir of swill
Open to night sky like in tenement hallways
The footfalls, and midstream a bargeman's lone call;
Sideways leading to her green, like black, like copper
Like eyes, on tide-lifted sewers and façades

Reading that, I want to stop at "floated gloze" and just linger there in wonderment but can't; the implicit collaging of perceptions and memories (how did that New York tenement with a broken skylight over the hallway get in there?) contains a lurching but unstoppable energy. And the immediacy! Schloss reflected that "Edwin taught me to use the near and not the far for poetry," but in *Mediterranean Cities*, Denby brought the most distant histories near, and lent intimacy a rare grandeur. Re-reading these poems now, I realize how much of what they achieve is what I've aspired to in my own poetry. It's strange; although I've admired Denby's poetry since I first read it in the late 1970s, I've never thought of him as one of my "influences," as I think of Mallarmé and Reverdy, Williams and Stevens, Celan, Levertov and Creeley, Spicer and Ashbery…and yet he has been as consequential for me as any of them.

Denby's *Collected Poems* were published in 1975, and a *Complete Poems* appeared in 1986 but has not managed to stay in print. Still available from Yale University Press is Robert Cornfield's 1998 selection of *Dance Writings and Poetry*, and as I write this, David Zwirner Books has just issued a smaller but similarly mixed selection under the title, *That Still Moment*, edited by Cal Revely-Calder—I quoted earlier from his introduction to the collection. To choose one poem as a representative of a life's work is a miserly task, even with a poet whose oeuvre is so small (about 170 pages) but today, the one I can't get out of my head is "Segesta"—though apparently it's not one of the entries from *Mediterranean Cities* that most struck either Cornfield or Revely-Calder, since it's not in either of their edited volumes:

Winter's green bare mountains; over towns, bays
And Sicilian sea. I sit in the ghost stones
Of a theatre; a man's voice and a boy's
Sing in turn among the sheepbells' xylophone;
From a distant slope sounded before a reed pipe
Sweet; a goatherd, yellow eyes and auburn down
Smelling of milk, offers from a goatskin scrip
Greek coppers, speaks smiling of a lamb new born;
Doric tongue, sweet for me as to Theocritus
The boy's mistrust and trust, the same sky-still air
As then; so slowly desire turns her grace
Across the years, and eases the grief we bear
And its madness to merely a powerful song;
As the munching boy's trust beside me is strong

Lisa M. Steinman

Listening to Varieties of Possibility: The Poems of Josephine Miles (1911-1985)

Years ago, a college classmate told me I would like Josephine Miles's poems. Although Miles mentored (among many other younger poets) the writer who first encouraged me to write, namely A.R. Ammons, I could find no books and only a few anthologized poems by her in the town where Ammons taught and I was a student, although the university's literary magazine, *Epoch*, did publish a special issue on Miles late in 1982.

When I then moved to the west coast, I found Miles was better known; she lived in California for most of her life. She was an undergraduate at UCLA before going to graduate school at Berkeley, where she taught for many years and was the first woman tenured in the English Department. Once I could find her books I began reading her work with increasing interest, not least because I had been and still am thinking about how she subtly featured the ways that cultural contexts change and affect language and relatedly how her poems incorporated different ways of speaking; to quote Miles: "I like the idea of speech—not images, not ideas, not music, but people talking . . . [the] active interplay of talk" (Larney 58). Representing people talking without condescension or a pretense of full understanding is something I believe Miles's poems achieve remarkably well. I will simply add that when I finally found myself running a reading series in 1985, I wrote inviting Miles to read, only to receive a note from Deborah Willis—Miles's aide—informing me that Miles had just passed away, a month before she would have turned 75. I deeply regret that I never had a chance to hear her read or, more, to experience the active interplay of talking with her.

Although it is her writing that interests me most, I will rehearse her biography and career, which in ways inform her views of both language and the world. While Miles is often thought of as a California poet, she was born in Chicago in 1911. Her father's work then moved the family to the Bay Area before she was one, and then moved them to Detroit before they settled in southern California due to her ill health (Larney 4-6). When she was four years old—following hip surgery—Miles developed rheumatoid arthritis that left her first in a body cast and then wheelchair-bound for the rest of her life. For this reason, she was first educated at home or by visiting teachers, and when she was accepted at UCLA, she was initially told she couldn't enroll because she'd not be able to register or manage the library steps without asking "too many favors"; however, she did find help and used the downtown public library instead of the university library (Larney 38-9).

Miles also found that, although she received a good education in earlier literature and scholarship at UCLA, as far as contemporary poetry went, she was "in a curious kind of limbo. . . . [having her] own makeshift world as far as modern poetry went" (Larney 39). This is not to say that she was not writing and even publishing poems from an early age, but Berkeley graduate school opened new doors for Miles; her work was published by Macmillan in a 1935 anthology edited by Ann Winslow titled *Trial Balances*. Miles's poems from that anthology won the 1935 Shelley Memorial Award (Larney 49). By 1939, her first full poetry collection, *Lines at Intersection*, was published by Macmillan, while her poems appeared in *The New Republic, The Nation, Poetry,* and similarly prestigious national journals. Within a decade, she was corresponding with John Crowe Ransom and other nationally known writers, while noticing what she called the "pull and tug" of those writing under the influence of Yvor Winters at Stanford; those who admired Robinson Jeffers; and those self-defined as San Francisco poets—as well as, later, the poets of the San Francisco Renaissance (Larney 52). Between her involuntarily makeshift world and her interest in diverse poetic practices, she forged her own style, or styles, writing both formal and "looser" poems, and ultimately published twelve full-length volumes of poetry as well as numerous chapbooks and critical books, some of the latter responsible for recent views of her as a pioneer in digital humanities and distant reading (Buurma and Hefferman).

Further, her critical books (including the 1942 *Wordsworth and the Vocabulary of Emotion* or the 1964 *Eras and Modes in English Poetry*) on how the vocabularies and stylistic features heard as typical of poetry change over time and place in ways anticipated Raymond Williams's 1976 *Keywords: A Vocabulary of Culture and Style*, especially in tracing how cultural change affects both the meaning of words and what counts as or in poetry.

That said, it is not easy to define a characteristic Miles poem. As I mentioned earlier, it is easier to talk about her styles (plural) than her style, which may be part of why she is under-rated (although poet-readers from Lyn Hejinian to Eve Kosofsky Sedgwick have admired her work): her shorter poems might at first seem too simple; her longer poems, in which subtle shifts in perspective are more obvious, might puzzle other readers. The common thread is a simplicity of language coupled with a complexity of points of view; as she wrote: "I like varieties of possibility. . . . It's just absolutes I'm questioning" ("A Letter from Josephine Miles" 67). She did have a clear sense of what she valued in poetry: linguistic energy, especially in spoken language; an awareness of the richness of ordinary speech-as-gesture; and the ethical and political implications of truly hearing different perspectives as a way of forging a cohesiveness that "will be hard won and complex," as she said in a late 1980 interview; in that same interview she noted: "We need to teach listening, to teach an honest responsiveness. The sense of the other person" (Clark 22-3).

Looking at a relatively late poem by Miles may help show the ways in which both everyday speech and the play of numerous possible perspectives inform her work. The poem—one of the few of hers widely available online—is "Family," from the 1974 *To All Appearances: Poems New and Selected,* a short sixteen line poem in two mostly unrhymed stanzas with lines ranging from twelve mostly monosyllabic words (only "family" in the first line is more than one syllable) to two words—"Holler, say"—and three syllables in line 6 (*To All Appearances* 40). The choppiness of the prosody and the use of pronouns underlines the poem's initial narrative: a "you"—there is no first-person in the "Family"—is caught in an undertow while out swimming as their family sits on the beach eating potato salad. That the potato salad (and the beach, "Seal Rocks") are specified, while the "you" and the family members (simply called "they") are not, sweeps readers into the poem, identifying with "you," just as the undertow sweeps the you "out away down/To loss of breath loss of play and the power of play." Syntax as well, specifically the lack of commas describing the predicament, again places a reader in the (breathless) position of the you as does the number of sibilants (swim, surf, Seal, sits, sand, and salad just in the first three lines) that echo the sound of the waves. There is also an exchange of familiar and familial language as the you tries to yell "help," and the family responds with "Hello," telling the you to "come eat potato salad." The second stanza, then, describes in somewhat more detail a young helicopter pilot who speaks only Swedish (but has taken off from an English and Spanish speaking island in the Caribbean), looking down saying (the poem emphasizes speech as much as sight) that someone is drowning. The poem concludes: "And he throws you a line./ This is what is called the brotherhood of man."

At first reading, the poem seems to be a simple ironic parable about how people who speak different languages might connect (or to use Miles's words, quoted above from her 1980 interview, forge a "hard won and complex" sense of community or brotherhood). On a second reading, however, the poem is more complicated. To throw someone a line or lifeline might affirm the kind of connection a first reading suggests, in which the family's inability to hear the you is contrasted with how the pilot hears the you say yes (that is, yes, they are drowning), but it also brings the colloquial expression of feeding someone a line (as opposed to feeding them potato salad) to mind. Further, poems throw or feed lines of poetry to readers, which calls into question how one is to take the ending: "This is what is called the brotherhood of man." The line seems, as it were, to call into question the tidiness of what initially appeared to

112

be a parable and invites questions about what it takes to have a sense of another person or how complicated forging community should be. That the interview in which Miles discussed developing coherence that takes diverse perspectives into account and insists on honest responsiveness also includes a paragraph that directly follows Miles's insistence on listening, in which she talks about how woman and girls are discouraged from complaining or talking. This suggests that a reader might reconsider the gendered language in the phrase "the <u>brother</u>hood [not a word Miles uses elsewhere] of <u>man</u>." In short, if we as readers dismiss the poem as too simple, too tidy, we are also invited to listen more carefully.

I do not have room to say much about Miles's longer poems, but I will conclude with a few comments on "For Magistrates," a poem in twelve sections first published in 1982 in *Epoch* and collected in 1983 where she chose it as the final poem in *Collected Poems* [hereafter, *CP*] and about which I have previously written at greater length (*CP* 247-53; Steinman 130-40). The poem juxtaposes various views, codifications, languages for and representations of justice and mercy, ranging from William Baldwin's 1553 *A Mirror of Magistrates* to Shakespeare's *Henry IV, Part I* (though Shakespeare, who drew on Baldwin, explores the relationship between mercy and justice in many plays), to the legal codes of Hammurabi and Solon (both represented in a frieze on the U.S. Supreme Court building), to the Watergate hearings, James Wright's poem on President Harding, Jiang Qing (Mao Zedong's fourth wife, active in the cultural revolution), as well as a long excerpt from Sam Kagel's *Anatomy of an Arbitration* . . . even lines from the lullaby "Sweet and Low." As the poem puts it: "The questions are obvious but the answers aren't simple" (*CP* 250).

Moreover, the poem's language shifts from section to section—the second stanza referring to Shakespeare resolves into a rhymed pentameter couplet (*CP 248*)—raising questions about how "justice" or "mercy" are represented or culturally framed while also suggesting that while language and categories inform personal choices, choices nonetheless matter. Or so it seems when after Howard Hunt asks that the judge temper justice with mercy—in language drawn from *Deuteronomy*—adding that his and his family's fate is "in your [the judge's] hands," Sirica responds: "His fate was in his own/ Hands . . ." (*CP* 248). The last two lines of the poem leave the questions raised open, citing Solon on how "the heart is merciless./ But renders justice, that it will survive" (*CP* 253). Not "*and* renders justice," thus implying that justice and mercy might not be opposed (and that mercy is not always the province of the heart). It takes a while to follow the syntax of the final lines; the period after "merciless" is a comma in the earlier version that appeared in *Epoch*, which I take to mean the period is purposeful, making it even more difficult to decide the referent of that final "it"—the heart? justice?—but at the same time suggesting what rides on making such decisions, which are ethical, political and poetically hard won as well as (like Miles's syntax) complex. It seems we are asked to listen with care and shows why Miles is well worth listening to.

Sources

Buurma, Rachel Sagner, and Laura Heffernan. "Search and Replace: Josephine Miles and the Origins of Distant Reading." "The Discipline" blog, Modernism/Modernity Print Plus, 11 April 2018. <https://modernismmodernity.org/forums/posts/search-and-replace>.

Clark, Naomi. "Interview with Josephine Miles." *Woman Poet Volume One: The West*, edited by Elaine Dallman. Reno, Nevada: Regional Editions, 1980: 21-23.

Larney, Marjorie, editor. *Josephine Miles Teaching Poet: An Oral Biography*, from interviews by Ruth Tesier and Catherine Harroun. Sausalito, CA: Post-Apollo Press, 1993.

Miles, Josephine, "A Letter from Josephine Miles," *Epoch* 31.1 (1982): 65-67.

_____. *Collected Poems, 1930-83*. Champaign: University of Illinois Press, 1983.

_____. "Family." https://www.poetryfoundation.org/poems/46822/family>.

_____. "For Magistrates." *Epoch* 31.1 (1982): 92-97.

_____. *To All Appearances: Poems New and Selected*. Champaign: University of Illinois Press, 1974.

Steinman, Lisa M. "Putting on Knowledge with Power: The Poetry of Josephine Miles." *Chicago Review* 37. 1 (1990): 130-140.

CIARAN BERRY

HYAM PLUTZIK (1911-1962)

"There is no conspiracy against us, unless it is a conspiracy of indifference," Hyam Plutzik writes, considering the fate of the modern poet in the preface to his second collection, *Apples from Shinar,* as he contemplates Federico García Lorca's murder during the Spanish Civil War. The statement seems prophetic given Plutzik's disappearance from the anthologies and the discussion of twentieth century American poetry. If truth be told, I probably wouldn't have come across his work if I didn't teach at Trinity College in Hartford, Connecticut, Plutzik's alma mater, from which he graduated in 1932 before going on to study at Yale University. Given the impressive list of accolades and acknowledgments he received during his relatively short lifetime (Plutzik died of cancer at the age of fifty in 1962) and the many wonders to be found in the poems themselves, this seems like an unfortunate oversight. It's to be welcomed then that Wesleyan University Press reprinted *Apples from Shinar* in 2011 to mark the centenary of this poet's birth, and that much of his work, as well as information on his life and career, which included a professorship at University of Rochester where he was the first Jewish faculty member, is now available via the website hyamplutzikpoetry.com.

It wouldn't be correct to place Plutzik among Louis MacNiece's minor poets, "who lived in the wrong time or the wrong place." His three collections *Aspects of Proteus* (Harper and Row, 1949), *Apples from Shinar* (Wesleyan University Press, 1959), and *Horatio* (Atheneum, 1961) were all finalists for the Pulitzer Prize with the second chosen by Wesleyan to launch their poetry series along with volumes by Barbara Howes, Louis Simpson, and James Wright. His work was also anthologized in 1956 alongside Elizabeth Bishop, Randall Jarrell, Robert Lowell, Theodore Roethke, Muriel Rukeyser, Delmore Schwartz, and Richard Wilbur in *Fifteen Modern American Poets,* and was chosen by Thom Gunn and Ted

Hughes to feature with Edgar Bowers, Howard Nemerov, Louis Simpson, and William Stafford in their anthology, *Five American Poets*, an attempt to introduce mid-twentieth-century American poetry to a British audience. In the foreword to *Hyam Plutzik: The Collected Poems*, published in 1987 as part of BOA Editions American Poets Continuum Series, Hughes wrote "Hyam Plutzik's poems have haunted me for twenty-five years…the best of his work seems to me marvelously achieved, a sacred book" while Plutzik's long list of admirers includes Richard Blanco, Anthony Hecht, Edward Hirsch, and Gerald Stern.

It's clear that Plutzik had a very successful publishing career during his own lifetime, but that, perhaps as a result of his premature death, his work has not enjoyed the same sort of afterlife as many of his contemporaries. This is a great pity given poems like "The Geese," which showcases what Blanco calls Plutzik's "declarative power" as it moves from the first tercet's sense work, aimed at conjuring that "moonward-flying squadron," through to the second's imagery of hunters marking "the crossing" before arriving at the direct, hard-earned statement of the third tercet and the blunt advice to the reader of the stand-alone last line:

The Geese

> A miscellaneous screaming that comes from nowhere
> Raises the eyes at last to the moonward-flying
> Squadron of wild-geese arcing the spatial cold.
>
> Beyond the hunter's gun or the will's range
> They press southward, toward the secret marshes
> Where the appointed gunmen mark the crossing
>
> Of flight and moment. There is no force stronger
> (In the sweep of the monomaniac passion, time)
> Than the will toward destiny, which is death.

Value the intermediate splendor of birds.

At times Plutzik's style seems to have less in common with English poetry than with poetry translated into English. We could speculate that his family background might have something to do with this. He was the son of Jewish immigrant parents from what is now Belarus and grew up in Brooklyn speaking Yiddish, Hebrew, and Russian before learning English at a grammar school near Southbury, Connecticut. What I'm trying to get at here though isn't any sense of approaching English as a second, third, or even fourth language, but a sensibility that reminds me more at times of the work of Zbigniew Herbert or Vasko Popa than say Elizabeth Bishop or Robert Lowell. Take these first three lines from "The Poetic Process" for example: "The poetic process is lonely but theatrical,/ Improvisation before an empty house/With the dread that prompter and stagehands will stay away." Or these lines from "Divisibility": "The limitary nature of a wall/Is partial only, to keep out dogs and insects,/ Contain the furniture, exclude the rain." The vision here, the shape of the ironies, the philosophical tilt, and the lack of adornment seem to me to have the feel of Eastern Europe, of poets like Holub and Syzmborska, and a particular way of telling it slant we don't usually encounter in American verse. In this particular guise Plutzik seems too perhaps a little ahead of his time.

Of course, the contemplation of walls in "Divisibility" also conjures the Robert Frost of "Mending Wall," that most New England of poems by that most New England of poets, and, here and there, we find echoes of Frost elsewhere in Plutzik's work too, for example in these lines from "Connecticut Autumn": "Then have come the sudden gusts of winds awaked:/The broken pageantry, the leaves upflailed, the trees/Tremor-stricken, the giant branches rent." Certainly, he leans more towards Frost and perhaps Yeats than Eliot, who he calls out as an antisemite in "For T.S.E. Only" ("You, hypocrite lecteur! mon semblable! mon frère!"). There's more though of Frost's old pal, Edward Thomas to be seen in Plutzik than Frost himself, particularly the Thomas of "Rain," the Welsh poet's most notorious poem with its directness and its more than intimations of mortality:

> Rain, midnight rain, nothing but the wild rain
> On this bleak hut, and solitude, and me
> Remembering again that I shall die
> And neither hear the rain nor give it thanks
> For washing me cleaner than I have been
> Since I was born into this solitude.

Like Thomas, who died at the age of thirty-nine in the battle of Arras, time is the central concern of Plutzik's work, and it's a concern that shows up repeatedly. Time is "the monomaniac passion" in "The Geese," it is what "runs out as the hook lashes the water/Day after day" in "The Last Fisherman," it is first on the list of "abstract demons" the poet's daughter must learn to deal with in "To My Daughter," and, most crucially, it is, in "An Equation," "The artist's damnation, the rat of time." Plutzik's poems often feel pursued by their poet's mortality and the pressure a finite lifespan places on the work, the effort to find what he calls, again in that preface to *Apples from Shinar,* "even one speck of the final distillate, the eternal stuff pure and radiant as a drop of uranium." Perhaps this is why he's such an economical and direct presence on the page. There's a sense in his work often of no time or word to waste, and of the poem as a place to instruct as much as evoke.

Sometimes, reading the work of Edward Thomas, or more recently, of Larry Levis, you get the feeling that the poems almost know of their author's ill fate before the author himself does (Levis died of a heart attack at the age of forty-nine) and this seems true at times too of Plutzik's work where there's often a strong sense of premonition. Perhaps, like Thomas, Plutzik's strong sense of mortality, and particularly his own mortality, comes partly from his service in the military. Plutzik enlisted in the air force after Pearl Harbor and spent most of the second world war in England, an experience that's at the center of "The Airman Who Flew Over Shakespeare's England" and also "The Old War" where a downed fighter plane is described as an "iron sparrow" that "blundered into the mother-barley." There's a strong sense throughout his work of our time being cruelly short and of our living in a world where "God is brutish life!/God is the living ether!" as he puts it in "The Mythos of the Man From Enoch." Yet, "Within these strange entrails/We must build our beautiful houses" as he asserts later in the same poem. Or, as he puts it in, "Requiem for Edward Carrigh," while "nothing can be done" about our always diminishing state of affairs, "something can be said at least."

The poem, for Plutzik, like so many others, is often a means to rage against the sudden dying of the light. And there's great pleasure to be found in how he goes about the task. Who wouldn't want to stop and admire a line like "My hand, too, scintillates like a strange fish" from "As the Great Horse Rots on the Hill"? Or the description of the milkman in the poem of that title as "A white ghost in an opaque body/Passing slowly over the snow." Who wouldn't want to be stopped in their tracks by the closing lines of "Portrait," where the reader, invited closer to the poem's subject, is asked to "Notice with what nonchalance, /The magazine in his hand and the casual cigarette to his lips,/He wears a shirt by Nessus." That unlikely sound-play between "cigarette to his lips" and "shirt by Nessus." The clever choice of preposition, which makes it seem like the mythical figure is a mid-twentieth century fashion designer. But mostly how, as happens so often in Plutzik's work, there appears, via a sudden shift in gears, a brief moment of hard-won understanding, that surprise for the writer that becomes a surprise for the reader.

In the opening of "On Hearing That My Poems Were Being Studied in a Distant Place," Plutzik, thinking of a faraway classroom, wonders aloud "What are they mumbling about me there?" It's a line that seems to cast itself not just across a vast spatial distance, but also a temporal one, illuminating this poet's (and every poets'!) anxiety over whether his work will outlive him. It would be a great shame and a great loss if, from our desks here in the classroom of the future, we were to continue to mumble about Hyam Plutzik and his poetry little or nothing at all.

Sources

Blanco, Richard. *Hyam Plutzik: 32 Poems*. Miami: Suburbano Ediciones, 2021.

Hughes, Ted. *Hyam Plutzik: The Collected Poems*. Rochester, New York: BOA Editions, 1987.

MacNiece, Louis. "Elegy for Minor Poets," *Collected Poems*. London: Faber and Faber, 1966.

Plutzik, Hyam. Preface, "The Geese," "For T.S.E. Only," "The Last Fisherman," "To My Daughter," "The Old War," "The Mythos of the Man from Enoch," "Requiem for Edward Carrigh," "As the Great Horse Rots on the Hill," "The Milkman," "Portrait." *Apples from Shinar*. Middletown, Connecticut: Wesleyan University Press, 2011.

Plutzik, Hyam. "The Poetic Process," "Divisibility," "Connecticut Autumn," "An Equation," "On Hearing That My Poems Were Being Studied in a Distant Place." *32 Poems*. Miami: Suburbano Ediciones, 2021.

Thomas, Edward. "Rain." *Collected Poems*. London: Faber and Faber, 1981.

BURT KIMMELMAN

WILLIAM BRONK'S HAUNTING BEAUTY (1918-1999)

"Is Oppen in it?" Celia Zukofsky was preparing dinner for the three of them, listening from the kitchen to Louie's conversation with their guest, Charles Tomlinson. Having settled in the living room of the Zukofskys' Manhattan apartment, Charles was telling Louie about the anthology he was developing, which he thought to title *Seven Significant Poets*. He'd accepted George and Mary's invitation to stay with them in the Oppens' Brooklyn flat and knew the matter of where he'd lay his head could upset his hosts. Louie and Charles got past any possible slight rather quickly—to his surprise. Celia's question was not an idle one. He was well-aware of the feud, now in its third year, between Louie and George.

Charles's sense of dread had to do with whether Louie would agree to have his own poems in the book. Without them the book couldn't work. The title said it all: *Seven Significant Poets. Seven*, not five. Charles planned to add William Bronk and James Laughlin to the five principal Objectivists: Louis Zukofsky, the acknowledged theoretician of their collective poetics; the older progenitor, Charles Reznikoff; Lorine Niedecker, Carl Rakosi and, of course, George Oppen. The book would sharpen readers' focus on what was, really, *the new American poetry*, by suggesting other ways to think about relationships amongst the innovative poets Donald Allen had included in his 1960, ground-breaking anthology he'd titled *The New American Poetry: 1945—1960*. This phrase was becoming widely familiar by the spring of 1966.

The Objectivists, the Allen anthology's spiritual parents, were a bridge back to Ezra Pound, H.D., and William Carlos Williams, who formed the bole of the Modernist tree. (Burton Hatlen would lovingly refer to them as "The Philadelphia Three" because they'd met, in adolescence, in or around the University of Pennsylvania.) Allen's tome appeared three years after *The New Poets of England and America* edited by Donald Hall, Robert

Pack, and Louis Simpson. They'd sensed the postwar poetry wars about to break out into the open. (No poet in one collection was to be found in the other.) Their anthology was dedicated to current mainstream tastes, which didn't necessarily comport with Modernist precepts.

Like his fellow Englishman, Basil Bunting, Tomlinson had taken part in the exciting cultural transformation giving rise to Allen's book. Its contributors read each other's work in the same journals where they appeared—like Cid Corman's *Origin* and Robert Creeley's *Black Mountain Review*. Bronk published there (as did, sometimes, Modernist poets like Wallace Stevens). Corman called Bronk the "thread that [bound] all the issues [of *Origin*] together" (*The Gist of Origin 1951-1971* [New York: Grossman/Viking, 1975], xxxvi). Origin Press published his first poetry collection, *Light and Dark* (1956). But Allen ultimately soured on Bronk. Taking advice from Charles Olson, he decided Bronk couldn't fit into the sections he'd invented (e.g., "Black Mountain," "New York School," and "San Francisco Renaissance").

Bronk was the final poet cut from the manuscript. The exclusion contributed to his self-imposed exile in Hudson Falls, New York where he'd live his entire life. It was the perfect place to protect him from the fierce infighting that continued all around him. Now Tomlinson meant to reinsert Bronk into the "official" avant-garde. As for Laughlin, he'd founded New Directions and been Pound's most famous student (the sole pupil in what he affectionately called "Ezuversity").

Two years earlier, Bronk's second book of poems, *The World, the Worldless*, was brought out by Laughlin's press—thanks to Oppen's half-sister, June Oppen Degnan, who then was an editor at New Directions. (George was to edit the Bronk manuscript.) Bronk gained a wider readership with the new book, which received enthusiastic praise. (Later books of his received a number of major awards.)

Longer, fuller assessments of Bronk ensued. Corman had published an adulatory book on Bronk years before. In the late 1980s, the journal *Sagetrieb* published a large collection of analytical essays on him. Several critical full-length books followed, along with scholarly books containing chapter-length critical discussions of Bronk's work. Various journals continued to run individual articles on it.

Paul Auster's pronouncement, in the *Saturday Review* in 1978, captures what many of Bronk's readers had been trying to articulate starting as early as the 1950s: "Bronk's poetry," Auster writes, "stands as an eloquent and often beautiful attack on all our assumptions, a provocation, a monument to the questioning mind" (30). Other poets had been drawn to Bronk's disturbing eloquence. Oppen initiated, in 1962 (recognizing how important silence was in his poems, as it was in Oppen's), what became a years-long correspondence with Bronk.

That evening at the Zukofskys', in 1966, Louie'd succeeded in calming his guest's nerves by consenting to have his poems appear in the new anthology. Alas, when he received the publisher's permissions form, he refused to sign it. Was this reversal because of Oppen? Or Bronk? Had Louie thought twice before saying anything about Laughlin? Louie'd impatiently derided Bronk, once told of the plan to include him in the book. "All that Stevensian bothering," he quipped. And, intending to elucidate this pungent remark, he explained it by quoting himself (from his famous 1930s essay "Sincerity and Objectification"): "You either '[think] with [. . .] things as they exist' or you give up" (Tomlinson 444).

Right about this time, Bronk took me and another fledgling poet, Sherry Kearns (née Moore), to visit Tomlinson for high tea in his Colgate University parlor (he was, then, poet-in-residence). I still picture these two poets seated across from one another, their cautious yet obvious admiration, possibly true affection. The pleasure each took in the other's company hints at how wrong Zukofsky was—not simply about Bronk, but about Stevens too.

Zukofsky, a great poet, mistook Stevens. Did he misapprehend Modernism itself? The concealed irony in Tomlinson's remembrance of his dinner at the Zukofskys' ("Zukofsky and Oppen, a memoir"), which becomes clear, is that Stevens and Bronk were not the only people, of their time, who composed poetry of ideas. For all its sensuous beauty, at times its baroque lavishness, Zukofsky's work ("A" most of all) compares well with Stevens's.

Yet who else, within the mid-century avant-garde, was making rigorously intellectual poetry? Here's a shortlist: Tomlinson, Oppen, Olson, Creeley. Bronk singles out Creeley's "I Know a Man" for praise (in a letter to Olson [16 January 1962])—in mindset, Creeley also challenged "all our assumptions" (in Auster's phrase).

The surface features of Olson's poetry were radically different from Bronk's, yet Olson's affecting blurb (for *The World, the Worldless*)—"I may have, for the first time in my life, imagined a further succinct life"—reveals their shared outlook, even their questioning of the *real*. Bronk's voice, prosody, diction *per se* constitute a softspoken grandiloquence readers have prized, which resides within his precise, "succinct" language. His restless existentialism is stylistically not that of Tomlinson's; nevertheless, there's a shared penchant for this quietude (which is something like what drew Bronk and Oppen together).

In a kind of ritual, readings of Zukofsky's and Stevens's work were juxtaposed as part of Zukofsky's ultimate *apologia*. It was the last essay Zukofsky wrote. Valorizing Stevens was a complete turn-about. The essay was a humble admission of error. The fact may have been that, in 1966, Zukofsky was unable to recognize Stevens's pose of philosophizing— mere posturing—which was Stevens's ultimate masquerade. In poem after poem, Stevens abandons a philosophical discourse he has begun, for the sake of his colorful, hallmark surrealism. Neither Stevens nor Bronk was a philosopher—yet in his poems Bronk closes the circle of thought.

Bronk's penetrating meditations were why, then and now, his poetry is not as popular as it should be: simply put, Bronk is hard to take. He leaves his reader no corner in which to hide, in stripping away all our comforting illusions. He's scrupulously existentialist, thoughtful, the most uncompromising of poets; Stevens is naturally lured toward the beauty of the sensual—while Bronk's quiet, steady, careful probing is aesthetically, intellectually satisfying due to the sheer elegance in which it's couched.

In middle age, Bronk had to throw out all of Stevens's books he owned. This strikes me as a classic example of Harold Bloom's *Anxiety of Influence*. Stevens had a great mind, was a great poet, but he just wasn't interested in working through the conundrums Bronk fully engaged: the unreality of consciousness, the intellectual inability to affirm human being. Zukofsky's symphonic passages, in *"A"*, disclose his penchant for something akin to Stevens's flamboyance, which in his poems manifested more intensely through imagery and diction. Bronk abjured such showiness. His style, precise sentences and prosody, support his epistemological forays, his interrogations of—not the nothingness to be held at bay but, instead— *worldlessness*. His poems' persona, in its enunciations, does not merely mount a philosophical inquiry; it finally finds *its raison d'etre* in cerebral persistence.

"If I am not central to the world," Bronk writes in the 1960s, "then it fails / to make any difference whatever I feel" ("Of the All with Which We Coexist"). This was not the paradox of solipsism. Rather, his philosophical *and* poetic enterprise is tautological—self-evidential. His precision is essentially epistemological, serving the further end of raising up a distilled language of inquiry.

In his poem "Of the All with Which We Coexist" he relies on a single image (a central one for both Stevens and Bronk)—that of the eye—which is meant to signify perception:

> Looking around me. I see as far to one
> sky as another. The limitations of the eye:
> we know the sky goes farther. Yet instruments
> give us the same view and absolve the eye.
>
> If I am not central to the world, then it fails
> to make any difference whatever I feel.
> The universe is large: to be eccentric is to be

nothing. It is not worth speaking of.

If I am anything at all, I am
the instrument of the world's passion and not
the doer or the done to. It is to feel.
You, also, are such an instrument.

You speak of justice and injustice, and well you might.
You speak of grief, of ecstasy. This
is a cruel world and a gay one. We are. Feel.
There is nothing to do, to be done, to be done to.

Bronk deflates the power of his images by being discursive. Linear, spare in his imagery, he objectifies and diffuses the very scene he depicts. In "Of the All with which We Coexist" his notion of centrality is more pronounced than Stevens's could ever be because he questions the propriety of eccentricity as it resides in the self. We choose—or we want—to move toward the center. Stevens feels incapable of such an option, going only so far as to wish for such a choice, or else he retreats as he mourns this loss.

In his poem "The Well Dressed Man With A Beard" Stevens mourns the lack of enduring images: "One thing remaining, infallible, would be / Enough. Ah! douce campagna of that thing!" (CP 247). He recoils from the total renunciation Bronk finds as solace, in contending that "to be eccentric is to be / nothing." The central image of the eye as perception becomes an emblem for the ego that finds value for itself in feeling; feeling is of value only when it is (when Bronk is) "central to the world."

The poignant story of Zukofsky finding Stevens late in life, belatedly finding himself, makes a kind of sense insofar as the two poets were actually kindred spirits. Bronk was right to disgorge all possessions hinting at Stevens; it was an impulse to survive. We cleave to Stevens's, or Zukofsky's, rich tapestries. They're a reprieve from our existential fate.

Bronk is not especially interested in mortality. The matter of *the real* is another problem altogether. Stevens uses it as an element within his overall poetic sensorium. Bronk's greatness relies upon his ability to resist that. He rejects what he calls, in "The Abnegation," "handouts, makeshifts, / sops for creature comfort." When Bronk claims in this poem "I am the world" he's refusing a compassion that might invite a subjectivism. "I refuse," he insists. "I will not / be less than I am to be more human."

Desire is persistent, unbending and universal. "I want to be that Tantalus, unfed / forever," he insists (cf. Kimmelman 110). Bronk's work is unnerving finally because its execution is undeniable. His greatness has as much to do with not being willing to indulge in illusion. Finally, in expurgating Stevens, Bronk was free to pursue his own, singular poetics. His greatness resides within this unalloyed integrity.

Sources

Bronk, William. "[Letter to Charles Olson, 16 January 1962.] The Charles Olson Research Collection. University of Connecticut. Storrs, CT.

Corman, Cid. *The Gist of Origin 1951-1971*. New York: Grossman/Viking, 1975.

Kimmelman, Burt. *"The Winter Mind": William Bronk and American Letters*. Madison, NJ: Fairleigh Dickinson UP, 1998.

Tomlinson, Charles. "Zukofsky and Oppen, a memoir." *Paideuma: Modern and Contemporary Poetry and Poetics* 7.3 (Winter 1978): 429-445.

Martha Ronk

Barbara Guest (1920-2006)

Barbara Guest was a member of the New York School of poets, similar to them in her interest in art, avant-garde experiments, the creation of multiple selves. Nevertheless, she was omitted from the famous *An Anthology of New York Poets* 1970 edited by Ron Padgett and David Shapiro and neglected by critics of the New York school. Her renaissance was fostered by women poets and critics in the 70s and after (to list a few: Rachel Blau DuPlesssus, Sara Lundquist, Lynn Keller, Kathleen Fraser, Marjorie Welish, Brenda Hillman), but her extraordinary vision of the lyric is still often unexplored.

Born in 1920 in North Carolina, Barbara Guest spent her childhood in Florida and California, graduating from Berkeley before moving to NYC where in the 60s she made a name for herself as a poet, wrote art reviews, and published her first book, *The Location of Things.* She continued to publish book after book, including *The Blue Stairs* (1968), *Moscow Mansions* (1973), *Countess from Minneapolis* (1976), *Herself Defined: The Poet H. D. and Her World* (1984), *Fair Realism* (1989), *Defensive Rapture* (1993), *Miniatures and Other Poems* (2002), *Forces of Imagination, The Red Gaze* (2005). Her *Collected Poems* was published by Wesleyan UP in 2008. In 1999 she received the Frost Medal for Distinguished Lifetime Achievement from the Poetry Society of America.

I urge attention to Guest for several reasons: the intellectual pleasure of "difficulty"; the purposefulness behind her unusual use of imagery; and the creation of a fluid "self." I am especially taken by the meta-poetic nature of so many of her poems. The first stanza of "The Screen of Distance" describes her poetic process: a wall becomes a screen for a projected mix of shadows, lights, words, images, "real" buildings, an imagined frame of a tilted girder which then holds a plot (of ground? of narration?), poetry, and a tree "casting language upon the screen."

On a wall shadowed by lights from the distance
is the screen. Icons come to it dressed in caps
and their eyes reflect the journeys their nomadic
eyes reach from level earth. Narratives are in
the room where the screen waits suspended like
the frame of a girder the worker will place
upon an axis and thus make a frame which he fills with
a plot or a quarter inch of poetry to encourage
nature into his building and the tree leaning
against it, the tree casting language upon the screen.

Guest's poems undermine linear narrative or argument. They can be difficult to track, to make clear sense of the relation of one line to another—they skitter and shift, align and oppose one another, introduce gaps and silences. As in cubism, objects are presented from multiple points of view, spaces are skewed and ambiguous. Robert Bennett describes her use of space, often domestic space, as "deliberately constructed both to unsettle conventional expectations about the nature of spatiality itself and to suggest instead intimations of a more complete world in which both 'proofs' and 'illusions of stability' are subverted by a profound awareness of the chaotic contingencies of modern life" (Robert Bennett "Literature as Destruction of Space: The Precarious Architecture of Barbara Guest's Spatial Imagination," *Women's Studies* 30 [2001]). One of my favorite titles from *Defensive Rapture* is the witty, "The Surface as Object," a poem that illustrates her use of space (the gaps are far greater in the published poem):

the visible

as in the past

subsisting in layered zone

refuses to dangle

oaths on marsh field

whitened or planned

memorial distance

rather than vine

Barbara Guest's poems fuse the concrete with the abstract, the mysterious with the knowable, using what she calls "invisible architecture" in construction. They *move* into the past, into nature and paintings, into myth, into two or more places at once creating a tension between location and unlocatabilty. Influenced by imagism, she then moved into literary abstract expressionism: "The necessary idealizing of you reality/is part of the search, the journey/where two figures embrace":

Also from "An Emphasis Falls on Reality" in *Fair Realism*:

Cloud fields change into furniture
furniture metamorphizes into fields
an emphasis falls on reality.

"It snowed towards morning," a barcarole
the words stretched severely

silhouettes they arrive in trenchant cut
the face of lilies. . ..

I was envious of fair realism.

I desired sunrise to revise itself
as apparition, majestic in evocativeness,
two fountains traced nearby on a lawn.

In another poem from *Fair Realism*, "The Rose Marble Table" (Matisse) she collapses a painted table with a "real table" with the igniting of shadows:

Creative soul you hesitate, I with my hand
on the marble table, like you a difficult creature
ignoring the universe, igniting shadows. Gulls
over porches, bamboo familiars mine.

And from the final stanza:

Supple nature declares texture lends
formality to words a flight of marble
can rearrange the speed of waters,
we pass hands upon its surface and embrace
the creative object, throbbing waves fly over.

Subjectivity appears here as variously located and ever-mobile: "Creative soul," "I" "like you," "we," "my familiars," and even "the creative object." In Guest's work there is a look of mutual recognition between spectator and artwork. She alludes to this in her essay on "Walter Benjamin in a Museum" in *Forces of Imagination* when she states that "one does not in any way enter into its space. Rather, this space thrusts itself forward, especially in various very specific spots." This infusion means, I think, opening oneself to the marvelous. In "Invisible Architecture" Guest writes: "Losing the arrogance of dominion over the poem to an invisible hand, the poet campaigns for a passage over which the poet has control. Yet the unstableness of the poem is important."

In ways both off-hand and serious, Barbara Guest's poems utilize images as, to use her language: definition, summation, what the poem means to say. As a poet I am drawn inexorably to trying to understand the ways in which they function, especially in *Fair Realism*. It is my contention that Guest radically changes the ways in which images are used. She does this by treating visual images as foreign substances that run counter to or athwart much that they seem to be connected to. As she says in "H.D. and the Conflict of Imagism," the image is a "foreign substance."

Often this sense of the foreign nature of Guest's imagery is created by her use of ekphrasis, since an extended picture in words clearly moves away from the body of the text into its own space, separate from the rest, and offering the pleasures of opacity by obscuring or contradicting or causing friction with other aspects of the poem. Guest describes this particular use of the image in her essay on H.D:

> Yet the image despite all its energy and activity has arrived as if it were a foreign substance. It is strangely isolated. This isolation or foreignness of the image from the rest of the poem exerts a fascination to which the poem is willing to submit, but not always the reader. The reader is apt to say, 'oh, another image,' or 'oh, another picture'—remember that Imagism is highly pictorial and visual. If you consider this, you realize the image has a lonely perch.

By employing ekphrasis, Guest creates the sense of another realm, seemingly related to the one at hand, but in some ways quite unrelated, a questioning not only of reality, but also of mimesis itself. Thus, despite their sensuality, one often questions what it is that one is "seeing," and realizes that often Guest's images appeal rather to the mind's eye. The illusion permitted by the word liberates the mind. As Murray Krieger claims, the poet is not a painter; because the linguistic sign does not resemble its object: "it therefore [is] free to appeal to the mind's eye rather than the body's eye. And the mind's eye, through which the intelligible is 'glimpsed,' is of course superior to the body's, restricted as the latter is to the sensible" (Murray Krieger, *Ekphrasis,* Johns Hopkins UP 1992). Or as Pound argues and as Guest twice quotes in her essays on imagism, the image may arise from external sources, but it is the rearrangement of various elements and aspects in the mind that creates the cluster of fused ideas, a cluster infused with energy.

Yet, more significantly perhaps, Guest's use of ekphrasis not only enables a movement beyond what she calls the locked kingdom of linearity, but also suggests the ways in which ekphrastic failure, a failure built into the very project itself, aids in producing certain desired effects. No matter what the effort, a poet can never bring the visual fully into language but is ever destined to confront impossibility and failure. No matter how detailed or extended the visual description, a poet cannot produce a visual object; and it is then the very apophatic nature of ekphrasis that has the potential to unleash the unseen, the mysterious, the hallucinated. Ekphrasis performs both impossibility and its over-coming in alternating fashion.

"Wild Gardens Overlooked by Night Lights," one of Barbara Guest's most famous poems, starts where the title begins looking over gardens, night lights, buildings, parking lot trucks. Stanza two begins with an enigmatic pronoun without a clear antecedent:

They urge me to seek here on the heights
amid the electrical lighting that self who exists,
who witnesses light and fears its expunging

What follows is an ekphrastic rearrangement in which the speaker removes a landscape painting from the wall and replaces it with a scene from "The Tale of Genji," the episode where Genji recognizes his son. This action rescues the speaker from immobility and allows her to be "mobile like a spirit," traveling in and out of the story, the picture, the emotional configurations of the episode itself; and it also seems as if the Genji move outside their reality into the space of the speaker, "that modern wondering space/flash lights from the wild gardens."

The use of ekphrasis here allows for mobility and exchange: one picture is exchanged for another dominated by the color black and the emotions of sadness and remorse. Astutely, Guest creates a literary device by literalizing it. Thus, the poem suggests a formal and temporary solution to the problem of locating oneself and things by suggesting that it is a question of position, and a position that can be and will be shifted even as one changes one painting for another. Foreign—here literally foreign—images are inserted and extended in a somewhat arbitrary way. The picture of the Genji is inserted into the poem, and it operates paratactically to suggest possibilities, opening up the poem's formal and emotional range. Imagery here is not mere color or design; it is the operation of the imagination in the poem; and such operation is underscored by the position of the line in which the scene of the Genji is inserted, coming as it does after the long pause indicated by blank space:

> I take from my wall the landscape with its water
> of blue color, its gentle expression of rose,
> pink, the sunset reaches outward in strokes as the west wind
> rises, the sun sinks and color flees into the delicate
> skies it inherited,
> I place there a scene from "The Tale of Genji."

Moreover, abstraction and synesthesia tend to blur visual description. Profiles detach from figures, become shapes and float. A line of green "displaces" Genji and his son. The shapes of the hair are rendered not by expected adjectives, but by the intrusion of color so that any pictorial image is, if not obliterated, rendered more complex as one struggles to comprehend black shapes:

> An episode where Genji recognizes his son.
> Each turns his face away from so much emotion,

135

so that the picture is one of profiles floating
elsewhere from their permanence,
a line of green displaces these relatives,
black also intervenes at correct distances,
the shapes of the hair are black.

As in other Guest poems, she calls attention to her use of ekphrasis by means of a frame, here the literal frame of a painting. Her repositioning of herself and her readers is highly self-conscious; she evokes an "I" who "actually" moves pictures around in her room, an imagistic rearrangement literalized; such a technique moves ekphrasis into a realm that is not only highly artificial but also fake and thus close to a kind of "failure," unless, as I am arguing here, this is what makes for Guest's obvious success. That is, the poem acknowledges the failure of ekphrasis by wittily creating it as a theatrical scene in the poem itself, thereby ensuring the potency of the Genji for all the readers of this extraordinary poem.

Martha Collins

Catherine Breese Davis (1924-2002)

I met Catherine Breese Davis in 1962, when, as a first-year student in the Iowa Writers' Workshop, she gave a guest lecture for a course taught by Mark Strand. I believe I was the only class member who was not enrolled in the workshop—who indeed was not yet writing poems—but I loved poetry and was impressed by Davis's lecture on plain and aureate styles, with its deep historical knowledge of English poetry. My then-husband and I soon struck up a friendship with her, based partly on the discovery that she had studied at Stanford, from which we had just graduated.

Davis had been at Stanford in 1950, as a recipient of what would later be called a Stegner Fellowship. This was one of several accomplishments that set her apart from her somewhat younger fellow workshop members. By the time she came to Iowa City, she had published poems in *Poetry, The New Yorker,* and *The Paris Review,* as well as the influential 1957 anthology *New Poets of England and America.*

None of this was predictable from Davis's impoverished background. Her father was sent to prison for robbery when she was still a baby, and she never saw him again. She lived with her mother off and on, but also spent time in foster care and lived with her aunt and uncle during high school. Her mother disowned her when she revealed at sixteen that she was gay, and Davis never saw her again.

Without financial stability, she spent the next twenty or so years dividing her time between school and work. She studied with Robert Penn Warren at the University of Minnesota, and at the University of Chicago with J.V. Cunningham, who recommended her to Yvor Winters at Stanford. She later lived and worked in New York and Washington, D.C. before coming to Iowa City at the behest of Donald Justice, who continued to support and champion her throughout her life. In later years, she taught briefly in California and Missouri, and for many years in Boston, but still

137

without much money and with emotional and physical challenges that included alcoholism and a mild case of cerebral palsy.

In Davis's early years as a poet, metrical poetry was the dominant mode, and she was a master of it. Her style was, in the terms of the Iowa City lecture, "plain," but this did not mean easy or conversational, but rather precise, exact, every word counting. Nor did it mean simple: committed to exploring deeply, Davis traced patterns of thought through what was often complex syntax. Contemporary readers may not be drawn to poems titled "Indolence," "Patience," or "Obsession." But using a complex interplay of prosody, syntax, and diction, and refusing to settle for less than a full expression of experience, those poems involve the reader in states of mind that are simultaneously states of feeling.

"Obsession," for example, addresses its subject as a "parasitic ghost" that eats the speaker's "substance," and continues: "You share my narrow bed; you make / My thoughts your own, your own my blood." Later, a compelling line break forces us to contemplate a striking simile before going on to an important "and": "You feed as shadow on the light / And grow—on what shall I subsist?" As the poem progresses, metrical variations and enjambment convey the disturbance that the growing obsession creates until its "loose shapes" become "Innumerable mouths."

Also notable in Davis's early poetry is an ever-expanding series of epigrams, no doubt influenced by Cunningham and Winters, which display a great deal of wit as well as metrical precision, sometimes in as few as two lines: "Love is not blind, but overmuch / Given to darkness goes by touch." The title of the epigrams ultimately became "Looking In and Looking Out," and there is in fact some chronological movement in Davis's work from one to the other. While many of the early poems, including "Obsession," rely on sustained metaphor, others at least begin in the perceived world. But observation becomes increasingly central to poems begun shortly before Davis moved to Iowa City.

"A Small River in Iowa and the Wide World," which I will discuss later, reflects that movement, and it also marks, with its intimate address to someone else, a shift into more personal matters. The sonnet sequence "*for tender stalkes,*" begun in Iowa City in 1964 and added to at least as late as the early '70s, also reflects this movement, taking as its immediate impulse an "unpromising" love "so wasting and distraught / It let me neither work nor rest." Davis had addressed love in general and sometimes witty terms before, as in the epigram quoted above; but the intimate address in these poems indicates a willingness to reveal feeling in more immediate terms and leads to some of Davis's most eloquent verse.

A somewhat later manifestation of the personal lies in the poet's exploration of the past, which, like love, had appeared in abstract terms in early poems but was not given faces and names until the 1970s. A poem originally dedicated to "C.D.M." is later addressed to "Dear Sister," and its concluding reference to "the past you fled" directs us to Davis's own past, which she explored in at least two finished poems and a number of unfinished ones. "Railroads" references her impoverished childhood by the railroad tracks in Sioux City, Iowa, and "She" depicts her mother in colloquial and unsentimental terms ("what a hell / on wheels she was / but / drive!").

"Railroads" uses a version of William Carlos Williams's triadic line, and "She" and other poems are clearly influenced by it. Although she undoubtedly knew his work earlier, Davis's Iowa City reading of Williams, as well as Robert Lowell's *Life Studies,* led her, like many of her generation, to free verse, although she continued to write formal poems as well. Surprisingly direct, many of the free verse poems display an increasingly far-sighted "looking out" at a wider world through what is often an overtly political lens. Davis read the newspapers obsessively during her Boston years, and at one point wrote that she couldn't see "in all I saw and heard / a single line of poetry." But she finally did make poetry from contemporary topics that include poverty, war, and race, which were not dominant in poetry at the time.

Nor did she limit these explorations to free verse. One of her most moving late poems, "The Summer That Never Was," reflects on the assassinations of Dr. Martin Luther King, Jr., and Robert Kennedy, while at the same time recounting Davis's own troubled stay at a mental hospital that same year. This long poem, written in rhyming lines of various metrical lengths, also employs the careful observation that had been apparent in her work for some time.

But starting in the mid-1970s, Davis didn't finish many poems. The notebooks from the late 1970s contain a number of unfinished ones, but after 1977 she apparently didn't finish any new work for seventeen years. She did put together several versions of a book manuscript over the years, beginning in 1970 when she sent *From the Narrow House to the Wide World* to Harper and Row; but the manuscript was lost, and the publisher didn't ask her to resubmit. In the 1970s, Donald Justice asked her for a manuscript for the National Poetry Series (which was not yet a contest), but after much delay she finally submitted two incomplete manuscripts, one of formal verse, one of free, which forced him to choose another poet for the series. Justice continued to encourage Davis, who in the 1990s submitted an ever-changing manuscript to at least three university presses and also sent a copy to Justice, "for safe keeping." But she didn't try hard to publish a manuscript, and in 1996 wrote: "I certainly don't want to have a posthumous book, but it may come to that."

It finally did, when in 2015 Kevin Prufer, Martin Rock, and I published, in the Unsung Masters Series, *Catherine Breese Davis: On the Life and Work of an American Master.* The volume includes a large selection of Davis's poetry, an interview with her last partner, a number of essays about her work, and miscellaneous material. This essay draws heavily on the work in that volume, and both paraphrases and quotes from the essay I wrote for it. By working on that book, and by writing this essay, I hope not only to bring the fine work of an "unsung master" to a larger public, but also to honor a poet who, by the example of her work and her tough encouragement of me as I began to write my own poems, started me on a writing career I might not otherwise have had.

"A Small River in Iowa and the Wide World" is one of the poems I came to know and love in Iowa City. Many re-readings later, it still offers me new insights, both aesthetic and emotional. An elegantly formal poem in rhyming iambic pentameter, it displays the mastery of diction, syntax, alliteration, and enjambment that characterizes Davis's early work. But it also omits punctuation in several of its many memorable lines, and beautifully relies on the outward-looking mode of the later poems. Beginning with the still image of "Three perfect oval mirrors" cast by a "homely bridge's arches" and moving through immediate time until "The sun is gone," the poem itself becomes a "reflection" on perfection and imperfection, permanence and impermanence, and, in its final phrase, "earth's both excellence and plunder." Throughout, Davis weaves observation and contemplation: "The fire-swept wings of the blackbirds, the flood / Of feelings that their shadows on the grass / Give rise to, as the day flames down, turns slate." The poem is both intimate and colloquial in addressing the object of an "imperfect love": "You are not here," Davis writes. But as the poem progresses, it's easy for the "you" that is the reader to feel both present and included as Davis asks: "Do you not feel with me . . .?"

I do and continue to do so as I read and re-read the poems of Catherine Breese Davis.

CATHERINE BREESE DAVIS

A SMALL RIVER IN IOWA AND THE WIDE WORLD

July, late afternoon. I sit alone
And look at only water; the still river,
On which the homely bridge's arches cast
Three perfect oval mirrors less than a stone
May break and break the stillness, soon will shiver
With life, be lost, imperfect as the past.

What of imperfect love? which wears perfection
A day an hour a moment—a moment's wonder
That fails as morning's dew, as mornings do.
This small river's a good place for reflection:
Its little hour, before the sun goes under,
Begins to change. Then what of me? of you?

We talked that other hour of love, but not
Of mine, of yours for someone else. Now all
This afternoon I've thought of love and you,
Who are not here. The wide world makes a knot
Of spirit bones flesh blood dark love loss gall.
And yet the grass, come night, is laced with dew.

This river, quick with carp as thick as mud,
Is a cool place where idlers like to pass
An hour or two and fish or contemplate
The fire-swept wings of the blackbirds, the flood
Of feelings that their shadows on the grass
Give rise to, as the day flames down, turns slate.

And O how fleeting the seasons are, how on
And on they stream! Do you not feel with me
How cold the grass is? Will you never fear
This chilling, failing light? The sun is gone.
The river's glassy now. Do you not see
How still it is again? You are not here.

No matter. All this will soon be done.
And I shall leave for good this riverbank—
Sleek carp the redwings this close-knotted earth
The bridge its mirrors the hours will be as one.
Before the air darkens and goes blank,
Where will the world have brought me? What was it worth?

When all these that were shimmer, shadow, or gloss
Are far from here, shall I remember then
The river as a world wide as wonder
That flows, entwines continuous change with loss?
Having once been, shall I be once again
Aware of earth's both excellence and plunder?

James Finnegan

A Poet Missed and a Misplaced Book: Encounters with the Poetry of Bert Meyers (1928-1979)

In my early twenties, living in St. Louis, I was just becoming a poet, and I was becoming obsessed with reading poets of all manner and stripe. But I missed my first opportunity to read Bert Meyers in those early 1980s. My first poetry teacher, Howard Schwartz, had co-edited an anthology that included the poetry of Bert Meyers. The anthology was entitled, *Voices Within the Ark, the modern Jewish poets* (Avon Books, 1980, H. Schwartz and A. Rudolp, eds.), and I recall I owned a copy. But somehow, I didn't catch Meyers. Then and now my reading habits tend to be flighty, with many a book opened, read in part, then set aside.

By the mid-1980s I was living in Northampton, Massachusetts, and I would often visit my favorite bookstore in town, The Globe Bookshop (long gone, I'm afraid). The owner Mark Brumberg liked to hire poets to help him mind the store. The poet Wally Swist was working there at the time and one day when he noticed me browsing the poetry section, he put in my hands a copy of *The Wild Olive Tree and Blue Café* (Jazz Press/ PapaBach Editions, 1981) with a recommendation that I'd like this poet. I prided myself on being familiar with many contemporary poets, but Bert Meyers was a new name to me.

I did in fact very much like the book and I read it through several times as one does when the poems are fetching. At the relatively young age of 51, Bert Meyers had passed away only a couple of years before *The Wild Olive Tree and Blue Café* had been published, so I had the feeling that I was reading perhaps the last work I'd ever see in print by this poet.

I kept the poetry of Bert Meyers as my own semi-secret. I say "semi" because sometimes talking to other poets about poets that should be read more, or have been overlooked by anthologists and critics, I would throw out the name Bert Meyers. When my poet-friend Dennis Barone and I were kicking around names of neglected or forgotten poets a couple years ago now, I inserted Meyers name into the conversation. Sometime after, Dennis conceived of gathering an anthology of neglected or lesser-known poets. His idea was to invite various poets to write a short essay about a favorite lesser-known poet. I quickly volunteered to do a short piece on Bert Meyers. However, when I started to write this essay, the book *The Wild Olive Tree and Blue Café* was not to be found on my shelves. (I still have hope it's only misplaced among my too many poetry books.)

I was completely unaware at the time I offered to write this piece on Meyers's poetry, that a new book related to Bert Meyers and his poetry was about to be published as part of The Unsung Masters Series: *Bert Meyers: On the Life and Work of an American Master* (Gulf Coast, Copper Nickel and Pleiades, 2023), edited by Dana Levin and Adele Elise Williams. Given my mislaid book, being able to refer to Levin's and Williams's tribute book was a timely gift to me, and I made good use of it for this essay.

The name of the series confirmed that I had selected an 'unsung poet' at least. And yet, I did wonder how I could have thought of Meyers as being overlooked when other contemporary poets certainly were aware of his poetry and its evident merits. Turns out I was just one among an obscure society of other poets already passing around Meyers's name with admiration over the years.

Almost all of Bert Meyers's previously published poetry is scarce or costly in out-of-print editions. I must admit here that, somehow, I don't own Meyers's *In a Dybbuk's Raincoat: Collected* Poems which was released in 2007 by University of New Mexico Press. That collected seems to be out-of-print as well, and what used copies are for sale command a dear price. All of which points to the fact that to call Bert Meyers a neglected poet might be a stretch. Still, Meyers's work didn't get gathered by the major anthologies of his time (the sixties and seventies), nor can his work be found in major anthologies published since his death in 1979—thus Meyers was, one might say, easy to miss.

Neglected or not, it's time to turn to the poetry of Bert Meyers:

"Imaging is, in itself, the very height and life of poetry," stated John Dryden. The preeminent attraction of Bert Meyers's poetry lies in his "imaging" and his command of metaphor. Examples abound in his work; what follows are three beauties:

At the close of the poem, "Funeral," mourners at the casket are described as: "tasting their tears, / naked in a dream / over the long drawer / they have closed in the earth."

"No one spoke to the sunflowers, / those antique microphones / in the vacant lot." ("Sunflowers")

"All around me, butterflies, / ecstatic hinges, / hunt for the ideal door. / A cicada's rachet / tightens a place in the yard." ("All Around Me")

Image is a key element in any poem that dwells on a single object or a thing. Meyers had a gift for the 'thing poem'. See "The Garlic," "Cigarette," "Pencil Sharpener," et al.

Meyers's poetry is an oeuvre of short, descriptively charged lyric poems. Even the poems that are longer are typically segmented into short, numbered sections. A few of the lyrics I most admire are: "Gulls Have Come Again," "Old," "The Dark Birds," and "When She Sleeps."

Images alone are generally not enough to make a poem. One needs to feel the poet's hand in the making of the images: in seeing, hearing, and sensing particular acts and certain things. And then one needs to feel the poet's sensibility as the images become implications of emotional importance to the poet, and thereby to the reader. "Images, however beautiful," said Coleridge (*Biographia Literaria*, 1817), "…become proofs of original genius only as far as they are modified by a predominant passion; or by associated thoughts or images awakened by that passion; or when they have the effect of reducing multitude to unity, or succession to an instant; or lastly, when a human and intellectual life is transferred to them by the poet's spirit."

As an example of how the imagery alludes to a poet's state of mind and enlarges the stakes beyond the descriptive brilliance, here's an excerpt from start and ending of the poem, "Spleen":

Sometimes, I just hang around
like a dead man's coat,
or a vacant lot that trembles
when the construction crews pass.

[...]

Evening begins with headlights
and a sound track of birds
that fades from tree to tree.
Behind a garage, a few
strange weeds, taller than men...

With their mix of mirth and melancholic resignation, many of Meyers's poems share aspects found in post-WWII eastern European poets like Simic, Popa, and Szymborska. As example, here's a very short poem in full:

They Who Waste Me

When I ask for a hand,
they give me a shovel.
If I complain, they say,
worms are needles at work
to clothe a corpse for spring.
I sigh. Whoever breathes
has inhaled a neighbor.

From what I know of Meyers's biography he seems to have been a good person, a family man and a dedicated, beloved teacher. Before he turned to teaching, Meyers worked for many years as a picture-framer and gilder for galleries and museums (see his poem, "Picture Framing"). Many of the poems do feel tightly framed, but never would they be called gilded. Of note is the fact that Meyers did not have even a BA in poetry or literature. He was an autodidact who was able to get a full-time teaching position at Pitzer College (now part of Claremont system in southern California) based solely on the strength of his poetry and his knowledge of poetry.

As I said at the start of this essay, I'd missed reading Bert Meyers as part of a Jewish poets' anthology, and so I've come to think of Bert Meyers as a 'secret being' doing good work for poetry on earth until his death. I assert that Meyers may have been one of poetry's *lamed vav* (Hebrew for the number 36), from a legend in Jewish mysticism: One of 36 unknown good-deed-doers who live and work among us—we don't recognize them, even as they are in our midst, nor do they call attention to themselves and would not claim to being good-deed-doers. They would claim only that their acts (writing poetry in Meyers's case) were no more than any person would do for another in his community. Meyers' poetry and his teaching were his good works. Though the greater community of poetry may not have fully recognized his talents and the demonstrable quality of his work during his cancer-shortened lifespan, now, decades after his death, my hope is that many more of us will come to recognize the simple human powers on display in the poetry of Bert Meyers:

Gulls Have Come Again

Gulls have come again
to consider another beautiful death of the sun.

People were flowers that grew by the shore;
twilight takes them home,
they fade together at their tables.

In the tall green shops the pulleys of birds
lower the last light,
the eyelid of a shadow shuts the hills,
The sound of the ocean walks over the land.

Nobody wants to die.

Aldon Lynn Nielsen

A.B. Spellman (1935-)

So teach us to number our days, that we may apply our hearts unto wisdom.
Psalms 90: 12 KJV

I would venture that when the majority of the Grammy Awards audience for the 2023 presentations heard the name of A.B. Spellman, their reaction may have been "who?" He was among the group receiving that year's honor for Best Classical Compendium, though he didn't play an instrument or conduct. Spellman was being honored for his contributions as a poet to the collection *Passion for Bach and Coltrane*, a title that might well describe the poet himself. He had not even been nominated in the recently established category for Spoken Word Poetry. That award went for the second time in two years (the award has only existed for two years) to J. Ivy, who had in fact authored the proposal for the creation of that award. Spellman took to the stage to accept the award with The Imani Winds, and Jeff Scott, who had created the oratorio on the recording.

There had been a long, though quiet, prologue. Spellman had first published a collection of poetry in 1965, with Poets Press, bearing a preface by no less than Frank O'Hara. But he had not published a second volume till 2008, in the interim becoming far better known for his book on Free Jazz, originally titled *Four Lives in the BeBop Business,* and for his work as a commentator on jazz, including work as the on-air host for a series of Public Radio concert broadcasts. Spellman was born in Jim Crow North Carolina to parents who were teachers. For college he migrated north to "the Mecca," Howard University, known as the flagship of HBCUs. It was there that he met the slightly older LeRoi Jones, and soon enough Spellman was following Leroy Jones's example and rechristening himself "A.B.," having been born Alfred Bennett. By the time Spellman had followed Jones to New York, he was known to his many artist friends as "Ben." He was active in the Civil Rights Movement and relocated to Atlanta, where he was a founding figure of the Atlanta Center for Black Art. This was followed by a move to Washington, D.C., where Spellman went to work for the National Endowment for the Arts. While he participated in readings and workshops during his many years of government service, he wasn't publishing his poetry to speak of. Upon retirement, he published his second collection of poetry, and he has most recently published *Between the Night and Its Music: Selected Poems,* with Wesleyan University Press.

Begin with a day without number. The first poem in A.B. Spellman's first book, *The Beautiful Days*, is titled, note the definite article, "The Beautiful Day." And yet there were days and days to come. Frank O'Hara's prefatory note to *The Beautiful Days* asserts that *because* Spellman is honest, his poems, or at least a lot of them, are perfect. Now, Spellman's writing, both here and in his works on music, is notable for its honesty, and whatever your notion of perfection may be, a lot of his poetry likely fills the bill. And while I may beg forgiveness for my skepticism about any inherent causal link between honesty and the perfections of poetry, in all honesty I do find Spellman's poems often an application of heart unto wisdom. Take that first poem, "The Beautiful Day," a poem not included, as indeed most of the "Beautiful Days" are not included, in the *New and Selected Poems*. Its opening description of getting high with two fertile women might strike many as indicative of a certain age and time, but the poem's introduction of peacock feathers that seem to float leads to the sort of perfections O'Hara may have had in mind. The floating feathers, as felt by one of the women, lead into stanzas balanced on the apex of metaphor. "The shadows in the room have such weight / they seem to float / a weight down the lids." The weight of a shadow, one that only seems to float; the eyelids, heavy with the high, perhaps, with the slumbrous movements of the afternoon. "My weight of emotion," writes the poet. Not the weight of his emotion, but his weight of emotion; a striking formulation. "Just how thick is love," he asks, "& what / does it weigh" and "does it have eyes?" These lines summon a host of proverbial emotions. "There is none so blind as those who will not see," for one instance. In the fifth chapter of Jeremiah, twenty-first verse, we read: "Hear now this, O foolish people, and without understanding; which have eyes, and see not; which have ears, and hear not." The weight of love lays heavy upon us, if we are fortunate, and yet it lifts us up. It takes us higher.

In the *New and Selected* we have no beautiful days until day five, at least to judge from the table of contents. So, we will not share the sharp observations of the street scenes set out in Day Two with its invocation of the poet's friend "White" (a reference to the William White whose drawings accompany the poems), though the poem "For White" is there, closing as it does with "the day moving away." Nor will readers find themselves invited, in "the beautiful day, III," into the obscene house of an imagined page. "The Beautiful Day IV" gives us an initial stanza sounding like one of the Objectivist poets of a preceding generation, sounding much like George Oppen: "up & down, in & / out, round &," then across a stanza break a shift in rhetoric: "which way do / you go, hugo." I don't know, and neither will you, who this Hugo is who rhymes so neatly in the poem with "you know," "window" and "showing." But Hugo is cool, "so white" he vanishes "into the ground / up & down. The / softest ice in town."

Which gives way to day five, the first beautiful poem of the beautiful days selected for the *Selected*. There are some minor revisions in the version in the *Selected*, small changes in punctuation, perhaps more significant alterations in lineation. The version that appears in *The Beautiful Days* consists of four three-lines stanzas. The new version alternates stanzas of three and four lines. Still present, though now enjambed differently, is one of those passages that demonstrate the way that an abstraction can be spectacularly concrete: "the night leaked into the room" seems a relatively standard image, but then the night leaks "into the 'idea' of the group." Scare quotes around the word "idea" are retained in the new version, but the revised lineation makes for a yet more effective enjambment: here night leaks "into the 'idea' / of the group," leaving readers a nano second to

152

be, as Stanley Fish might have it, surprised. In *Surprised by Sin*, Fish finds the reader's own fallen state as the true subject of *Paradise Lost*. Spellman's fifth beautiful day, by pointing a second person pronoun directly at us, herds us into this idea, groups us with the actors of this lyric. "What a soft / lie your silence is," lines that remain the same in both versions, lines that impale us on the page.

"Beautiful Day 6," appears identically in the original book and in the new *Selected*, aside from its Roman numeral in the title being replaced by an Arabic. In *The Beautiful Days* of 1965 we are given an eight-day week of Beautiful days. Number seven presents a terrifying assault, sharp contrast to the loving atmosphere of what preceded. We do not know who the "wild man" in this poem is, and probably would rather not know. But the eighth Beautiful Day, which is the closing poem of that first book, returns us to the moods of the first, a man and a woman, seemingly alone in intimacy, but in "a world where war breaks / like a day in my conscious mind". There is no terminal punctuation here, suggesting a serial chain of beautiful days to come.

Did they come? In the most reflective verses of the newly *Selected*, the poet is often found looking back to the period of that first book. "I often think of the sixties in mystic terms," he notes. Maybe you had to have been there; that's assuredly how they seemed at the time. But then, "I wrote no poems for twenty years." Many of us wondered if he was writing but not publishing during the years he spent working for the Expansion Arts Program, imagining that perhaps the potential conflicts of interest stood in the way. But at the close of the often mis-dated millennium, it appears the poet finds himself "alive in the subjunctive," following the "cadences of the tensions & releases of art / & history." And this is where we discover the tenth Beautiful Day. Was there a ninth? Is there an eleventh? A hundredth? On the tenth day the poet recalls painter Bob Thompson, ignored mostly for decades but enjoying a reputational rejuvenation, complete with gallery showings, today. A note informs readers that number ten was composed in 1996, long after the eight that we know preceded

153

it, and that it was revised in 2020. The epigraph is the song "Oh, didn't he ramble," a song copyrighted in 1902 by the great Johnson brothers, J. Rosamond and James Weldon (not to be confused with The Brothers Johnson), a song much loved by poet and critic Sterling Brown (not to be confused with Sterling K. Brown of *American Fiction* fame), the Howard University one-man brain trust Spellman had known long before I met him. The song was first recorded in the year of its copyright, by Arthur Collins, and has never left the playlists. It is perhaps best remembered in the 1939 recording by Jelly Roll Morton, but was also waxed by Kid Ory, Louis Armstrong, in later years Peggy Lee, and even later by Dr. John, who seems to have been in the right place at the right time.

Another student of Sterling Brown's, known at the time as Leroy Jones, has also written poems to and about Bob Thompson. Jones's first, "Tone Poem," from the book *Black Magic Poetry 1961-1967,* proceeds from the same era as Spellman's first book of poetry, and commemorates the beautiful days when Jones, Thompson, and their friend drummer Elvin Jones would roam the streets in concert. The second, an uncollected piece titled "The Occident," bears a note in manuscript reading "A Poem To Be Read at Bob Thompson's Funeral." Thompson died in 1966, and so Spellman's first draft seems to arrive three decades later, perhaps itself rambling through the decades to arrive at now. From 1957 to 1958, Thompson was studying at the University of Louisville, under a trio of prominent European and American artists: Ulfert Wilke, Charles Crodel, and Mary Spencer May. He had then moved to New York, where he quickly fell in with such musicians as Charlie Haden and Ornette Coleman, and such poets as Allen Ginsberg and LeRoi Jones, and, presumably, A.B. Spellman. He was an associate of Red Grooms, Mimi Gross, and Allan Kaprow and is reported to have been a participant in the early adventures of "Happenings." He and his wife moved to Europe on a fellowship, but Thompson's death from a heroin overdose cut short one of the more prolific and promising careers in the sixties art world. His painting of the LeRoi Jones family is but one overt sign of the intense and productive interactions in the arts communities of the time.

"Oh didn't he ramble," asks Spellman, echoing the song. "He rambled" the poem ends, but again, and appropriately, without a full stop, without terminal punctuation. Wedded to the song in this poem is a fresco painted by Piero della Francesca, "Procession of the Queen of Sheba; Meeting between the Queen of Sheba and King Solomon." "O sheba / look around you" urges the poet. Though Sheba may not actually have existed, given that the Midrashic account of her journey suggests that she came from modern day Yemen and Ethiopia, and that the Quran's Sura 27, the "Chapter of the Ant," reports that Solomon had written to her there to invite her visit, it's unlikely that Sheba looked much at all as Piero depicts her. Thompson, one of whose purposes in going to Europe was to see first-hand the European masters, may have had thoughts about that. In any event, Spellman advises: "ramble a little most slandered of queens." The poem's second half turns to Thompson himself, who:

opened up his pores to the music
he moved inside of fickle as the day
Bluegrass / blues umbilically fed
east third street hard bop
downed with a straw
rhythm and blues force-fed with a spike

I like the way this segment, beyond being a tribute to the openness of listening among these friends, this hearing of all musics, also reminds readers of the intimacies of relation among the genres, and of the African Diasporic origins of most of what is today marketed as "Americana." Bluegrass is often termed the "jazz" of country music; country has been termed "three chords and the truth," a more than apt description of the Blues—and any guitarist can tell you a minor scale in the Blues is at the same time a major scale in country. But then there's that spike. Around the time these men were arriving in Bohemia, a movie titled *The Man with the Golden Arm* was playing in theaters. It was an adaptation of the Nelson Algren novel and featured a score by Elmer Bernstein. The protagonist of the narrative, named Frankie, is played by Frank Sinatra, and is an aspiring jazz drummer fighting to stay clean after a life of addiction. The spike is not a golden spike.

"So much music his heart moved over," writes Spellman, a line carrying generational weight. The tragedy of Thompson's end can never be compensated for by the triumphs of his art, but there is his art, and "oh, didn't it ramble." In remembering the many friends A.B. Spellman has memorialized in these beautiful days, we not only pay tribute to the generations who opened paths for us, but we also return to some of the great art of the past decades. Spellman is still rambling among us, and so we may apply our hearts unto his wisdom.

A. B. SPELLMAN
DEAR JOHN COLTRANE
—WITH ACKNOWLEDGMENTS TO MICHAEL HARPER

dead night has me writing poetry
in another hotel room. j.s. bach
is on the radio. The keyboard concerto
in f minor: the one you also hear
on oboe or violin. The largo
second movement begins
& the book in my hand drops
the room fades
& i put my reason down
to trail the bach of endless line
along this earthless path, each note full
& bright, a brilliant footprint on the dark
through beauty, past knowledge, into
that state that shines too much
to be wisdom, is too transparent
to be art. i catch a fear of the place
where he will lower me when
this transporting melody closes
then it closes on itself & here i am
dear john, back at the beginning, better

later, different station, cold room dimming
it's you, john, *trane's slow blues*
now it's your line that opens, & opens
& opens, & i'm flying that way again
same sky, different moon, this midnight
globe that toned those now lost blue rooms
where things like jazz float the mind

this motion the still & airless propulsion
i know as inner flight, this view
the one i cannot see with my eyes
open. i hear the beginning approach, &
i know the line i traveled was a horizon
the circle of the world. another freedom
flight to another starting place

if i believed in heaven i would ask
if you & bach ever swap infinite fours
& jam the sound that light makes
going & coming, & if you exchange maps
to those exclusive clouds you travel thru
& do you give them names?

Patrick James Dunagan
A Portrait of Poet Richard Tagett (1936-2024)
(w/ debt of thanks to Brian Lucas)

Rich was born in 1936 onsite at a corner pump station in Ashtabula, Ohio; but fully realized his calling upon a North Beach bar stool in San Francisco listening to Jack Spicer hold court during that poet's infamous final tragic years; and later swishing verse with the likes of poet Hunce Voelcker (author of the magnanimous work of poetic engagement *Hart Crane Voyages*) atop his pet cow up along the Russian River. Earlier, during the Korean War, Rich served in the Air Force. While stationed in Japan, he played piano in smoky jazz bars as he also would later on during trips into Los Angeles while living in Riverside, CA.

From an early age, Rich delightedly understood and openly accepted he was queer. In the 1960s he came to San Francisco and alongside local figures such as poet Robert Duncan became involved in the pro-gay/lesbian group Society for Individual Rights (SIR). In 1969 he co-founded *Manroot* magazine with Paul Mariah. Although he always downplayed his role, Rich was an instrumental force in every essential *Manroot* project from the phenomenal Spicer issue to publishing Lynn Lonidier's *A Lesbian Estate* (1979) with iconic wraparound cover art, a paste-up by the artist Jess.

For many years he lived with his partner Jose Laffitte, a Cuban painter of visionary realism scenes of fantasia who passed away too young of AIDS. A cataloging librarian by trade, Rich worked for many years in downtown San Francisco at the Mechanics Institute; eventually settling into a semi-isolated marijuana and Johnny Walker Red infused routine of poetry blues/jazz listening reading and movies in his two-bedroom apartment bordering San Francisco's Noe Valley/Mission neighborhoods. He ventured out for beers and playing pool, swims and passionate rounds of ping pong at the Y, along with playful gazing at younger men whose ambience he has always fancied. Having rather drifted away from poetry—joining a Marxist reading group throughout the 1980s—shortly before his retirement in the late 1990s, he befriended the several decades younger sui generis artist poet mythos figure Brian Lucas whose company sparked a renewal of social interest in poetry and art that blossomed in over twenty years of ongoing friendship. Rich was writing and publishing poems again, attending readings, and generally reengaging, if with arch trepidation, into the San Francisco poetry scene.

In a 1969 review of Robert Creeley's *Pieces* published in *Manroot* Rich opens with a description of the overall circumstance of a Creeley poem being "a 'locus of experience' wherein some queer honesty, simple/good taste, and the worldly & moral commitments work together toward a compact quality of proportion." As with any good review-writing by a poet about another poet, this statement is likewise fittingly apropos of Rich's own work. The concision found in his poetry arises from a sought for absolute clarity based upon principled intent: he means for the poem to contain nothing more and nothing less than exactly what is necessary. Ever tidily circumspect about his person and his home he is the same with his poetry. Going over the lines again and again through the years Rich was ever trimming and refining not only individual poems but his oeuvre as well. No doubt he has tossed aside as much work as he has retained.

As with his editorial work for *Manroot* Rich, never interested in showboating, placed little emphasis in seeing his poetry broadly distributed. In this he in part followed Spicer's lead in keeping things local in terms of publishing his work. With his re-emergence into the San Francisco scene local small press Ithuriel's Spear published the slim yet comprehensive and weighty *Demodulating Angel: Selected Poems 1960-2010* (2011) followed by *Somatic Messages* (2020). When he shared his work over the years it was always with particular friends or influences with whom he felt the poems had an immediate connection.

It was via Brian Lucas I came to know Rich. My wife Ava and I joined Brian and his wife, Nan, one Thanksgiving weekend for a festive potluck over at Rich's place. Along with food, there was some smoking plenty of music beer and whiskey. As the evening grew on there was some dancing as well; Rich with his tambourine giving himself a whirl. We got on. That night led to several more over the years, all of a similar nature, though the company might change now and then, be just Brian and I, or maybe us with one or two other poet pals, and we would order Chinese delivery or a pizza.

Some nights we also shared poems, reading them aloud to each other. Always there was discussion of poetry, art, and music. Later, I brought Rich a copy of Larry Kearney's *Testamentality, Transcryption: An Emotional Memoir of Jack Spicer* (Spuyten Duyvil 2019) which Rich immediately took to. Kearney recalls how he connected with Spicer: "Then we looked at each other, purely as a matter of recognition. By recognition I don't mean anything to do with status of any sort but merely the deep 'oh, yeah, I know you.'" Something similar passed between Rich and I on these early visits. That ease of recognition. You either have that or you don't. There is no fabricating it.

In an introductory note to a recent chapbook *Objects in the Square: The Shape of a Moment* (Bird and Beckett 2022), finished just as his latest health issues were driving him out of San Francisco and likely ending his capability to continue writing poems, Rich details some partial poetic lineage asserting basic principles guiding his work:

> The imagists and French symbolists were among my earliest attractions, while most contemporary poets were loosely defined as lyric. Today there's no such thing as lyric poetry, or modernist or American modernist poetry. One is left to define oneself. So call me new imagist—not *neo*-imagist as derived. Working *from* the image while eschewing narrative, I'm intent on realizing the essence of things through personal feeling while highly conscious of form and structure (Oppen), culminating in a synthesis of sensations and affect toward a subliminal clarity—as it were a syntax of the mind itself (Reverdy).

Once again as meticulous as possible Rich withheld or—as will most probably prove to be the case—abandoned as many recent poems as he included in this likely final collection.

In early 2021 as San Francisco began the slow emergence from out the pandemic shutdown Rich entered a series of illnesses resulting in multiple hospital visits. It became increasingly clear that living alone in his apartment was no longer sustainable. His extended family made arrangements to move him out of San Francisco to Detroit. His niece Becky flew in from Michigan and scooped him up declaring her willingness to look after him at her home. He took few things with him. I have his pool cue. A number of his books and cds, along with his 5-disc cd player stereo system which he wished for Ava and I to have if we liked.

Although his days had seemed perhaps numbered, once he was with his niece, Rich sprung back to health. I last saw him when I passed through Michigan for a book release reading in Nov 2022. We had dinner together in Ann Arbor and he came to the reading, his niece joining us with some local friends of hers. Though his movement was somewhat restricted by his needed use of a wheelchair, Rich was alert and tuned in as ever. He noticed a familiar ring on my pinky finger, one of his own he had left behind in San Francisco. I immediately offered it back, but he simply shrugged in a relaxed manner, remarking "I have no use for it." Just as in his poems, Rich remains ever efficient and direct; he recognizes the stark reality of his situation and requires nothing less. As he put it a few years back in an emailed statement discussing a recently published book of my own poems: "I was a communist gas station attendant." He knows the score.

Dec 2023
Rich passed away at 10:03 am Friday June 30, 2024.

RICHARD TAGETT

DOWN

At the hip
The body draped
Over the hot fender,
An elbow of vim,
Life instinct
Against the thick
Glass, rubbing

Wet
Cotton . . .

Where were the
People headed

Happy
Held in a snapshot
Behind the
Eyes, the lava
Hands

An ever crystal blue
Crystal clear
Containment

Down—
Down to the real,
The good.

Richard Kostelanetz

N. H. Pritchard (1939-1996)

N. H. Pritchard was a Jamaican-New York artist/writer whose *The Matrix Poems 1960-1970* (1970) has the dubious distinction of remaining the most innovative one-author collection of poetry ever published by a commercial house here, in this case Doubleday. It was probably valued at the time not for its typographical and verbal departures but for its author's dusky race, as fifty-five years ago, in the wake of Civil Rights protests in 1968, American commercial publishers were more open to black authors than they had been before. (So, what's new?)

Its cover had a knockout black and white photograph of its author, looking perhaps black, with half of his face in shadows, wearing a collared shirt with a tie and jacket. Pritchard looked elegant, much as Ralph Ellison was elegant; but whereas Ellison emerged from a fatherless family Pritchard's father was a physician who immigrated to New York City from "the Antilles," as his son so elegantly put it. At his death in 1972, Dr. Pritchard was remembered with a *New York Times* obituary as a department chief in a Harlem hospital. Much like other educated Jamaicans, the Pritchards were culturally BASP, which is to say a Black Anglo-Saxon Protestant, as Afro Caribbeans are as different from African Americans, strictly defined, as, say, Israelis in America are from American Jews.

Whereas Ellison didn't finish Tuskegee, Pritchard went to prep schools before taking his B.A. with honors from New York University and continuing with graduate school in art history. (He claimed in an interview to have gone to Downtown Community School, a legendary "progressive" institution on the Lower East Side, where I went as well from 1947 through 1951. Though Norman's birthyear was one year ahead of mine and DCS offered only one class for each birthyear, I don't remember him there.)

When I first met Norman, soon after *The Matrix* was published, he greeted me in his darkened studio apartment on Park Avenue in the 70s. He had received from the Abraham Woursell Foundation (in Vienna, Austria) one of those unpublicized grants designed to keep a young writer solvent for five years. Though only a year older than me, he seemed not just more sophisticated but unique in all the ways that a creative person can be unique. Pritchard's personal letters resembled the illuminated manuscripts of William Blake. To my copies of his printed texts, he added not just a personal inscription but the handmade enhancement of colors and lines that I treasure.

The poems in *The Matrix* appeared in several formats that would still look alternative today. Words were crushed together; some were printed upside down. Weighty phrases were repeated within the page. Words both familiar and unfamiliar had extra spaces between the letters. While some pages had just a large single letter, on other pages the print ran to the outside edges, suggesting that they might have continued beyond it. First of all, *The Matrix* challenged how a writer's "Collected Poems" should look.

As for the texts themselves, they approached the limits of semantic comprehension, as Pritchard's ideal was the "transreal," as he called it, reflecting his awareness of mystical, supernatural modernism in the visual arts. On an opening recto page was this epigraph for himself: "Words are ancillary to content."

On page 46 is "Gyre's Galax," whose fourth page repeats the phrase "above beneath" from its top to its bottom, sometimes amended by the words "it" and "in," because Pritchard wanted to take poetry into a domain previously unknown—that was indeed *above beneath*. For a remarkable acoustic experience, listen to Pritchard's own recitation recorded for *New Jazz Poets* (Folkways 1967).

The following year, 1971, a second Pritchard collection, *Eecchhooeess*, appeared from New York University Press, and to this day it has another dubious distinction as the most radical one-author poetry book ever to appear from an American university press. Repeating many of the same challenges posed by *The Matrix, Eecchhooeess* is no less brilliant, if somewhat lesser. *Eecchhooeess* should have included a brilliant long poem, "Hoom," that I first read in Ishmael Reed's anthology *19 Necromancers from Now* (Doubleday 1970), as well as other shorter texts deposited in fugitive places that should be collected. These books ended Pritchard's career as a publishing poet: he was 32.

He began to teach in his home city, first at the New School, and later at the Friends Seminary, which is a downtown institution that was culturally different from such uptown preppies as, say, Collegiate or Brearley. Soon after his father died in 1972, he changed his public name to Norman Henry Pritchard II and moved to Gradyville, Pennsylvania, west of Philadelphia where he died two dozen years after his father. If a cache of unpublished poems exists, they haven't surfaced.

The most unusual quality of the recent reprints of Pritchard's two books is that they appear intact, with their original front covers duplicated, each totally devoid of any new preface or afterword. Only the title and copyright pages are different, though the back cover of *The Matrix* reprint has blurbs appearing only with authors' names and no sources. Not even Pritchard's bio note is updated. Whether such authentic recycling represents smart republishing, a whole half-century later, I'll let others decide.

*

I had assumed that no more books would appear by this author. I was wrong. Primary Information, which reissued his 1970 collection *The Matrix*, has published his manuscript of *The Mundus,* which I would characterize as the first masterpiece of typographic abstract "graphic" fiction. I emphasize abstract because it differs from Emmett Williams's *Sweethearts* (1967), likewise a typographic fiction and likewise a masterpiece (composed only with words made from the seven letters in its title), but explicitly about love. Considering himself to be a spiritual "transreal" artist, Pritchard regarded aesthetic abstraction as superior to,

166

say, representational portrayals of religious themes.

While the publisher presents *The Mundus* as a single continuous text, it may also be read as a sequence of shorter narratives, each with its own typographic signature that changes visually from page to page, thus suggesting narrative, before skipping onto a different typographic signature. If this book is "a novel with voices," as Pritchard reportedly suggested, then it could be read as monologues by several visually distinct visual "voices," some of whom speak words and pseudo-words, others just certain letters. For instance, the book opens with over forty pages of the letter O—just the letter O—both upper case and lower case, distributed over the page's entire field, occasionally with the addition of a few short words. Another voice says "sh" in a single horizontal line without spaces continuously over eighteen pages.

As innovative as Pritchard's narratives still are, what marks this book as belonging to the 20th century, rather than the 21st, is that all the letters are roughly the same size, because they were produced on a typewriter. Had Pritchard survived into this century, he surely would have exploited the enormous typographic opportunities now offered the visual poet composing on a home computer.

Now that *The Mundus* has (re)appeared, one wonders if other extant Pritchard material—work only published in magazines and anthologies (such as the aforementioned long poem "Hoom") or work previously unpublished—might be collected and released. Until then, *The Mundus* must be seen to be read, let alone believed.

Sheila E. Murphy

On Gerald Burns (1940-1997)

The overall work and career of Gerald Burns reflects his classical education. His was a life lived in books. He spoke of being "18th Century trained" (Burns, *A Thing About Language* vii) indicating that real life is lived in volumes. One irresistible feature of Burns's work is a studied confidence in his subject and the courage to offer an always brave and surprising experience for the reader.

Gerald Burns is a difficult poet while immensely rewarding for those who seek and appreciate his depth and range. As the consummate reader, Burns's voracious appetite for thinking delights the reader who cares. Anything is fair game: the arts, versification, the field of magic, and more. Always with amazing generosity of spirit, Burns pays attention to the tangible realities of daily living, opening our minds to areas deserving of our attention.

What Burns was and always is about is the company of writers and artists, Creeley reminds us in the Foreword to *A Thing About Language*, a volume delicious with rich observations that delve into the hardware and spirit of poetry. Structure, stamina, and interest infuse the work of Burns. One observable phenomenon of his poetry and prose is a fascination with the well-made thing, how things work, all with the commitment and devotion to the sensuous while precise detail that creates a universe.

Imagine a writer known by those in the know as the real thing. I was privileged to have met Gerald quite accidentally by way of Jim Haining's Salt Lick Press / Lucky Heart Books at an early point in my writing career. A good friend of mine, John Beck, advised me to send something to Jim. His words at the time were "Go ahead and send him something. At the very least, he'll send you a couple of baseball cards." Oddly and happily, Jim wrote back, "Like your work enough to print." Little did I realize at that time how special and important this event would be.

Salt Lick Press / Lucky Heart Books represented the nexus of an important group of writers in Dallas, Texas, foremost of whom was Gerald Burns. As with geographical clusters of writers in San Francisco and New York City, the Dallas-based writers formed the core of writers who transcended geographical boundaries. So much of literary history encompasses groups of committed writers who were mutually inspiring. Jim Haining had a vision for the writers he wanted to represent. He worked slowly and deliberately. "Busy all the time" was the motto emblazoned on the table of contents for the 1989 Volume IV, Numbers 1 & 2 issue of Salt Lick Press, the twentieth year since initial publication. The care and artistry yielded a satisfying and surprising result, a work of art, mixing visuals alongside Gerald Burns, and other featured writers and artists including Robert Creeley, Michael Lally, Martha King, David Searcy, Tom Cassidy, Paul Shuttleworth, and Blaster Al Ackerman. Included in the Lucky Heart Books referenced in this issue were several volumes by Gerald Burns, including *Letters to Obscure Men, A Book of Spells [first third]*, and *Boccherini's Minuet 2nd Edition.*

Sadly, Leland Hickman was to have published *Longer Poems* by Gerald Burns as the first book from Temblor Press ("nearly all of its poems first including all 888 lines of *A Book of Spells II* appeared in his magazine *Temblor*" (*Longer Poems*). Hickman's death of AIDs at age 56 in 1991 changed literary history.

David Searcy's Barnburner Press took up the mantle. Most of the volume was typeset by Hickman. Burns alluded to the collaborative nature of this work. Burns, always enamored of the fact of typesetting, appeared to recognize that act as finishing a text. In the volume Burns offers a generous rendering of the "map" inherent in the poems themselves (London, Paris, New York, Dallas, Santa Fe, Austin). Each of these cities figures in the content of the longer poems.

It is a further testament to Burns's commitment to creating complex, challenging longer poems that necessitated substantial time and energy to create. Burns acknowledged that longer poems are harder to place in

169

literary publications. Keep in mind that all 888 lines of *A Book of Spells II* that appeared in *Temblor* involved considerable effort and care. Robert Trammel invited Burns to give a reading within three months' time and Burns took up the challenge. It is worth noting that Burns engaged in an intentional plan for each of the longer poems included in the volume. "A Chain for Madeline" took Burns nine months to write. "Socrates Dying in Widener," ten months and ten weeks (*Longer Poems*). The craft is always signature, and Burns acknowledged the difficulty of achieving the sumptuous result of each of the longer poems.

Burns intended a pairing of shorter and longer poems. Constantly in touch with Creeley, Burns kept him in the loop regarding the matching set of shorter titles. It is worth nothing that few literary events and selections occur in a vacuum. Aware of the richness of the *Shorter Poems*, Creeley selected the volume for the National Poetry series in 1992. The collection would undoubtedly have been different from other contenders for the award. The poems included in-depth perspectives associated with richness of the highest order. He moves among laps of erudition almost unimaginable and (dare I say it?) fun. The reader who willingly enters any given swatch of prose or poetry comes away surprised and often grateful. There is a careless quality placed side by side with hard-won, indisputable learning.

Boccherini's Minuet is a relatively gentle and straightforward series of poems in contrast to the more complex pieces in *Longer Poems* and *Shorter Poems*. After considerable reflection, I have decided to include #10 of the title-poem (Burns 10) for its contextual beauty that bespeaks Burns's popular collection. It should be noted that this was the first second edition of Burns's books.

10/
A green glass bottle with beer in it
sunk under water
is the color of the water on
a warm day on a lake in Michigan
living water, warm beer
yellow green and brown

a rich, silty heady liquid loam
what smells of old rope and gasoline
the kind of water that you know
is full of live things
little perch, and long pickerel
and the great Muskie I have seen
mating off my back lot
and the secret clam
which no one seems to eat in Michigan
though I am told they are good with pepper
and the lake I remember most
is Torch Lake, so clear
the bottom sand shows grain-perfect
through 20 feet of water, air on air—
ringed with round flat stones
Lake Superior
so cold it numbs the feet against stones
a shore rich in exoskeletons
of little crayfish, blue-white
thinner than eggshell
and Lake St. Clair, the lake I grew up on
which may have eaten as many freighters as Erie
in its spare time in tornado weather
the color of steel beer
and having risen early once one morning
stumbled on a Purgatory dawn
sky and lake one pearl
and heard *In exitu* . . .
to grow upon on Michigan light on Michigan water
makes every other place Pontus.

Unlike the more abstruse work by Burns, this collection reveals pure unadulterated poetic prowess. If I am not reading too much into the work of Burns, I recognize his own tendency to show off his scholarship (deservedly so) in much of his work. This, in stark contrast to his signature gift for perception and true, deep poetry of the finest order.

When reading Burns, I say to myself, "Try to keep up." It takes work. The difference between reading generous Gerald Burns and other rarified authors is that, in the manner of a great teacher, he is able to understand deeply and broadly a vast array of human experience and shape it. His mind was interested in everything. Further, I note a consistent commitment in Burns to place value on utility. Often, this encompasses a field of endeavor that spills out into metaphoric application. Witness his love of useful things, calling to mind the obvious and important draw of utility when referencing "My favorite barn" in *A Thing About Language*. Burns reveres utility "on the workbench the hearth idol was a very good, a very heavy vise, in coffee cans and old drawers now open boxes such iron filaments as I found in my farm rounds. They were sometimes useful, especially the metal straps and hasps, bendable in the big vise, with effort . . .". "There was charm when the bits were old enough (rusted spark plugs are still boring) and potential utility, as in a time-game of potential utility" (1).

Nothing effete here, in stark contrast to the rarified air of Eighteenth-Century learning. Like good teachers, Burns sees through and into the meaning and value of any starting place for learning with ready admitting where value may lie and apply.

Hanging in my closet is a beautiful off-white t-shirt with an original drawing of a flute in blue and gray by Gerald Burns, sized large as was my preference. I keep that affectionate gift among my most sacred possessions. Gerald wrote the introduction to my books *Teth* (Chax Press, 1991) and *Falling in Love Falling in Love with You Syntax: Selected and New Poems* (Potes & Poets Press, 1997). His attention paid to my poetry came at a time when his appreciation lifted my work for the central place in my life it continues to occupy. The greatest gift of all to me was Gerald's own

172

work, which I regularly revisit and at which I marvel. Any single passage of Gerald's work lives as testament to his brilliance.

Sources

Burns, Gerald. *Boccherini's Minuet*. Dallas: Salt Lick Press. 1981.

_____. *Longer Poems*. Dallas: Barnburner Press. 1994.

_____. *A Thing About Language*. Carbondale: Southern Illinois University Press. 1990.

T THILLEMAN

GEORGE F. BUTTERICK (1942-1988)

Butterick's short life and his collected output, though only a couple hundred pages, forms a body of awareness onto itself. The poems exemplify seriality punctuated not merely by the physical, nor the materiality of subject matter, never resting in textualized experiment. They are *indexical*, that is, interior to the poem's sequential event. The work expands an understanding of time and tempo. As Ed Dorn wrote in the opening to his own longer poem, *Gunslinger*:

> Time is more fundamental than space.
> It is indeed, the most pervasive
> Of all the categories
> In other words
> Theres plenty of it.
> And it stretches things themselves
> Until they blend into one,
> So if you've seen one thing
> You've seen them all.

Butterick's was the work of a longer, serial or sequential composition, and if he had been allowed to continue past his 45th year, the volume would have comprised more notoriety to his name than as the well-known and thorough editor and compiler of Charles Olson's *The Maximus Poems*. In contra-distinction, Butterick's work does not take place in one city or specific era, per se, but leaps toward form in its struggle between plasticity and subject.

A central device in Butterick's seriality (not unlike that utilized by Proust in *À la recherche du temps perdu*) presents itself through a constant criss-cross with verbal digression, momentary word-choice alongside textual "precision." This method for the writing is made into a kind of statement in "A Visit from the Whisper Woman." Its six stanzas move through the world and thus many guises holed up within existence. Existence, totality, that is, or "She," the first word of the poem : "When she came she had so many boxes / she could have used a slave." A breakdown of that personified many as momentous glimpse, he writes, attaching to a "celestial region...."

> What spilled wasn't my hopes or even my breath.
> Her lips a grapeskin thick, reluctant to let all
> the smoke out. Whisperette. ...

This eke of meaning "inside" and held within the poet is preceded and followed by a flat assertion that there is nothing below this region "to cause or warrant" a glimpse at its final meaning. There is a "rival culture" at work from both ends— "hollows of her neck" as well as what is "lying out there." Breath and speech intertwine through her region, as much as the material world does, yet superseding its presumptions.

So the final stanza in such a glimpse or sudden insight, the "whisperette," the Muse who holds creation in her thick-lipped seeming, appears and asks the poet a question which reflects this two-fold, mirrored and non-mirroring rival of inner and outer culture. Her quotes sit on the page as two apparitional speeches. The effect of celestial as well as textual, mortal, earthly reading—the hollows previously mentioned—take on complete amplitude ("whispered" to ourselves) has the poet bathing under a "dripping, buttery moon." A level of success (we are told) no one minded as long as it "got the job done."

And what, then, is the job, of poet and poetry in this close hearing?

The sequence "Protein" conjures a night scene any such domicile might entertain.

From my bed
somewhere, somewhere the soft night
creaks of burglary

But what house? We've been brought to the expansiveness of night so as to enter a blackened sky. What burglary? The idea of words stolen as they compose themselves on the page transmutes the composition into relations of stars as opposed to mere human neighbors.

In his youth, in the classroom, he would seek a
path on the marbleized cover of his notebook,
and so be free. He would also blacken squares in
the "times table" on the back cover,
instinctively seeking pattern and control.
The smallest conceivable details recoverable.

Here the night composes the poem and human agency is out of the equation, even as it voices from a person. What poet, then, writes what we hear? It's a matter of measure and the magnetics of the vocabulary set from the first lines of "Protein."

What kind of man would refer to his hat
as his "vehicle"?

The incongruous meaning that adheres more to a pun than to an analogy? Butterick is constantly at the equivocal sound and meaning of what could become a pun factory let loose through the vestiges of the sequence and is always at the ready to see what else is at work—not grammar in ruins but a thought house in shambles. The displacement within this struggle against received knowledge, over against a larger measure and mean, shows a symbiosis of subject and the "plastic" reality of "hat." Representation here is no longer one of a received, or too easy, metaphor for thought or mental transport; rather the actual being who might think his existence could swing from one insight or hearing to another, residing in the life of one symbol, Butterick questions again and again. The spaces, the cornering of the poem's progression becomes one of pressure. The steam, as it were, always let back into the poem itself, unhung as it is in the urgency of the struggle to continue.

> There are too many facts living on this planet.
> Control their population.
> Take heed, take wing, take Tahoe, but
> don't take notes for an answer.
> facts with a little chin drizzle, facts flaking
> front and behind, affronted facts,
> fact aplomb, scattered termites of splattered facts.
> Too many; too mean.

There is no one place the poem comes to rest within. That is, a doing away with "facts" as they would be used to win an argument. Here the actual is "inside" the entry. Further than that entry is the fact of its break with a fact-based scheme. What phonemes, what sounds collide within the subject the poem has raised from the first as protean articulation. Every reflexivity is attracted toward an interior that seems to vanish, the poem comprising a pressurized mercury from an increasing vacuum. In other words, the poem asserts its own vocabulary, and, through that assertion, a view through reality. We are experiencing Night.

Butterick is experiential. No part of his output was unrelated to the experience writing offered.

> …Franco banned Catalan, saying
> bite, don't bark, your tongue. A ruthless muzzle
> do you know the etymology of embezzlement?

No, but I certainly know the consistency of
entitlement. What kind of men are these?

They are not merely men, of course, but consistently rigid identities
who cannot understand modulation. The disappearance of dialect and
language can track alongside these kinds of identities as well. So the poem
struggles in that equivocal range of subject and object, finding its own
parameters in expansion and contraction.

> Stretch marks glistening like snail tracks. Too rough
> for you, babe? Like getting in the back seat with
> a bottle washer. A golden arch for the vomitorium.
> I'll give you description, your academic heart
> will do a nosebleed in the snow. It has been so long,
> her pubic hairs clung together like Velcro fasteners.

Direct transcription of a sexual act does not use the same words as its
social construct. Do not, the poet warns, take yourself into a permanent
separation of time and space based on social convention; don't change
your face if you are not willing to understand time in unending sequence.
You are facing an extinction brought not from your self (though you've
reasoned an extension of willpower) but from dead nodes of symbology
passed around through conformity. But the poem is a conformity as well.
The struggle is this:

> ...Please, choose the dark,
> the silent, the subtle over the bold,
> the active, and forceful. Only in this way
> is the natural order of events
> disturbed as little as possible.

Believe in yourself as part of a larger Night. The fundamental orders of time—as Dorn references at the beginning of *Gunslinger* in order to riff on Parmenides' injunction "all is one/ for I return"—necessitate a reality that is all pervasive, no matter its trend or guise. We are moments of insight, yet in the black of night, where no easy measure can rest, there is slippage, a fall, a struggle and continuation that cannot be violently burgled out of the house.

> Rub the hyphens out of your eyes! Learn to smell.
> We live in very preoderant times. Improve your spelling
> or
> turned sidewise, you'll be infinitesimal.
> Quicken your erasers! Insert
> your skills, insist upon a label.
> You wouldn't say Meet me to dinner
> would you? Then why do you say, meet me
> to plan a menu? Can't you cook yourself?
> You can, if the pot is big enough.

No one is going to change your mind about the poem if the outer—the world we assume outside the advent of the poem—is doing all the defining of reality. We have one chance, one lifetime, in order to get this say right. Choosing a larger realm, one not trapped in preconcepts of imagination, that is, received landscapes, gets us past an infinity of one finite mistake.

> What I hate are poems
> that have only one good moral to give
> or people with only one meaning. The unexamined wife
> is not worth leaving.

Why would anyone object to reality, say, only to find themselves in the surround sound of reality even so? Change your name: you are, still. Modified, perhaps, but hunger sets in and one has to go out again and

179

forage. Or go in and forage. In other words, the tenets we live by, untested, might be the most dangerous, even if they're ethically prudent. Test them again; do not simply discard.

> Make mud a miracle, and even
> the police will go topless.
> What kind of talk is "from before?"
> Subordination is an aid to unity.
> Insubordination means you never
> drank the kool aid.

Keep the poem alive, keep the composition, keep the vocabulary whirling in the mind, in and out. Even as the indexicality of the poem goes from word-trope to experiential trope, there's an obligation the hearer, the reader, needs to travel through the reality the poem is uncovering. Certainly, the circularity of such a statement is never a *real* end. Assumptions pile up into the circle of circularity. Breath and the "whisper" of the poem turn themselves over to an academic trope, a continuum that only mimics. It is in the respiration of a living, contemporary poem, the true understanding, never far from its assertion in the unknown NOW, comes to mean what the various sequences are pushing forward.

> Check the dumb puns—
> seize her, Caesar—
> before they do any more damage to one's discipline.
> Whip them back, like fanged droolers.
> Let only the entendres metaphysically true
> pass the brittle gates. Hold in steel
> your command of mind, gaze that shares
> the prowling area with puff of warm laughter;
> pad around a theme, rise to towering nod
> over it, bow soulfully, as profoundly as the

soulful bow, the greeting that honors as
it obeys.

Again, the received language that forms in the mouth might capture the thesis of the poet's thrust, but it cannot be entertained for long. The mind is a value not to be wasted on mere words. *Theoria* has no life without its others: *Phronesis*, or practical wisdom, but also *Thanatos* and *Arete*. What about *Episteme* and *Nous*; in short, what about the others? The names are endless but interiority of their use is a terminal of awareness coupling action with experience—and experience is what the poem means to honor.

Professor Mickey Moment visits the Terminal Chamber.
He pads and pads and pads,
the right side of his head always slicker
where he pats it, wets it down with his
own nervous palm.
Eyelid twitch steady now, had been
Creeping up after twenty years of office hours
Denying student pleadings.
In conversation, he refers to "they"
a lot. Once he pinched my cheek and hung
On there. I put my hand in my pocket
not to hit him. Not a misplaced ethnic hair;
shaves deep down his neck so that nothing bursts
forth there, either.

There is the idea that knowing and form (in a Platonic sense) are at work in Butterick's cascading vocabulary, its use and plasticity. The subject may begin with one simple, say "night," but it can stretch and reach every other form, so the poem becomes a long wind-tunnel to measure the entirety of evolutionary time. Certainly, there is this leap from the present, even in its global socio-political, back into paleo time, a kind of parallel vision of writing, one that sees it not as product of any class or kind, but a plumbing of any and all form.

THE NEOLITHIC BROTHERHOOD

Restore Jerusalem to its original citizens.
Eliminate all Jews, Moslems, and Christians.
We were there before David. We were there
Before Dj'ru-salaam.If Vietnam vets are still
Howling 15-20 years later, and Holocaust survivors
40 years later, Armenians 70 years after,
Cherokees 150 years, the Irish, the Afro-
Americans—how much more do we remember!
We are known to each other; look for the signs
And ask yourselves,
Are you one of us?

The selection that follows, "Photons and Epigrams," continues to play at this criss-cross of textual realism alongside momentary glimpse.

You don't write poems by polls,
An image is not a consensus.
Isolated cars pass like the moons of Jupiter.
The poet is in his condition like a dinner jacket.
Who ever said it was his responsibility
to renew the inquiry?

There is, at the end of "Protein," emblematic of his serial thematic, the final lines, the sense of sight and verbal counterpart which make much of the interiority of the poem. We might say: *content*, but there are no boundary markers in this struggle with subject matter, gone thru its plasticized revolutions, exiting again into the reality of all human artforms:

Every sentence must be, or supply, its own transition.
Laughter is the oxidization of meaning;
meaning is the laughter of the mind.

George F. Butterick

A selection from "Photons & Epigrams"

Like sitting wrapped in a wet sheet,
sitting in the car wrapped in wind
and speed, itself not speed
but producing speed-that relative
causation by which one person becomes
his other in the same period of time.

*

Do you hate the saying "quite a nest egg"
as much as I do? Would you run your grandmother
into the ground for using it? When a policeman
chases you, do you hear sweaty pistons, is there
the thud of breath and the creak of leather
like a horse's cinch, jangles dulled by sweat,
and down you go into the concrete or against the bricks.
It isn't pretty.

*

"Smell that!" he said, suddenly
extending the clenched fist.

And each enjoyed the privilege
of a smell at the fist of power.

*

All her love
in a flappy fire.
Cheap things
burn cheaply.

*

He/ she stood before the mirror and looked at his/her
figure, but all she/he asked him/her was the size of
his/her figures of speech.

*

She had a snack for a brain
and went to bed hungry.
At Point Lobos, the land licks
its own fingers, whatever the sea
throws up. The eating habits
of continents are indelicate
but deliberate, and costly,
not to mention forsaken.

*

His hot breath
in her ear. Fear,
is there room in there
for me?

Charles Bernstein

Leslie Scalapino (1944-2010): Rhythmic Intensities

The poet dies, the poet's work is borne by her readers.

When I first encountered Leslie Scalapino's work I was hard hit by its psychic intensity, formal ingeniousness, and rhythmic imagination. I felt I came to the work late; the first book I read was *The Woman who Could Read the Minds of Dogs,* which while published in 1976, I didn't read till around 1981. The psychosexual dynamics of the work and its ability to make dislocation a visceral experience immediately became, once I had taken in the magnitude of Scalapino's project, a capital point on the mapping of poetry associated with L=A=N=G=U=A=G=E magazine, one that deepened and enriched that survey. When North Point published *Considering How Exaggerated Music Is* in 1982, Scalapino's work became an indelible part of my poetic firmament, that imaginary company each of us chooses but that also chooses us. That is, I feel as much chosen by Scalapino's work as that I was doing the choosing; her work entered into and changed my consciousness about what was possible for poetry, changed the terms for all of us working along similar lines.

Every-once-in-a-while I would say something to Leslie about *Considering how exaggerated the music is.* She would shake her head, slightly laughing, "Oh Charles not *the* music: considering how exaggerated music is." As in her music, the music of her poems. Not exaggerated in the sense of hyperbolic or overstated, but as in *extravagant,* wild and wandering.

Starting in my earliest conversations with Leslie, when I would try to describe qualities I found in her work, she was adamant in resisting interpretations she felt countermanded her intentions. When I would say, but you know, Leslie, readers will respond in many different ways to a poem, she would give no ground; for her, how a work is to be interpreted was part of the poem: not just her intention, but part of the integrity of the work itself. I felt her rebuke to my more porous view of interpretation to be magnificent and improbable, for as much as Leslie set the bar for interpretation a bit higher than actual reading practices will ordinarily sustain, she demonstrated her fierce commitment to poetic meaning and also the truth in the form and materials, sincerity in Zukofsky's sense: that reading was a social bond that necessitated the reader's recognition of the formal terms of the work. So there was a right way to read, not in the moral sense but in a very practical one, as in a right way to operate software so it works, does the job for which it was made.

And you could say that Scalapino created a new and thrilling poetic software, allowing for a phenomenologically unique experience, something like a 3- or 4-D poem. Her overlays, repetitions, and torques enable proactive readers to enter the space of the poem as something akin to a holographic environment. The present time of the work is intensified by her echoes (overlapping waves of phrases) of what just happened and what is about to happen, so the present is expanded into a temporally multi-dimensional space. Her undulating phrasal rhythms are in turn psychedelic, analytic, notational, pointillistic, and narrational. Think of it as deep-space syncretic cubism. And Scalapino's performances of her work, many collected at PennSound, are crucial guides to entering this hyperspace.

Scalapino's poetry was central to my poem/essay *Artifice of Absorption,* which I wrote starting in 1985. In *Artifice of Absorption*, I noted that Scalapino's rhetorical repetitions create a disabsorptive/affective charm: the slight, accented, shifts in similar statements operate as modular scans of the field of perception, building thick linguistic waves of overlay and undertow, the warp of a thematic motif countered with the woof of its torqued rearticulation.

When I visited Leslie and Tom in Oakland a few weeks before Leslie died, her luminous and effervescent stoicism, the nobility in which she acknowledged death lurking in her garden, was fused with her refusal to give up on life and her urgent, tragic recognition of the work she still had it in her to do that she would not be able to do. She spoke of how much she wanted to come to New York to read her new work, and so together with Stacy Szymaszek and Tracy Grinell we made plans for her to read at Saint Mark's Church. In Oakland in May, we laughed together at the moment's literary gossip and we talked about her just finished book, *The Dihedrons Gazelle-Dihedrals Zoom*, written in the late style of *Floats Horse-floats or Horse-flows*; she knew it would be her last.

I sent her my response to this work just days before she died, trying to do justice to the work and hoping that she would accept my description as apt, which Tom tells me she did:

The Dihedrons is an ekphrastic implosion inside our severed human-body/animal-mind. "Memory isn't the origin of events," Scalapino writes early in this magisterial work, which restores the synthesis of events to its place as meanings' origin. *The Dihedrons Gazelle-Dihedrals Zoom*—as much a work of grotesque science fiction as a poem—cracks open the imaginary reality astride reality. In the stadium of its visionary composition, the everyday floats vivid strange: *in* time, *as* time, *with* time, *beside* time.

Scalapino's poems, from her first book to this last, probe politics, memory, perception, and desire, creating hypnotically shifting coherences that take us beyond any dislocating devices into a realm of newly emerging consciousness. Like a sumo wrestler doing contact improvisations with a ballerina, Scalapino balances the unbalanceable poetic accounts of social justice and aesthetic insistence.

Every once in a while, I'd say something to Leslie about her book series, calling it O Press; she would shake her head, slightly laughing, "Oh Charles not *oppress*, O Books"! "Oppression is our social space." Leslie, with the support of Tom White, created one of the great small presses of our time.

I keep thinking about her titles, which are among the most amazing, fantastic, and unexpected of anybody ever ... And her essays, which are models of a non-expository, exploratory style remains foundational for

188

any activist poetics.

Like a ballerina doing contact improvisations with a sumo wrestler.

The poet dies, the poet's work is borne … by us, in us, through us, as us.

It's the longest day.

Considering how exaggerated music is.

LESLIE SCALAPINO

FROM CHAPTER 1,
FLOATS HORSE-FLOATS OR HORSE-FLOWS
(BUFFALO: STARCHERONE BOOKS, 2010)

The green speechless and languageless fractionators and whirlabout but which appear transported not stationary anywhere are. Yet shimmying sieves vast on cobalt they roil audibly driven only—but uncontrolled where the cobalt is uncontrolled also but quiet. But the cobalt is *their* condition? Precluding blowholes without ground they are divided from action yet a dag is walking on the road alone. How can he be charming if he's alone, he is still charming. Yet is future. A hastate is completely silent whereas the huge whirlabout has feathery entrails emerging from their bending poles daggling the cobalt by a leaping speechless hartebeest who is small by comparison. Though there can't— one thinks—be comparisons because the dag doesn't make any, doesn't think of it, in not either seeing the hartebeest or hearing it? Guess. A hartel is occurring. Yes. The closing of the shops but the dag doesn't work in the shops or anywhere, and since the workers there don't come to work, the hartebeest wandering, the vast shimmying fractionation is heard from the cobalt. Four (acting as a verb, four shops aren't passive resistance) I'm surprised. The people's action *is* passive resistance having closed the shops. The green fractionate antimatter, the shadow stretched (outside is transient) not one and not passive or resistance *then*. Arms out the stretched flat tummies hit the water of swimming pools. Having closed the shops, yet they are without work at the same time. They halve the water everywhere at once. They have either and the fractionators grind the delicate cobalt future once. How can it (what) be the same as sound? They only remember the sound of the dew approaching almost at dawn, in that the dew is not there now. Before the two conceiving birds singing by the two bound people who're also conceiving and speaking, paired in the condition of the quiet cobalt attacked by blasting motion, they're hearing it.

Beside deduction the black guiltless cattle are like dogs in someone's description, the uselessness of speaking, the same person says suddenly recognizing the one-box-fits-all words he's used that act making even plants indistinguishable from people. The doctors could burst out start off in garveys on the waves. They hope. At night the doctors go on house calls and being targeted they're being assassinated, many fleeing decimating, assassinated because they treat the people the assassination of the entire people is intended by "insurgents oar resistance" who are not centrally directed? The 'insurgents' oar' is grinding the quiet cobalt. Asleep the dag appears walking a dog in the future it's on a leash but very large, it's from the herd of cattle and is bawling incipit walking with the dag because it is guiltless light its feet hardly touching. Seen. The cars fractionate or some decorticate a single blind area. The road is filled with apparent dogs bawling incipit in waves above the ground then. A worker in the shop district where there's still grass is speaking to plants calling them Betty as he waters each one where the dag passes. It happens this was the single name given to the cattle who bark at night so they could be quieted by someone calling once. Betty. I hear rain. See. Inceptor, the dag has entered a single day on the basis of one incompliant silent word not named, not known by the dag subjectively, though it is *only the dag's* basis, since there is no basis except inclinatory—so, T wakes and says Why is it raining? He addresses the air. Colorless cars waving, they're impinging Rrr fractionators of the rain which only falls and waves distinguished from hearing dew a teal garganey flying. As sound travels clearer in rain the car motors incoherent dust there, is no dust anywhere in rain here, the wave lacking unity or harmony *is*. Caaah caaah. Above is the rain, it is waving on the street then the cattle halving the rain everywhere they puncture walls of the neighborhood. They are apart. Bawling since (oar after) the dag is silent. Calm, apparently mad (angry) at one ("the vast black cattle"), the two beings indistinguishable are there also. After the mother died. A corpse lightly grinds the motionless cobalt-fractionator of a deaf spot. One is heard thinking *passing that day* the dag who's watering the cattle, now dogged, the water pouring from them. Above them the cobalt still motionless *as* (acting as a verb) their own fractionation (thinking), (of the cobalt oar grinding the quiet).

PETER BUSHYEAGER

GOOD LUCK ON THE LONG DRIVE HOME:
AN APPRECIATION OF LEWIS WARSH (1944-2020)

The publication of Donald Allen's 1960 anthology *The New American Poetry* was a major event for many young poets. Lewis Warsh was among them. Allen's anthology presented an extensive body of post-World War II poetry that was outside the official canon and delineated new areas of exploration. A cursory look at Warsh's bio shows an early and ongoing commitment to work initially inspired by the anthology's then-novel blend of first-generation New York School, Black Mountain, San Francisco Renaissance, and other influences. Warsh took these influences, honed his own unique voice, and became a leading poet and influential editor, publisher, and teacher who inspired readers and helped guide poetry developments in the coming decades.

Warsh grew up in New York City's Bronx borough, began writing poetry in his teens, and attended the legendary Berkeley Poetry Conference during the summer of 1965 where he met many other like-minded poets, including Anne Waldman, a future collaborator. He subsequently attended City College of New York where he received undergraduate and graduate degrees in English. Early in his career he moved away from New York and spent time in California, Massachusetts, and New Hampshire, establishing a broad literary network and collaborative relationships with notable poets including Joanne Kyger, Robert Creeley, William Corbett, and many others. However, for most of his life, his primary location and point of reference was New York City.

He was an integral part of the Poetry Project community at St. Mark's Church in Manhattan's Lower East Side, which included Ted Berrigan; Ron Padgett; Waldman, with whom he founded the publishing venture Angel Hair; and Bernadette Mayer, with whom he co-founded United Artists Books. Warsh's work includes 24 volumes of poetry and 10 books of fiction or autobiography. His awards include grants from The National Endowment for the Arts, The New York Foundation for the Arts, American Poetry Review's Jerome Shestack Award, and the Editor's Fellowship Award from the Coordinating Council of Literary Magazines.

Mentoring younger poets was a significant, ongoing focus in his life. He taught at Naropa University, Queens College, Fairleigh Dickinson University, The Poetry Project, The New School, and at Long Island University in Brooklyn where he was the founding director of the MFA program in creative writing.

Lewis Warsh's work is sometimes classified as second-generation New York School. However, that label is at least as much a function of his physical location and the company he kept as any commonality with Ashbery, O'Hara, and other marquee names from the first generation. For accuracy's sake, one should also include among his influences Reznikoff and the Objectivists, and Whitman's quest for the universal via intense listing/naming. Warsh's poetry wields vulnerability and a quiet, steady power. No aesthetic theories shouted from the ramparts. No career-savvy minting of a colorful persona. No Olson-like stentorian musings. Warsh identifies classic human behavior and revels in the quotidian, which often, surprisingly, gives way to the sublime. Nostalgia and pathos are leavened with deadpan humor. Mundane details accrue energy and meaning as they relentlessly scroll out on the page. In short, he shares the gossip of life and is often as surprised as we are.

...You see,/I'm trying to draw/on all my resources/in an attempt to portray/ a feeling for who I am, draw/on my feelings like a scanner picks/out stars in the midnight sky . . .

(Warsh, "To Have an Eye to," *Information from the Surface of Venus*).

Lewis Warsh is about "the personal," but he presents a skewed version of it. He is not, strictly speaking, a confessional poet. He hints at explosive facts that must never be divulged and lets the reader know he's holding tight to the details. No photos here. Only rough sketches, and you fill in the blanks.

> Use words to describe feelings?
> I wouldn't if I were you.
> Tracing back the history
> of a symptom to its source, the
> world of memory beckons and
> we turn it into feeling
> rude as the heart quickens
> for fear some stranger
> might intrude, some presence
> like a court filled with jesters
> and fools performing a masque
> Ben Jonson might have written.

(Warsh, from "4/13/79," *Information from the Surface of Venus*)

Nostalgia is often key to Warsh's work. But with the exception of very early poems, he doesn't present painful, sentimental recollections, which can be rife in many poets' work. For him, remembering is a fertile field for the imagination. Past events are replayed for new perspectives and possibilities. This lends a speculative air to poems that can present an immaculate surface of reportage while emotionally loaded material roils beneath the surface. As a result, the reader is an ardent eavesdropper and investigator.

> Write
> about your life for awhile
> then change the tune. You stay
> the subject as long
> as it's you writing, I guess,
> the same way St. Augustine's Confessions

are as much about you and me as they are
Brad Fisk, local butcher . . .
(Warsh, "Forest Park Store," *Blue Heaven*)

Lengthy sequences of short, pithy, prose lines of "information" that build and morph are a hallmark of Warsh's oeuvre. *Methods of Birth Control* (1983) presents this mode in a largely conceptual context and serves as a precursor for later, more emotionally driven work that shares this tactic. The book includes "Eye Opener," an 85-entry disquisition on vision, the 72-entry "High Fidelity" about sound systems, and the 79-entry "Methods of Birth Control." The fact-based entries in each work are marked by Roman numerals, formally underscoring the book's conceptual focus. It's interesting how even factual information can attain a certain resonance in the hands of an astute writer/editor like Warsh.

In the '90s, nearly 30 years into his career, Warsh streamlined autobiographical elements in his poetry even more, tooling them into unresolved, collaged, elusive, jump-cut narratives that reverberate, create overtones, and encourage the reader to participate. In *The Origin of the World* (2001) he made an entire collection of these machine-gun poems, which deploy disparate, prose-like segments in a fierce way with an acute, knowing awareness of diction shifts. Flat reportage, irony, over-the-top simile ("her voice is the sound of a wood thrush in the abyss"), officialese, genuine emotional expression, and advice merge and swirl, creating a beneficent but mysterious assault. There's a 360-degree mountaintop viewpoint, with the observer/notator standing center stage, making a circular sweep, quickly moving from observation to observation, then doubling back.

After the movies we go for a drink at Babette's
This place is sacred because a child was born in it
The house was haunted by the child who died in her crib
Tell all your friends about the new restaurant on 14th Street called Babette's

196

The husband returns home early from the party & assaults the babysitter
Everything you do is a crime in someone's eyes
I left the muffin in the toaster & the smoke alarm went off
  (Warsh, from 'Work in Progress," *The Origin of the World*)

In *Elixir*, a posthumous collection published in 2022, Warsh brings all of his technique and experience to bear, once again outlining life's vagaries and dramas in his distinctive style. Given the open-ended nature of his work, *Elixir* doesn't necessarily feel like a grand summing-up, but rather the latest installment in his decades-long examination of memories, those that are retrievable as well as those fragmented or lost. There are, however, inescapably haunting overtones to the book. The title poem, which is set in a hospital room only months before Warsh's passing, includes a list of poet friends—Larry Fagin, William Corbett, Bill Kushner, Joanne Kyger, Bill Berkson, Lee Harwood, and Bill Berkson—who have passed on. One of the book's poems calls language a "painkilling drug"; others include lines like "I am not talking /about myself necessarily/but someone I used to know," and "the hours in between feel like nothing at all, like years." Warsh's elegiac stance permeates the book.

> It was 1940-something, believe it
> or not, and I was wearing a bib. I probably
> spilled some food on my shirt, as
> I sometimes still do …
> . . . you are some old
> gray-haired dude who's lost his way or
> who had too much to drink at dinner …
> be careful not to spill any
> down the front of your shirt, and good luck
> to you all on the long drive home.
> (Warsh, from "Not Far," *Elixir*)

The quality of Lewis Warsh's work begs the question: Why hasn't he yet been recognized as one of the most notable American poets of the late 20th/early 21st century? Perhaps his quiet, steady approach hasn't adequately underscored his substantial achievement. It wasn't his nature to make attention-getting aesthetic statements or adopt a high-profile personal stance that would reach beyond those in the know and attract a broader audience. He simply worked hard, produced an impressive body of work, mentored many other poets, and contributed his discernment to the poetry conversation of his time.

LAYNIE BROWNE

WIND, OR "THE WAY TO KEEP GOING" IN FIELDS OF VIOLET & DANDELION TIME IN THE WRITING OF BERNADETTE MAYER (1945-2022)

The more-than-human-world is one through-thread in Mayer's work that serves to stitch—not to separate. From "wind" comes the movement of pollen, plants and more specifically weeds, medicinal wildflowers: violets and dandelions—boisterous actors and instigators in several of Mayer's books.

Beginning with wind in *Studying Hunger Journals*, Mayer writes:

"It's certain the wind blows unsteady. . . . What a blast of power I feel just for an instant, or is it: when you are gone, but it's awful, a curse, how does the wind get in here, here that should be, here that ought to be sealed, how does it enter, can I do that, or is it me, I am sensitive, the wind a knot of it has pushed me too hard I am hurt, pushed into you where I belong, I am keeping a secret, I am not speaking, I am hurting, I am stoned, I am a bubble, I am seen, so many winds, some of them in knots, such sinking motion, always sinking in my mind, I am high, now that I'm sure you're near. . . " (37).

The many ways the wind moves through Mayer's writing make it impossible to link to only one impulse, or as is relevant to *Studying Hunger,* states of consciousness. Wind is often meta, a mirror to writing, or a movement which suggests a written momentum, including the ruthless and unpredictable, the ecstatic, the unpleasant and the urgent as well as every large looming, or miniscule quotidian thing.

There was no wind before I turned to Mayer's passage on wind. Her book blew onto the page. Wind is immaterial, yet acts as a catalyst, precursor to consequence. We could say this about writing, that it has no body or substance, the act is mostly invisible. The wind and the line or sentence move invisibly leaving little trace but riotously shaking up landscapes, the mind, and various paths through libraries, pages and lives.

Can words be both material and immaterial? This non-separation of being from doing, where nothing is ever hierarchical, is one way Mayer's signature whorls—as disruptor, radical world collider.

*

Wind loves a field as in a place of games, a place we cultivate, or better, wildcraft. In this way Mayer is both a classical poet and its opposite. What is the opposite of classic? Aren't all classics their opposites first, interlopers, unprecedented? We invent a field in a classic wind. Yet wind decides the meaning of class. We may in a disorderly way arrive and see what's already growing or invisibly moving through. Mayer is a poet of change, willing to both revere and toss aside mantles all the while improving upon sturdy forms making them tremble, break apart, glow.

*

One element in a field: wind. Stein writes: "What is the wind, what is it?" (*Tender Buttons*, "A Long Dress")

In the poem "The Way to Keep Going in Antarctica" she writes:

"And then I panicked most at the sound of what the wind could do / to me" (128).

And in her collection, *Milkweed Smithereens,* she writes:

"it's the wind i'm hearing next day, 2 stinkbugs, 1 fly, 1 sun that doesn't make much warmth on the still-green field, can you feel sorry for a field. i feel sorry for myself though I'm smarter than the field, maybe, but not as smart as nabokov, as we both go around criticizing everything, but poor nabakov didn't understand about whale's memories of the future, how come?

a memory is nothing
nothing is a memory"

Can the most brilliant poet in her field be smarter than an imaginary field, a field of her own invention, the field of the poem? Field day. Field guide. The opening of the field. A fielding of questions.

One way to read "it's the wind i'm hearing" is that the sound of the wind is the "sound" of all that follows, observations made, and every question. As if the wind were no different than the chain of associations made in mind, no different than the poet thinking, or—consciousness. She writes, "it's the wind i'm hearing next day" which also suggests she is hearing the wind from tomorrow—today—inverting linear time, which suggests no separation, of one day from the next, one element from a thinking body. The wind as a thinking body. And the poet not separate from that.

This makes poetic sense when returning to Stein's "what is the wind, what is it" and the question of a person who is "maybe" smarter than a field, and the implied humility, a nod to the intelligence of a "field." A physical field and also a metaphorical field, or a field of knowledge (astronomy or brain science). Elysian fields. Fields and what is below. Darkness. Gestation. Seed time. That invisible cultivation on which survival depends. What soil knows. The unsaid. What we cannot show. And also what the wind makes visible—the movement of the field.

Then we get to "a memory is nothing / nothing is a memory" which works like a koan. This Cagean-Steinian-Mayeresque moment, in which we don't know what anything is made of, we don't know any *thing*. A memory is not a thing. What is a memory? A memory has no substance, yet can be entirely gripping, like wind. If nothing is a memory we can read this as experiences only existing in the instants they occur. We can also read "nothing is a memory" as a way to read time as only happening in the present, which makes "it's the wind i'm hearing next day" happen now. Wind as participant in subverting straight notions of time.

*

What are the effects of reading *Milkweed Smithereens*, described as a "bouquet of poems" meaning to say, gathered against time?

The title poem is an astonishingly bright elixir stating clearly the powers and intelligence of the plants. She writes "the home of the plant was in heaven / under its influence Indra / fixed the earth & sky in their place, / the Soma plant / removes death) / a common roadside weed (syriaca)".

A plant that overcomes death is truly outside of time. And in the next breath, that it is the common roadside weed, that which is abundant, free, and overlooked, like violets and dandelions. She writes, in her letters (in *The Letters of Rosemary and Bernadette Mayer*) that violets were her mother's favorite flowers. What is the significance of favoring what is mostly ignored? These concepts recur throughout Mayer's work, an ethos of examining and re or un-calibrating attention. Why are the things most vital to our survival (for instance, water, air, soil, trees and herbs, insects, pollinators) considered of no or little value? Outside the field of the poem. Outside the field of her poem. Poetic sense meaning to say the field of the poem creates an alternate ethos composed here of wind, soil and the invisible flowers below the soil, delicate heads not yet pressed through earth.

To exist outside of time is another attempt to defy human notions of time. The phrase "violet and dandelion time" occurs (75) in a later section of "The Covid Diary." Surrounded by quotidian tasks, like making lunch and looking out the window to see birds and white violets. Violet and dandelion time is the arrival of spring in the way that wildness renews inner and outer landscapes in spiral time. Humans do nothing in order to receive these reminders of purple white and yellow. So color is time, and repeats in ways humans can only attempt to tune—into flowers as frequencies.

Why gathered against or in contrast to time as it ordinarily flows in books, as opposed to lives, and how is that subverted here? In *Studying*

Hunger she writes, "I dream the book I am writing about my life, I just tell you I'm up to the dangerous part, who's gonna stay" (46).

Wind is another way to describe the movements which are mostly unseen, akin to invisible vibrations.

She writes:

"i'm 73 now it's the 14th of may, it's only violet and dandelion time, i will empty the dishwasher, make lunch, make a snack for phil, no orioles yet. rocks, flowers, birds trees. mushrooms, atmosphere, ghosts, supernatural things, would that be ghosts? otherworldly things, it's a wordy yet worldly word or word, but why do i live in it?"(Milkweed Smithereens 75)

*

Another evocation of wind and the more than human world comes in the short poem early in *Milkweed Smithereens*, "From All Sides" (16).

From All Sides

her hand's on her hip
she looks, maybe down
the window trembles

she looks down while
the window trembles
but she's become a tree
out of her head comes
a tree that begins at the roof
safest place to be is the past

+

What does the title reveal or conceal. A female figure is deluged from all sides. Deluged with what? Is the reader presented with the figure from all sides? Not exactly. What is meant by "all sides." The figure could be deliberating something, unspoken, from every angle, thus the deluge is in invisible thought. We don't know where her gaze is since the poem tells us "she looks, maybe down." What we know for certain is that she is standing near enough to the window to sense the trembling of the window, which could be the glass or the frame or both. The elements, or precisely again, we return to the wind. Relation of wind and window. A window begins with and contains the word 'wind.' A window meant to keep the wind out, or open allow the wind in.

Again echoing a line from "The Way to Keep Going in Antarctica"

"And then I panicked most at the sound of what the wind could do to me"

The wind has a profound, trembling effect. Does the window tremble or does the "her" in the poem simultaneously tremble along with the window. Is this a poem which is a pre-amble to transformation, becoming other than a frightened figure standing near to a window. Frightened in that she is about to surrender her grey matter, her skull, hair, eyes, teeth, mouth, nose, forehead, ears—and become tree. She is about to become a person with a tree growing out of her head and this may be less than convenient, possibly brilliant, yet also catastrophic. Her head becomes "a tree that begins at the roof" so perhaps the "her" in the poem is also stretched, grown by imbibing a botanical potion. Thus the final line of the poem, "safest place to be is the past" because she's already survived that. The window has survived its past. The plants have something to say, and this tree, about to become her, or her mind, is 'violet and dandelion time.' Mind as wind, a useful misreading or realigning.

Yet the "she" has become a tree. Aligning person or "she" with the

204

evolved consciousness of tree, the more than human world—this necessity to survive, not the past, which has already occurred, but the devastating present in which a figure troubled by wind is then moved. The field of the poem moves not only indoors, but into the poet, transferring the speaker into a present in which the heads of flowers emerge from darkness, from darning old notions of souls—not only—and no longer—human. A present in which it becomes possible to think—with and from and to— blossom and tree—by virtue of wind—and all above and below the field— and moved with the field—is the way to keep going.

Sources

Mayer, Bernadette *Studying Hunger*
Mayer, Bernadette *Milkweed Smithereens*
Mayer, Bernadette, *Poetry*
Mayer, Bernadette, *The Formal Field of Kissing*
Stein, Gertrude, *Tender Buttons*
Mayer, Bernadette and Rosemary, *The Letters of Bernadette and Rosemary Mayer*
Poetry at the Railpark, podcast,https://media.sas.upenn.edu/pennsound/podcasts/Railpark/Mayer-Bernadette_Poetry-at-the-Railpark_Laynie-Browne.mp3

Joseph Lease and Mark Statman

Genius:
The Vision and Voice of David Shapiro (1947-2024): A Conversation

<u>Mark Statman</u>

Why would being smart lead one to be underappreciated?

<u>Joseph Lease</u>

It's sad: unfortunately, there is a (strange) bias against active thought in mainstream U.S. poetry, and to make matters worse, there is a bias against both active thought and direct emotion. David is brilliant, and he is also sincere, passionate, a psalmist and visionary and surrealist. He could of course be very funny, but he always resisted smarmy irony, which was such an easy sell that it (for a while) seemed to become the only "acceptable" way to be an actively (radically) smart poet in public.

<u>M</u>

So: brilliance, sincerity, passion, vision, wit. His politics?

<u>J</u>

That too. Music.

<u>M</u>

Yes, music.

<u>J</u>

David's poetry is in the mode of psalm and prayer and love poetry and devotional poetry.

<u>M</u>

Voice of the father, the mother, the sister, the friend, the teacher.

J

He made all of those voices extraordinarily elegant, and the elegance is magical, not mere (store-bought) elegance.

M

David as Old Testament psalmist. One who praises, who warns, who describes.

J

He creates these voices in ways that are both complex and beautifully simple and direct. He enacts the voice of a child and the voice of a great philosopher.

M

He heard in the voices of children what he thought we should hear. For instance, David's *Daniel* poems—the ones David and Daniel [his son] wrote together and the ones David wrote for Daniel.

J

And he does it without condescending to the child or mystifying the philosopher.

One word we need to mention is maximalism. I have never heard anyone use that word the way David used it: what I took him to be saying was *not* that maximalism was the opposite of minimalism, but that maximalism meant that reality is very complex, and so poetry needed to be (and more importantly could be) made of different kinds of meaning, different kinds of power, including multiple poetics that others might see as mutually exclusive. In David's work those different possibilities, strengths, magics sang together and became a single amazing thing.

<u>M</u>

Would it be fair to say that David is more theologian than philosopher?

<u>I</u>

David was a spiritually visionary poet. I think he was a poet in the mode of Walter Benjamin, and there is a great deal of great theology in Benjamin. David had a way of getting a remarkable fullness of representation into poetry, not in the sense of conventional realism but in the sense of a maximalist humanity.

<u>M</u>

That's David and Whitman: containing multitudes.

<u>I</u>

Yes, but with Dickinson's musicality, and her compression (distillation) and metaphysical wit—what one critic called nimble believing.

From the essay I wrote about David years ago: "When I first read Shapiro's amazing 'The Night Sky and To Walter Benjamin' I was immediately certain: the poem is a psalm (a kind of love poem) and an uncanny, evocative ritual celebrating spiritual and intellectual work (poetics)":

Best to use a dead and nervous language
The extraordinary effort will do nothing
The sun is so close to us
The moon of Pluto even the newspaper's moon of Pluto so far away
The one thing Hamlet did not mention is that things might get better
In the clear sea a little glass pulverized for my pleasure
You do your griefwork, dreamwork, like homework
Someone lost his money in the night sky

Someone cut into the shape of dice threw the dice against unbounded odds light from falling dice.

"Lyric structure and poetic language become dramatic action. The poem enacts and embodies and answers the double impulse to represent and not to represent—that's one of the reasons the poem can enact making so powerfully and evocatively—the poem needs to represent the world and the work, and it needs to refuse to represent the world and the work falsely." The poem is "a new response to multiple traditions and genres that makes fullness of representation actual and active (a primary language, a roller coaster ride rather than a description of a roller coaster ride)."

M
I am thinking of "Untitled," which embodies what you're saying:

Lord
I have fallen in love with the harp again

vaguely, I saw
that the waves
were turning black

it was a friendly ferry

that night you were born

The poem begins with the invocation (Lord), locates itself with intimacy (love) and the moment (again), creates a sensation of uncertainty (vaguely), of biblical action (black waves), longing, reassurance, and hope (friendly ferry). It ends with affirmation (birth). Which could be seen as a repudiation of death, but, as we see in "Friday Night Quartet," David

209

doesn't know the story quite like that.

J
So beautiful.

M
It's astonishing language: light and airy, nothing wasted.

J
Which shines.

M
A theology of hope, longing, regret.

J
Which also shine.

M
But tempered regret: the ferry as an image of crossing (faith) is key. The poet calls on the Lord, but only to witness.

J
When I interviewed David in 1990, he said, "There is an aspect of my poetry which irked the parodistic in poets such as Ron Padgett and Ted Berrigan, the part of me that's perhaps too involved with seriousness, but I was very taken with the idea of Rilke that one should not be merely ironic, and I always told my students to dig past mere irony"—and of course the poet who said that was tremendously funny and ironic and could play self-consciousness like a violin.

M
He talks about a moral seriousness: "achieving the kind of depressing,

massive sense of melancholy that one gets again and again in Jasper Johns."

J

I think he could make that massive sorrow (and beauty) appear in a very small lyric space (lyric brevity), then turn on a dime. That happens again and again in "Friday Night Quartet," one of David's great elegies for his mother.

M

Part one of "Friday Night Quartet," "St. Barnabas," is an intense, long-limbed monologue, sustained (details of disease and surgery), layered, fragile and focused, familiar in its sadness and humor.

J

Sitting and crying, she said this is not Chekhovian or Tolstoyan, David.
This is annoying.
--
My mother said, The worst words in the English language
Are these, David—Don't move.
And what do you think the best words are: Here's some water.

M

Part two, "Those Who Must Stay Indoors," gives internal and external landscapes (imagined/real)—invocations of childhood/dream that are neither childhood nor dream; down the path, to another landscape of pain, loss, and still hope:

"Upside-down bird and twirl-around-a-twig describe antics
Apparently liked by those who do not know your name
A visitor and beloved
By those who must stay indoors"

J:

It's extraordinary that the inner and outer landscapes are in balance: both landscapes are portrayed with beautiful precision and finesse so that the poem can be, well, Chekhovian and Tolstoyan. On one hand, it's realism, and on the other, the lyricism becomes a sort of postmodern song.

M:

In Part three, "Orange-colored Sky," forward motion: the child enters the room, the story told the way a mother would tell it, David in the poem but it's what she thinks worth remembering.

So we wrote a letter to him, and I wrote it for you

J:

The child's voice and the mother's voice are braided—distinct but braided.

M:

Part four, "Friday Night Quartet," parallels the interior/exterior of Part two:

When we dead awaken we'll play chamber music Fridays

--

Dear flower, destitute and household god, my enormous youth beneath

The poem moves from the we of mother and son to the poet's I—a centering and inertia.

The fish rose up in a transparent bloc against me

Inertia because we can't go where the dead are going. David writes

212

about death in the most extraordinary way, with compassion; unafraid, he is able to empathize with Death.

Then, in Part five, "Fountain," we have water again (old life giver),

my mother was dying in her sleep like a cloud
that has slipped out of place
and rolled down
the canvas sky
Dizzy, wavery, asleep,
How could she die?

Hades-like, the vision of waiting.

J:
That water is amazing here, overdetermined, almost polyphonic.

"Laugh loudly, love, as my voice laughs in the grey water."

M
Part six, "Sestina": what would be the greatest gift? A new form of heavenly verse.

The tension of a new form that has no language:

like magic marker on a lake:

_____
_____
_____
_____
_____

Writ in water. The poem begins with his mother speaking. She ends saying done.

I:

David reaches silence, finds a new way of embodying that dances between the domestic and the visionary.

Another perfect example of that dance is one of David's greatest poems from his 2017 book, *In Memory of an Angel,* "For the Jewish Objectivists":

Seeds or snow
Not everyone can tell
There is a blessing for being blessed
And a blessing for catastrophe
But is there a blessing
For a house split open by
Seeds of snow
So that everyone sees through you
As if you were a grey door

M

There is a blessing for it. What we just read. It's another of David's images of destruction leading to creation: a house split open by seeds of snow and leading us to a new awareness of space and possibility (blessing).

I

I love that in this poem snow can be a seed, and that seeds of snow blossom into new awareness. That's the creation, and the awareness makes us—or the you—transparent, so that everyone can see through you.

M

There's grey again. Which we get in "Friday Night Quartet" at the end.

I

A grey door is and is not and is transparent.

<u>M</u>

David has faith that the world can be transformed, made into something better. Seeds or snow becomes seeds of snow. David as poetic alchemist.

<u>J</u>

Oh, absolutely: the change from *or* to *of* is alchemy.

<u>M</u>

He's constantly working on transformations.

<u>J</u>

In David's poems, the transformation is the soul.

<u>M</u>

His vision for poetry is both fierce and gentle, like the Archangels and Blake's Lamb. His poetry seems to encompass all poetries, aesthetically, historically, without apology.

<u>J</u>

His poems are brilliant, wise, passionate, and as inspiring as any art there is. Put simply, he is one of the greatest poets of our time. His work makes poetry better, and makes us, as humans, better as well.

Sources

Lease, Joseph. "Afterword," *Burning Interiors: David Shapiro's Poetry and Poetics,* edited by Thomas Fink and Joseph Lease. Madison, NJ: Farleigh Dickinson University Press, 2007.

Lease, Joseph. "After the New York School: David Shapiro Interview," *You Are The You: Writings and Interviews on Poetry, Art, and the New York School,* edited by Kate Farrell. Asheville, NC: MadHat Press, 2024.

Shapiro, David. *New and Selected Poems, 1965-2006.* NY: Overlook Press, 2007.

Shapiro, David. *In Memory of an Angel.* San Francisco: City Lights Publishers, 2017.

Carla Harryman

Ron Allen (1947-2010)

Ron Allen touches the core of the meta-experience and at that core is 'word sense'.

Ron's is the poetry of sensation. All of those sensations that defy containment of mere utterance. ...And those couched in the intricate rhythms of ghetto diaspora.

—Faruq Z. Bey

Biography and poetry

Ron Bodhidharma Allen was a Detroit avant-garde poet, a dynamic music-text performer, a playwright, and director and producer of radical poets' theater experiments. He was also an instigator and sustainer of community, a teacher and advocate for addicts, and, from the late 1990s to the end of his life, a practitioner of Buddhism. In a crucial period, poetry was for Allen a means of becoming a politically conscious and self-knowing being. His early poetry arises from the onset of schizophrenia in the late 1960s and was spurred by his first lessons on the subject of American imperialism, received at the age of 17 in Vietnam where he served his military time as an army cook. In the mode of a vernacular surrealism, Allen's poetics short-circuited objectifying or simplifying social and cultural logics in a grammar he codified as "weightless language." A term that resonated with his Buddhist practice, *weightless language* was deployed by Allen in an array of discursive contexts, including a Blogspot established after he moved to Los Angeles in 2006:

> Weightless language—noun—1. The space before form. 2. Triangular tongues gripping the wind. 3. The category of moisture refined in the pineal gland refracting midnight. 4. A conjoined occurrence of aggregate sound and rapture, resonating on high frequency like ether, the tangible jive

of the wind. 5. To speak, to utter a language that congeals
the historic conundrum of fancy and dark experience of
the light.

In addition to a medley of poems written in the last years of his life,
some of which are posted on the *Blog*spot, examples of his poetry can
be found in two of the most prominent anthologies in English of Black
experimental writing: Franklin Rosemont's and Robin D. G. Kelly's *Black
Brown and Beige: Surrealist Writings of Africa and the Diaspora* (2009),
where we find him in the company of American diasporic surrealisms
of Ted Joans, Jayne Cortez, and Bob Kauffman; and Aldon Nielson's and
Lauri Ramey's *What I Say: Innovative Poetry by Black Writers in America*
(2015), where we find him in the company of a multi-generational array
of American poets, including Detroiters Kim D. Hunter and Geoffrey
Jacques as well as Will Alexander, a cherished interlocutor after Allen's
move to Los Angeles in 2006.

Otherwise, little if any of his poetry is currently available to new
readers. *HIPology*, an anthology of Detroit poetry, which he co-edited with
Stella Cruse (Broadside Press 1990) and his three books *I Want My Body
Back* (1996), *Neon Jawbone Riot* (2000), and the visual-text collaboration
with Shaq Kalaj *The Unborn Muse of Shadows* (2004), are long out-of-
print as are his two music-poetry-performance CD's *Painted Mind Code*
(with electronics composer VisionEar and ensemble, 2004) and *Code
Zero: The Frequency of Nothing* (with vocalist Sarah Cruse and ensemble,
2008). None of his striking poets' theater plays have been published, even
as fourteen of these have been staged and with many of them produced
several times.

In the early 1980s until his move to Los Angeles in 2006, Allen resided
in the Cass Corridor, a civic hub renowned for its bohemian scene
and counter-cultural ethos located near the urban campus of Wayne
State University. In the Corridor he made a living as a restaurant cook,
immersed himself in a life of artmaking, community engagement, and

spiritual practice and study. In addition to surrealism, the poetics of Allen's early period are seeded in a plenitude of attunements to Western and Eastern philosophy, Black Arts, experimental poetry and performance art in the Detroit scene, blues music and out jazz, church rhetoric, and the innovations in popular music and dance in Detroit of the post-war period. As the description by Detroit musician and composer Faruq Z. Bey (above) suggests, much of his language registers the gritty zones of the city's sensorium. In this excerpt from an early poem, "Do You know the Blues," lyric conventions are incorporated into polyvocal voicings and torqued urban rhythms that work a satirical edge, with and against traditional blues modes:

Do you know the blues
Stop jar hammer bar
Bacon grease on yr sheet
Jelly and bread
Fertile and loud
After hour posing
Suck on a pig bone blue
The Blues
Bent in the melody (19)

The citational game of Allen's syncopated lyrics throughout his writing flickers with the present and history of embodied experience: a performative game-groove where defamiliarization is joined to the dance-sense. One can hear currents of early hip hop in the beats and stresses of some of his poems, but he largely resisted spoken word style, discouraging his Horizons in Poetry workshop students from adapting modes oriented toward prescribed form or sound.[1] As his writing developed, Allen's poetic language increasingly reflected what Leroi Jones/Amiri Baraka describes with regard to musical technique in avant-garde jazz as use "of what important ideas are contained in the residue of history or in the now swell of living" (Jones/Baraka 72). This "now swell" for Allen brought the ontological into proximity with events of instigated *change*: such as the consciousness altering education he received from South Vietnamese women about American Imperialism while serving in the army; a surrealist practice of poetics that "mines the Black male experience" as a practice of liberation from archetype;[2] and his seminary study of religion which led him away from "patriarchal ideologies" to the practice of Buddhism under the guidance of a woman teacher. Ever responsive to what was current within the zones of Detroit's downward-spiral material realities as well as its cultural vibrancies, Allen's vision of the city was often unflinchingly focused on the violent effects of capitalism on the everyday life and consciousness of its inhabitants. In "Merchant of the Open Grid" one encounters a vision of the collective body as part of the city's circuitry, or grid.

> The wall is Detroit. It is invading you with cellular truth.
> The cell is a grid; it bites. It tastes of rind. The rind is
> a tether. The tether is a word. The word is a prayer. It
> does not know itself. The rind is knowledge. It knows the
> grief of your mouth. Detroit lives inside. It is solid with
> industry. Smog is the image of the cell. It is billboard cool.
> We walk the high porn casino riff, solid as your teeth. (18)

Meeting Ron Allen and a few remarks on his poet's theater plays

It is through the wildness, lyricism, humor, and aggression of his poet's theater plays that my friendship with Ron Allen begins, in 1997, when he attended a performance at the Detroit Institute of Arts I directed of *Car Men*, a feminist and anti-racist poet's theater play by Detroit-area poet Chris Tysh. Taken by the non/narrative poetic language of the performance-writing, the language-forward defamiliarizing style of the performance and the transgression of racial and gender binaries in the casting of roles, Ron responded to it by delivering to me the draft of a

220

play manuscript titled "Word Knowledgy Prison." Never produced and apparently unknown by anyone else, I read its nonnarrative "cornucopia of want the title of rush monkey speed in second binary motion of cool slip," as an inspired harmolodics through which sounded influences such as the poetic idioms of Black surrealists Ted Joans and Bob Kaufman jamming with the avant-gardisms of Jean Genet, Samuel Beckett, and William Burroughs. The gift of the play launched a conversation often focused on performance that lasted to the end of his life. For me, this first meeting marked the unfolding of an *oeuvre*, which, as it developed in a swift succession of works from the mid-1990s through 2009, emerged as a multivalent attack on racism and capitalism's holds on the mind, rendered in modes of linguistic rebellion that would signal the possibility of personal and collective liberation.

One of the experimental aspects of his plays involves the ways in which poetic language is focalized within symbolic or conceptual figures (instead of traditional characters), or words that perform as characters, including metonymic entities such as "eye," "head," "cage," and "mouth." For instance, *Eye Mouth Graffiti Body Shop*, produced in collaboration with visual artist Tyree Guyton and choreographer Kim Boyd and presented at the Metropolitan Center for Creative Arts, is a work that plays out the antagonism, collaboration, and eroticism of the city and its subjects through the entities of "Eye" and "Mouth." In this passage the entities create together a pungent litany of sensation imbued in ambient violence:

Mouth: the first official act was the mouth/ the taste of
    cucumber it drained the rosemary in us/
    it was thyme the eye of rosewood
Eye: the first official act was the eye/ a gridle cake of history/
    juniper paper onions of deliberate corruption/ it was
    rancid foiled sheep and deep wounds of game

The *Ron Allen Project* website, created in 2023-2024 by a cadre of cultural workers who had variously worked with Ron, documents productions of thirteen of Allen's plays;[3] beginning with *The Last Church of the Twentieth Century*, which premiered in October 1996 at the Red Door Theater in the Cass Corridor, and ending with *My Eyes are the Cage in My Head*, a production of the Los Angeles Poverty Department that played in several downtown venues and a café-theater in Culver City in December 2008. Other of his plays include *The Tibetan Book of the Dead: The Great Play of Natural Liberation from the Understanding in the Between*, a work he wrote and produced as part of his graduation to Buddhist priesthood, and the *Aboriginal Treatment Center*, a play that was revised and reperformed several times and that became emblematic of his performance poetics, which includes the radical querying of identity through placing female performers in the role of the Black male protagonist. *Hieroglyph of the Cockatoo*, Allen's last, and to some his most personal play, is a manifestation of his experience of schizophrenia as well as an astute, mostly satirical, reflection on medical and cultural responses to "madness." A staged reading of the play was featured in a posthumous exhibition-tribute to his life and work at the Hannan Center in Detroit in 2023.

The obscurity of Ron Allen

Contributors are asked to comment on the reasons why their selected poet remains remote or obscure to public notice. I can offer only a few speculations at the conclusion of this brief account. For health reasons, and to a lesser extent, economic reasons, Ron Allen did not have the physical mobility that might have led to a national dissemination of the majority of his poetry and plays in his lifetime. In addition, his unpublished plays would require varying sorts of editing, research, and archival investigation, and possibly complicated permissions—none of which would be impossible—for publication and performance outside of the communities that know the work. At present there are not enough supporters of his legacy who can afford the time or money to do this work. It is possible that given the renewed attention to his work that came with the Hannan Center exhibition and the community effort to keep his words and memory alive in an annual memorial reading and through The Ron Allen Project, his poetry will find its way back into print. What will happen to his plays and whether or not they can be distributed or interpreted to new audiences in Detroit and elsewhere are not easy questions to answer. Yet, what I have surmised here has a pragmatics that I believe does not begin to address the whole situation. Ron Allen was an iconoclastic Black avant-garde poet and playwright whose work combined perspectives and practices that counter the cultural practices of our niched and category-oriented times. Allen was thinking about revolutionary universal transformation in a raw, often transgressive, and bold fashion that incorporated surrealism and its concept of the revolution of the mind, Buddhism, anti-racist activism underscored by class consciousness, and a critique of capitalist ideology that resisted, in Buddhist fashion, an attachment to the politics of "isms." Even as, and especially because, it is based in an ethos that arises out of Black liberation of the 1960s and the emergence of gender critique in the 1980s and 1990s, his work speaks across decades to our troubled present.

Ayler (there is no closure on space)

the taste in my mouth
is ayler tripping on steel
cloud mushroom bandit
kissing dolphins on pristine madness
spitting him out of my mind
new as pennies
on the floor of healed toes
crushing wind over my gender

I explode dark
jasmine elliptical skulls
smiling day-glo music

Revolution is space
kemetic exits of thievery
enshrined rings of smoke
inside blackness
sacred sins of melody

is this definition schizophrenia
bone deep diasporas
are operas of murder
pushing blue weed
scales of mind space

This is god's food (32)

Notes

[1]In 1982 Allen confounded (with Wardell Montgomery and John Mason) Horizons in Poetry, a community-based poetry project that included workshops and reading events.

[2]*Metro Times*, June 26, 2006. The reviewer discusses Allen's undermining of archetype through non/narrative linguistic tactics and through non-conforming representations of gender in his poet's theater play *Aboriginal Treatment Center*.

[3]The Ron Allen Project is Ruby Woods a.k.a. Anita Jones, Jim Perkinson, John Jakary, and Carla Harryman along with Richard Reeves, curator of the Kayrod Gallery, Hannan Center and documentary filmmaker, and Daniel Land, documentary filmmaker. The website for the project is at https://ronallenproject.org/

Sources

Allen, Ron. *Weightless Language*. 2010.
https://weightlesslanguage.blogspot.com/p/welcome.html
_____. "Do You Know the Blues." *I Want My Body Back*. Detroit: Ridgeway Press, 1996: 19.
_____. "Merchant of the Open Grid." *What I Say: Innovative Poetry by Black Writers in America*. Aldon Lynn Nielsen and Lauri Ramey, editors. Tuscaloosa: University of Alabama Press, 2015.
_____. "Word Knowledgy Prison." 1996. Manuscript in the personal collection of Carla Harryman.
_____. "Eye Mouth Graffiti Bodyshop." 2001. Manuscript in the personal collection of Carla Harryman.
_____. "Ayler (there is no closure on space)." *Neon Jawbone Riot*. Detroit: Weightless Language Press, 2000: 32.
Jones, LeRoi (Amiri Baraka). "The Jazz Avent-Garde." *Black Music*. Brooklyn: Akashic Books, 2010 (reprint edition): 70-80.

Suzanne Frischkorn

Discovering Maureen Seaton (1947-2023)

I love poems born of chaos and into hybridism. I love popular culture, subversive styles, feminizing and queering traditional forms.
—Maureen Seaton

In an interview with *Writing Commons* when asked how she discovered her love of writing, Maureen Seaton replied she had been writing her entire life, *plotting a novel in fifth grade, winning a poetry contest in eighth grade, editing the high school newspaper, acing papers in college,* until she married; and that when her marriage ended, she began writing again.

Seaton was born in Elizabeth, New Jersey, on October 20,1947, and raised in New Jersey and Long Island. She attended a Catholic women's college, and she left college in 1968 to marry and begin a family in Westchester County, New York. The couple divorced in 1979.

Single, and raising two young daughters, Seaton thought she might be able to support her family by writing short stories for *Redbook* magazine. Her short story attempt was soon whittled into something she hadn't expected. She shared the text with a writer friend who told her: *Sorry Maureen, that's a poem (The Rumpus)*. Seaton went on to write a dozen poetry collections including *Fear of Subways* (1991), winner of the Eighth Mountain Poetry Prize; *Furious Cooking* (1996), winner of both the Iowa Poetry Prize and a Lambda Literary Award; *Venus Examines Her Breast* (2004), winner of the Publishing Triangle's Audre Lorde Award; and *Sweet World (CavanKerry)*, winner of the 2019 *Florida Book Award* for poetry. In addition, she wrote a dozen collaborative collections with Denise Duhamel, Samuel Ace, Neil de la Flor, Carolina Hospital, Nicole Hospital-Medina, Holly Iglesias, and Kristine Snodgrass. Her memoir *Sex Talks to Girls* (2008) also won a Lambda Literary Award. Additional honors include an NEA fellowship and two Pushcart Awards.

In 1992 Seaton moved with her daughters to Chicago. She taught poetry workshops, served as Artist-in-Residence at Columbia College Chicago, and taught in the MFA in Creative Writing program at the School of the Art Institute of Chicago. In 2002 she joined the faculty in creative writing at the University of Miami. She was voted Miami's Best Poet in 2020 by *The Miami New Times*.

I discovered Maureen Seaton in a literary journal. I had been searching for contemporary haibun poems and came across Seaton's "Once I Was a Witch." I remember being stunned by her syntax, her images, and I was deeply moved by the joy she employed in an elegy. The way her haiku expanded the prose was breathtaking. I looked Seaton up and found her impressive body of work—I couldn't believe I had not heard of her. This experience, I soon learned, is not uncommon. Many readers stumbling across her work are astonished to be discovering it for the first time.

According to the poet Denise Duhamel, longtime friend and Maureen Seaton's first collaborative partner, Seaton was not someone who courted fame (*Pleiades*). In interview after interview Seaton subverts speaking of her work, often turning the question back to the interviewer. She was uncomfortable in the spotlight. She loved her students and was more forthcoming and enthusiastic when speaking of teaching—*I've learned, through working with artists and poets, writing with my students in class, observing the results when my students collaborate with one another—that a fractal expands outward when two people breathe on it together. I've also learned that collaboration sparks fresh language in a way that delights and restores.* When pressed for her writing credo Seaton quoted *Uses of the Erotic,* an essay by Audre Lorde, "But when we begin to live from within outward, in touch with the power of the erotic within ourselves and allowing that power to inform and illuminate our actions upon the world around us, then we begin to be responsible to ourselves in the deepest sense." She said it guided her work (*The Rumpus*). Asked about writing for marketability, or accessibility, Seaton confided that while she did think about her reader, she chafed at the thought of having to write a certain way for any reason (*Indiana Review*). She never let readers get in the way of her poetic impulses. She was a poet's poet.

Reviewers described her work as melodic, exuberant, layered, and praised her wry wit, her intimate poetic landscapes, and agile sense of play. "A streetwise, postmodern alchemist," wrote the *Publishers Weekly* reviewer of *Furious Cooking*.

There are many reasons a widely published, accoladed poet like Maureen Seaton would seem like a secret outside of her immediate communities—she was beloved by the LBGTQ+ community, as well as her students and friends in Chicago and in Florida. Perhaps it's because she came to poetry in an untraditional manner; although she did go on to earn her MFA at Vermont College, most of the acclaimed American poets of her generation went to Ivy League schools and the Iowa Writers Workshop. It may have been because she was a woman. Gender bias against women authors in American literature has been widely researched and documented. Possibly, it was because she was a lesbian. Her book *Fear of Subways* was published in 1991. America was standing in the long shadow cast by AIDS. In a time of gay bashing, racism, and tokenism, Seaton wrote about her relationship with Lori Anderson, the black woman she loved, and her experience of black culture by proximity. Anderson turned out to be the great love of her life and the couple were together for 35 years.

I suspect it was because she was consistently innovative. Very few poets achieve stylistic mastery and leave it behind to try something new. Early on she wrote from a narrative, or lyrical impulse, her poems would build on-line, or image in a linear fashion. She soon turned to collage. Her interest in collage developed at the same time she was questioning her heterosexual identity, *Queer to me means pushing against boundaries, disregarding them. It's taking the idea of poetic license to the nth, both in poetry and in identity. My collage impulse grew at the same time I was questioning my hetero self....I think the "queerest" poem I ever wrote was that first one .... because I wanted it to be a story and it transformed itself into a poem (AWP*

228

Denver 2010).

Seaton's work grew increasingly hybrid. She shattered received forms and made them her own, she utilized language substitutions, deft associative leaps, and surprising image juxtapositions. She invented her own form, pi, where she chose ten words and used them as substitutions for the first 100 digits of pi. She incorporated prose and sometimes visual art. Seaton had a particular love for writing fractals, she wrote fibonacci poems, and as recently as 2022 she had started writing rondelets.

Seaton was also profoundly inspired by place. When I began reading her work her images resonated on a level I had not experienced with other poets. After reading her memoir I learned it was because we shared landscapes—my formative years were spent in Miami and the Hudson Valley—we had even moved to the same town, Ossining, NY, in the same year. She wrote about these landscapes often, and in ways that dazzled me.

Undersea (2021) is her love letter to Florida. The table of contents alone reads like a poem: "Sautéed Barnacles," "Bigly in the Wild Weed," "Jesus on the Beach," "Lemon Bay," "Salt," "I Swear There Were Oceans." These lines from the long poem "The Mystery of the Direction of Time - *Gulf of Mexico*" are an example of Seaton's ability to instill a sense of place with surprising images and sound.

She will draw a map and leave her body for a certain time.
She will prepare a sarcophagus under the porch and slip inside where the
    iguana owns the right of way.
She will hear firecrackers deep in the mangroves. They will burn the roof
    of her mouth.
She will look at the water some call the Lake of Mexico and absorb its
    poisons and serenity.
She will read that Pisces rules the feet and paint her toenails blue.
She will adorn her neck with egg cases and tiny whelks.

I began corresponding with Seaton in the spring of 2021. I reached out to her letting her know I was a huge fan of her work and asked her if she would send some poems to a new poetry journal where I was an editor. She was warm and gracious. She sent us outstanding collaborative poems she had written with Sam Ace. When I learned we would be press-mates later that year I was overjoyed and she, too, was overjoyed. Although I never had the chance to meet her in person, I still felt embraced by her. We corresponded through 2023, and I was devastated to learn of her passing.

Seaton was diagnosed with 4th Stage Cancer in 2017 and lived to see three poetry collections and three collaborative chapbooks to publication. She completed three more to be published posthumously. Seaton's life and her life's work taught me how to be a poet in this world; she taught me to stay true to my own vision, and my short acquaintance with her showed me the impact a beautiful, generous spirit brings to a community.

Maureen Seaton died on August 26, 2023, in Longmont, Colorado. She was 75. This poem is from Seaton's book, *The Sky is an Elephant* (2023) published a month before her death.

Maureen Seaton

The Days to Come (Reprise)

They say that Earth harbors clarity in her compass,
that whichever direction she points to will come true.

I used to live in New York City where poets ran around
like unplugged felons shouting in the wind, exhilarated.

I've dug up opals, feldspar, dust of stars, and plucked
lights from the oceans that no longer exist, but they did.

50 million years ago the horse, *Equus*, was 9 inches high,
weighed 9 lbs and had 3 toes. (I am not making this up.)

When I look at you, you shift between left eye and right,
changing pathways in my brain, rerouting the way I love.

"I love you my brothers and sisters. I fuckin love you"—
front and back of a handheld sign in Albuquerque, NM.

I wrote a song in C-sharp minor and played it in the key
of D-flat minor as if I'd never played capriccioso before.

This has to be a good sign for the days to come, I said
to every goddess and renegade. This has to be symbolic.

Sources

"Maureen Seaton," *Academy of American Poets* https://poets.org/poet/maureen-seaton

Denise Duhamel, "Introduction Maureen Seaton Tribute Folio," *Pleiades* 44. 1 (2024): 179.

Seaton, Maureen. "The Rumpus Interview with Maureen Seaton." Interview by Julie Marie Wade. *The Rumpus,* Dec. 2013.
https://therumpus.net/2013/12/11/the-rumpus-interview-with-maureen-seaton/.

Seaton, Maureen. "Interview with Ms. Maureen Seaton." Interviewed by Katharine Westaway. *The Writing Commons.* https://writingcommons.org/article/maureen-seaton/.

Seaton, Maureen. "Exquisite Flotsom & Kismet: The Making of Literary Collage (and Collaboration) — An Interview with Maureen Seaton." Interviewed by Esther Lee. *Indiana Review* (Aug. 2005.) http://www.maureenseaton.com/Views.html.

Seaton, Maureen. "(I've had) The Time of My Life," *Queering Desire: Queer Poets' Aesthetic Libidos.* AWP Denver, Apr.l 2010. https://pankmagazine.com/piece/maureen-seaton/.

"The Extraordinary Maureen Seaton." Obituary, *The Natural Funeral.*
https://www.thenaturalfuneral.com/the-extraordinary-maureen-seaton/   : accessed September 22, 2023), died 26 Aug. 2023.

Timothy Liu

On Frank Stanford (1948-1978)

You.
Frank Stanford.
Lost Roads Publishers, 1979, 2008.

Hidden Water: From the Frank Stanford Archives.
Michael Wiegers & Chet Weise, eds.
Third Man Books, 2015.

The Light the Dead See: Selected Poems of Frank Stanford.
Leon Stokesbury, ed.
University of Arkansas Press, 1991.

They say you die three times. Once when your heart stops. Again when they put you in the ground. And then a final time when there's no one left on earth to say your name.

*

Chinamen. Injuns. The plural N-word. Does diction alone disqualify, cancel genius in 2023? This by a man who shot himself three times through the heart on his way out. Triggering indeed.

*

At the Brigham Young University Bookstore, my mentor's first collection of stories, *A Woman Packing a Pistol*, was for sale, but you had to ask the manager for it. The thing was kept behind a counter, and when you paid for it, they handed it to you sleeved in a brown paper sack. That's how we'd pass it around to one another, my cohort and I drunk on the hooch of my mentor's words. I don't remember much of Darrell Spencer's debut published by Dragon Gate (defunct for decades now), but I remember a woman twisting sprinkled donuts on her titties like makeshift pasties. Samizdat.

*

This summer, a copy of *You* turned up on the used poetry cart at the Strand Bookstore. Six bucks for a slim volume. Clocking in at exactly 48 pages including front and back matter, the thing read more like a chapbook than a book-book even if it made the minimum of three "signatures" (16-page bundles in printing parlance). The first posthumous book from Lost Roads in 1979 after Stanford's suicide, this second printing had a pub date of 2008, almost three decades later, with a printed cover price of $15. Six bucks felt like a steal! Still, I sat right down on the floor between towering shelves of steel and read the thing straight through first. Ever done that in the dusty stacks of a library or holed up in some corner of a used bookstore faintly reeking of mildew and cat piss?

Ever feel like you can't believe what you're reading cuz it's so good? Words you've never seen put together by anyone else casting their dark spell:

Nights and days floated
Over the whorehouse
Like webs on the lake,
A monastery
Full of noise and girls

(from "Instead" p. 24)

She is dizzy from the light

Swimming through the reeds
Like shadows of minnows.
She is sad from sipping the flat beer
Of her own voice.

(from "Epiphanies" p. 40)

Verbs and nouns are the engines driving these poems stripped down to their bare-ass strangeness where "there is sadness in bed for twenty centuries / And everyone is chewing grass on the graves again."

(from "Circle of Lorca" p. 11).

Stanford's posthumous shadow seeps into all the proceedings, not only because of the suicide and his indelible means, but also that he died just a little after missing admission into the 27 Club (Janis Joplin, Jim Morrison, Jimi Hendrix, Kurt Cobain, Amy Winehouse). What else all these voices might have produced with their talent and genius we will never know. Keats. Plath.

*

Ever carry around a stack of books in a used bookstore only to put them back, one by one, onto the shelves where you first found them?— the ambitious appetite of our roving eyes checked by our actual bank accounts, the towers of books already erupting from every available square inch of floorspace in our abodes groaning under the weight of "No more!"

Our feelings never quite fit the forms, as my therapist liked to say.

Carrying around a stack of books like that feels like greed, a hambone too big for a loon-dawg's jaws, desire and hunger at its most aspirational.

By the time I was six feet off the Strand linoleum on a stainless-steel ladder, *You* was the only volume that remained in my clutches. I was determined to plant this one on my nightstand when I got home, let its wild verses seep into my dreams.

And what was I doing high up on a wobbly ladder under ugly bars of fluorescence? Looking for a possible mate.

*

As it happened, I got lucky. Stumbled across two pristine copies of *Hidden Water: From the Frank Stanford Archives*. And from the almost empty back cover, I read:

Lord, he had a way with him: His eyelids were like louvered shutters. When he looked at your face, he looked at your face.

(from "The Lacuna.")

Sho nuff, there he was on the front cover, his nakedness wrapped in a hand-sewn quilt with his icy blues capturing my gaze while a black panther sat under a full moon next to our shaman, looking off into the distance. The Strand had knocked five bucks off the $17.95 cover price, another steal. I would soon discover that the cover image had been painted by the poet's widow, Ginny Stanford, who along with the poet C. D. Wright, became trustees for Stanford's Estate. They were both present in the kitchen of the house when three shots rang out from Stanford's bedroom, this on the very day Ginny found out about the ongoing affair between Stanford and Wright. A trifecta.

*

That day at the Strand, there were no used copies of *What About This: The Collected Poems of Frank Stanford* nor Stanford's epic of 15,283 lines, *The Battlefield in Which the Moon Says I Love You,* the first printing from 1978 long out of print, and the 2000 reprint (both from Lost Roads, the press Stanford and Wright founded) thankfully easier now to track down online. That hardly mattered as both titles were already sitting on my shelves back home (though never fully digested, only nibbled on). What mattered was to chance upon what else I never quite knew existed. To score something new.

*

More than half of the books I own, I have not read.

When I turned 50, I decided to read Proust's 3000+ page magnum opus in the Moncrieff translation. It took me about 18 months. It was worth the wait, though what I had been waiting for all those decades, I can hardly say.

I have never read the *Aeneid.* Never made it through the *Divine Comedy* (let alone the *Inferno*!). I like the feel of Ashbery's *Flowchart* in my hands but have no intention of slogging through it. This past year, I did read the *Oddysey* four times all the way through in two translations (the Robert Fagles and the Emily Wilson). Why read this book and not that book remains a mystery.

Roland Barthes once said, "A classic is a book everyone has heard about but no one has read."

Something like that.

*

Here's how *The Battlefield in Which the Moon Says I Love You* came into my life. At the start of grad school in 1989 in Houston, I met Robin Reagler in my cohort. Queer and fresh from the Iowa Writer's Workshop, she seemed to me wisdom's very font! At some point, she mentioned *The Battlefield*. This was in the days before the internet and sites like www. bookfinder.com. Those were the days you carried a title around in your head like a missing Grail as you roamed from bookstore to bookstore across country, a time when kifing a volume from a university library was sometimes the only recourse, "borrowing" a book for a long stretch till an actual copy could be found/had/owned.

Fast forward seven years, and I woke up one morning in Providence at the home of Forrest Gander and C. D. Wright and Lost Roads Press. At breakfast, I mentioned how impossible it was to track down a copy of *Battlefield* over the many years since grad school! C. D. said to me, "Be right back." When she returned from the cellar, she was holding a slightly yellowed and warped (and not quite waterlogged) copy of the book and asked if I wanted it. It had been used for a doorstop.

*

I have lived in towns where marathon readings of *Battlefield* were given. I have admired the fervor and devotion but could never bring myself to go.

The thing is: I'm not sure I've ever been able to read more than a single page of *Battlefield* in a single sitting. The richness reminds me of not wanting to eat an entire Dove Bar, throw some of it out. Or make the thing last as long as possible.

If I read one page a day, it would take me 1.48+ years.

If I read one page a week, it would take me 10+ years.

Maybe Stanford dying so young makes me want to never finish?

Stanford is buried in St Benedict's Cemetery in Subiaco, AK. I read somewhere online that his tombstone reads:

Frank Stanford, Poet
It wasn't a dream, it was a flood.

*

Hidden Water: From the Frank Stanford Archives is a compendium, a kitchen sink of a book edited by Michael Wiegers and Chet Weise. This joint publishing venture between Third Man Books (Nashville) and Copper Canyon Press is a 200-page culling of rare treasures and ephemera from the Beinecke Rare Book and Manuscript Library donated to the collection by the Estate of Frank Stanford.

If one doesn't know Stanford's work, is this volume a good place to start or is it better to end up here only after long last?

The book's frontispiece includes a detachable perforated bookmark of the poem "Stars":

Slices of

cold butter

the lovers

are spreading

over their

toast.

Stanford's genius is everywhere apparent. One can dive in almost anywhere and pull up pearl after pearl:

I don't have flat feet
Or a new barn to hide death in
My rump isn't unclean
Like the bottom of a swamped boat
I have enough credit to buy shirts
But I still wonder

(from "Blue Yodel in Paradise")

*

One can try to collect all nine of Stanford's books. By my count, it would run one upwards of 10K if you want to include first printings from Mill Mountain Press and Lost Roads Press. Here are the titles one can recite like a mantra, a rosary:

The Singing Knives (1971)
Ladies from Hell (1974)
Shade (1975)
Field Talk (1975)
Arkansas Bench Stone (1975)
Constant Stranger (1976)
The Battlefield Where the Moon Says I Love You: A Poem (1977)
Crib Death (1978)
You (1979)

*

The first book I ever bought by Frank Stanford was *The Light the Dead See: The Selected Poems of Frank Stanford*, a relatively slim volume edited by Leon Stokesbury and published by the University of Arkansas Press in

1991, more than a decade after Stanford's death and right smack in the middle of grad school hijinks when I worked three jobs, buying poetry at the Brazos Bookstore being my favorite calling. For many of us, *The Light the Dead See* was a crash course, a primer, a sampler culled from all nine of the aforementioned orphans plus a half dozen previously unpublished poems. Can't think of a better way to drop twenty hard-earned bucks. That is, if you don't want to lug around a tome. Otherwise, for twice the price and more than nice, the no-brainer would be *What About This: Collected Poems of Frank Stanford*. A fine doorstop of a book that one can prop up in one's cellar, awaiting the right moment that just might change someone's life.

*

My mentor Richard Howard once said to me: "Every poet, no matter how famous or celebrated, enters a literary limbo upon death, awaiting to be resurrected by readers who never knew them while they were alive. Most are never revived."

Ladies (and Gentlemen) in Hell: Mr. Frank Stanford.

Frank Stanford

In Another Room I Am Drinking Eggs from a Boot

Hans Richter

What if the moon was essence of quinine
And high heels were a time of day
When certain birds bled
The chauffeur is telling the cook
The antler would pry into ice floes
Swim with a lamp
And we'd be shivering in a ditch
Biting through a black wing
There would be boats
There would be a dream country
The great quiet humming of the soul at night
The only sound is a shovel
Clearing a place for a mailbox

Eli Goldblatt and Julia Blumenreich

Why Read Gil Ott?

ELI

Recently Julia Blumenreich, Gil Ott's widow, and her second husband Drew Miller were clearing out their basement. They found four boxes of books marked "Ott/ Returns." Turned out, those boxes didn't contain books that had been sent back by book distributors to his Singing Horse Press. They held books he'd collected from friends and correspondents, poets who ran or published in independent presses and had sent him books to read or review. Poets in his circle wanted Gil to know what they were up to.

Gil Ott lived for poetry, supported poets fiercely, but he could be just as fierce if he thought you were writing without pushing boundaries or exploring the art without utmost integrity and commitment—and that meant rejecting styles he regarded as too slack or overly conventional. He was softening in his final years, becoming more forgiving of human frailty. Kidney disease and dialysis had something to do with that transformation; he developed a kinship within the disability community and edited *No Restraints: An Anthology of Disability Culture in Philadelphia* (New City Writing 2002), which was ahead of its time. Julia's kind and generous ways helped him to see the world more hopefully. I think his utter devotion to his daughter Willa also made a substantial difference in all his relationships. She was 12 when he died at 53 in 2004.

The "Ott/Returns" boxes contained all kinds of treasure. Burning Deck, Sun & Moon, Segue were only a few of the presses he collected; *Sulfur*, *Abacus*, *LANGUAGE*, *Shearsman*, and especially Cid Corman's *Origin* were magazines edited by people he wrote to regularly. I encountered the work of many of these authors and editors through him. Gil's publishing ventures connected him to people all over the world—San Francisco and LA, Detroit and New York, but also Malaysia, Japan, England, and

Australia. He was associated with an impressive array of avant-garde poets, but never considered himself a part of any group. His international associations broadened his appeal as a poet and a publisher; he developed strong poetic principles, but he was not dogmatic. Among his books I found Charles Bernstein, Bob Perelman, Lyn Hejinian, Ron Silliman, Rae Armantrout as well as Frank Samperi, Rosemary and Keith Waldrop, Leslie Scalapino, Harryette Mullin. He was interested in what poets could do with words at the extremity of linguistic structures and at the edges of spiritual and physical breath.

Gil had an inclination toward Buddhism and mysticism, but he was also practical, wary of poetry too far from common life. He was even warier of the tendency for poets to seek employment and acceptance in the university. Although he read extensively in literary theory and philosophy, he resisted seeing poetry in abstract terms. He was interested in scrutinizing what language could do as it unfolded under innovative procedures and surprising conditions, but he was neither "experimental" for the sake of novelty nor "academic" for the sake of critical power.

So why read Gil Ott today? Some of his work may seem difficult to enter, willful in its tendency to frustrate semantic decoding or paraphrase. Not unusual for a poet who published special issues on Jackson Mac Low and Charles Bernstein, but Gil's work had a different texture from others at the time. As I read his *arrive on wave: Collected Poems* (Chax 2016), I'm struck with the sense that the poems press toward a truth, a presence, that resides just out of reach. Witness what happens in "Reading," published originally by Cid Corman in *Origin* 20 (1982):

a reflection of hands
that wavers
up the street with
suppressed

the interruption

244

between us
time

of year when transport,
the thin shoots to
lapses
to wake
on the ground with leaves
gone from it,
two

as two at once, but from
oneself curiously

performing.
fingers
and the other
spectator
dress the daughter
stands
and fills.
(*arrive* 64-65)

Hard to quote only a piece from that poem, as with many of his other poems. Urgency keeps flowing on, the syntax searching for what is suppressed, interrupted, "curiously // performing." The "two" can be writer and reader or self-seeking-self, performer and spectator simultaneously. This poem was composed years before his daughter was born.

I was living in a group house with him in 1982, and he certainly didn't seem like a family man at the time, more like a grumpy monk for poetry. And yet, even his most terse lines imply a yearning for intimate connection, for rigorous kindness. As he says a few poems earlier in that same *Origin* sequence:

> it is in gratitude
> these words are written
> a man a complex
> of the between
> coherence
> (*arrive* 57)

I never read Gil's poems without finding lines I admire for their sound, for their elusive wisdom, for their playful shadows.

The poems are well worth reading again and again, but I want to point to another reason to read Gil: his larger publishing project. His magazine *Paper Air* is available at http://eclipsearchive.org/projects/PAPER/paper.html, and it is a wondrous catalogue of poets and innovative procedures developing at the margins of American literary respectability between 1976 and 1990. The journal started out as a handwritten publication, reflecting his experience with the street poet Kush in San Francisco during the years before Gil returned to Philadelphia. The early poems are rooted in wild '60s discourse—anti-war and pro-ecological, anti-authoritarian and pro-wonder—a bit tie-dyed and yet not New Age or druggy. The poetics of the first issues was closer to Kenneth Patchen and Jerome Rothenberg than to the Diggers in Haight-Ashbury, but his language did reflect the time:

> Paper Air opens its pages to artists actively engaged in the expansion of revolutionary perception. That sounds have lives beyond our utterance of them is evident in the inevitable progress of the image toward physical manifestation. Emotion becoming the word I speak is born as a bird becoming stone through flight. As technicians of the imagination we build new avenues of consciousness.

That's from volume 1, number 1, which features mostly Gil's own writing and drawing. But he's soon branching out: the anthropological visionary poetry of Nathaniel Tarn and Janet Rodney, early poems from Ron Silliman, and work by Rachel Blau Du Plessis, Toby Olson, and Harryette Mullen.

I don't have the space to review the fascinating publishing history of *Paper Air* and the even more expansive reach of Singing Horse (still publishing under the able editorship of Paul Naylor, singinghorsepress. com). The point I want to make is that Gil was always growing and reading for his own work, but he was also an agent connecting older and younger generations of poets, corresponding in earnest with people who sent him poems even if he never published their work, grasping beyond the edges of settled poetics for what could NOT be said or written but must be uttered anyway. Like his mentor and friend Cid Corman (but, I think, a better poet than Corman), Gil Ott the editor demonstrated a profound commitment to the indispensability of poetry. He was a bright node in a network of culture-makers, a sponsor for those who would use the imagination to surprise and confound us, uncover spaces occluded by capitalism, religious verities, and private sorrows.

In short, the boxes of books Julia and Drew unearthed in their basement tell much about who Gil was and what he was doing on this planet. The range of poets he published and considered his friends and colleagues always amazed me. In retrospect, all those titles feel less like a cavalcade and more like a brocade. When you appreciate Gil, you wrap yourself in the vibrant and activist literacy fabric of one collective poetry moment.

JULIA

Around 300 people showed up for Gil's memorial at the Painted Bride, the art center in Philadelphia he helped found decades before. The audience was diverse in every way: especially reflecting the wide arc of the lives his too short life had touched. The program included songs like the one he would often begin his poetry readings with:

Night and day will pass away
But love will always win
Night and day will pass away
But love will always win

Moon and stars fall from the sky
But love will always win
Moon and stars fall from the sky ay ay
But love will always win

Imagine being at a reading of Gil's and he walks to the front of the stage singing in his deeply resonant voice this simple yet profound observation to the audience. You settle into your chair, ready to hear more conventional, accessible writing, but you are quickly facing a writer who, in that same, assured and beautiful voice, presents you with poems that are like none you have ever encountered before:

beginning
the beginning
of the book

What is the best thing to do *now*? The book is looking forward, with empty hands, toward you. It is grounded in the failure to begin. Death is little, dying large.

(*arrive* 230)

I think of sending this poem from his book-length series *Traffic* (Chax 2001) to our daughter, Willa. Now, 20 years after his death, she follows her own compelling reasons to write, to remember that we all must begin to tell our own story or die *large* by not honoring our unique way of voicing who we are in the context of the world. Like her father, she wants to push the boundaries of language in order to discover in the resonance of this fearless exploration -- something unknown. What Gil, Willa, or any writer for that matter, does with this rupture of the known, is what defines their work. The result for readers who are willing to follow a route that the GPS does not choose, is experiencing the unexpected: the gift of a field that *could* stretch beyond the horizon. I believe finding oneself transported to this place that offers the reader meaning that is not fixed, edified, or pedantic is one of the rewards of reading Gil's poems.

Every time I open any book of Gil's, in this case *arrive on wave* his collected poems, I am able and sometimes even challenged to connect to the poems as the reader I am at that moment. Take for instance, "UNTITLED" the penultimate piece in the book:

From the silence she has filled
and from all measurement turning
space, blank space of a room enduring
promise, what is to have begun
begins, vibrant, beneath hearing.

That she distributes other airs
figures little in the composition
time has made, alternatives to freedom
falter, pale, equivocate her.

And in her transience constitute
philosophy, all that speaks in poetry

249

driven to light, reddening what secretly
warms the obdurate hear and keeps
in memory death's transparency
(*arrive* 326)

As today, I am writing this piece to introduce or perhaps remind readers of the effect of spending time with Gil's work, I landed in the above poem and found, "blank space of a room enduring/ promise, what is to have begun/ begins, vibrant, beneath hearing." His writing helps me hear what exists beyond sound, "all that speaks in poetry/ driven to light, … and keeps/ in memory death's transparency" I've found in reading this poem and much of Gil's writing, a voice that calls me to what we can and can't comprehend as humans. It's as if his voice is a piece of music whose time signature is malleable depending on whose listening. At this description, Gil might shake his head both "Yes" and "No," and then laugh at the pleasure of "what secretly/ warms the obdurate."

Sources

Gil Ott. *arrive on wave: Collected Poems*. Edited by Trace Peterson, Gregory Laynor, and Eli Goldblatt. Tucson: Chax Press, 2016.

_____. *Traffic*. Tucson: Chax Press, 2001

_____, editor. *No Restraints: An Anthology of Disability Culture in Philadelphia*. Philadelphia: New City Press, 2002.

Jacqueline Vaught Brogan

Recovering Melvin Dixon (1950-1992)

When, once again, one of the most formidable political leaders on earth is about to insist upon a tragically myopic (and prejudiced) vision for our country, Mel Dixon—and most particularly, his genuinely *remarkable* volume of poetry entitled *Change of Territory* (1983) is critical for us to recover, not only for Dixon's actual artistic skill, but for the very broadening of geographic and historical perspectives the title of the volume implies, and even demands. It is horribly ironic that just as he was coming to be recognized as a major voice in late 20th Century poetry, Dixon unexpectedly died from complications of AIDs, only one year after he lost his life-partner Robert Horovitz.It may be that Dixon's untimely death and relatively slim creative productions account for his now relative obscurity. But then, we could say the same of John Keats, whose name and work remain deeply imbedded in the canon.

Actually, Dixon was the recipient of several prestigious awards before his death, and so impressed by his work were my colleagues and students that for a brief period in the 1990s, the volume just mentioned was required reading for students seeking to earn a doctoral degree in American Literature at the University of Notre Dame. However, he became most known in the 1990s elsewhere as a novelist, particularly as an African American gay writer, whose back-to-back novels earned the major awards including the two listed below.

Yet this immediate recognition for his talent in prose seems to have faded radically over the last three decades---a fact that I attribute, quite ironically, to the then (and continued) great outpouring in American letters at the time of previously unheard voices across many gendered and ethnic lines. In particular, his melding of the past and present and his multi-narrated "novel' approach in *Vanishing Rooms* (1990) now rides relatively unseen among the wave of other works exploring a similar

251

aesthetic during the latter part of the 20th Century.(We can think of Sandra Cisneros' *The House on Mango Street* [1983], Louise Erdrich's *Love Medicine* [1984], Sherman Alexie's *The Lone Ranger and Tonto Fight in Heaven* [1993] --or even the luminary Toni Morrison and her singular *Jazz* [1992]—as obvious examples that all went on to have greater popular and commercial success.)

Yet Melvin (Mel) Dixon deserves recovery and recognition, perhaps now more than ever, as a genuinely important poet of the late 20th Century landscape, as our nation quite literally considers what it means to "preserve" our traditions and territory.

Brief Biography:

Born, May 29, 1950, Stamford, Connecticut—Died October 26, 1992, Stamford, CT

B.A., Wesleyan University, 1971; Ph.D., Brown University, 1975

Professor of Literature, Queens College, 1980-1992

Selected Awards:

Charles H. and N. Mildred Nilon Excellence in Minority Fiction for *Trouble the Water*, 1989

Ferro-Grumley Award for LGBT Literature for *Vanishing Rooms*, 1992

Major Publications:

Change of Territory (poetry), 1983

Ride Out the Wilderness: Geography and Identity in Afro-American Literature (textbook), 1987

Trouble the Water (novel), 1989

Vanishing Rooms (novel), 1990

Love's Instruments (poetry), 1995—posthumous

(Recent reprinting of certain poems from *Love's Instruments* as Featured Poet, *Poetry* [April 2024])

Critical Source

A Melvin Dixon Critical Reader (collection of essays), 2006

Overview of *Change of Territory* as a volume, with particular attention to "Bobo Baoulé," which encapsulates the work as-a-whole in a single suite of four totally integrated poems and perspectives.

Without question, Mel Dixon's work in general, and this volume of poetry in particular, bear traces of many influences and influencers—among them, blues and jazz, or Ralph Ellison, Romare Bearden, James Baldwin, and Richard Wright (to name only a few), as well as Alice Walker, Zora Neale Hurston, and Sherley Williams.He is certainly influenced by his family background in the Pee Dee area of South Carolina, his father's family move to the North, his years in France and West Africa and the Caribbean (and elsewhere). But the biggest weight bearing on and curiously controlling his work is quite literally the erased yet omnipresent history of what we might call questions of territory. Where, for example, is that territory? Is it one? Who decided? When? Who is asking the questions? Who is answering? Are the answers in our books? In our genes? In our memories? Must we travel backwards and forwards, over and over, to recapture what we perhaps never once had, owned, even knew? Are the answers in our language itself? What—who decided—is our language, anyway? Is it African? Southern? Rural? French? Urban? "General American"?

Such escalating questions barely begin to prod the myriad of the-forgotten-the-as-yet-to-be-answered troubling shards that disturb *Change of Territory*, from its opening "Hungry Travel" (in the first of four sections, called *Climbing Montmartre*) to its apparent resolution in "Coming Home"—the last section, of the last poem, in the fourth and final section of the book. For, "book" it is. This is not a mere collection of poems, but a genuine narrative of the poet's psychic journey through his personal history, time and space—all of which involves us as well (needed, as we are, to be active participants in recovery our collective history).Among the

253

most painful yet beautiful poems is the opening one, where the father is worn beyond giving, where the son (Dixon) knows his mother's "broken breath sung solo," and where all three "hunger for any words that cure." (To satisfy that need is the implicit task of the volume at hand.) In one of several poems dedicated to Richard Wright, we find that "One man lifts his wings"—perhaps a regular trope for the poet at large, but perhaps also an allusion to the "myth of the Flying Africans" (a myth disrupting the fact of slavery with the fable of freedom).

And myths, and fable, and actual facts are all crucial to the conflating, troubling, perhaps liberating words of *Change of Territory*. But as Dixon insists, to change, we must travel—physically, psychically, emotionally, historically, questioning all that defined or confined any given territory. (As the Masai elder tells Dixon, as recounted in the last poem, "'The hardest thing about it . . . ./ is leaving the ground." So, fittingly, even the final poem—with its initial resolution—is fraught with ambiguity. When the narrator/poet returns home, after travels through France, through Africa, through hemispheres, the mother (glad to see her son) immediately asks, "When you leaving," ending the volume with this sad question: "'How long this time,' she asks, 'How long you staying?'" (Only to us the speaker says the unspoken to his mother— "I can't answer for the years/ away or how I've grown"—a silent liberation that is of course a burden, unless we can share—precisely the hope implicit in the lessons learned over the course of the work's many layered "travels" and travails.)

Of all the poems, "Bobo Baoulé," a four-part poem (too lengthy to cite in full here)—itself one of the actual four sections of the entire volume--best encapsulates this major accomplishment by Dixon. While each section of the poem is set in a different place and time, and while each section could be read alone, the impact of the poem depends entirely upon our reading the vanishing history and the present (looming ever larger into perverse "fact") as one disturbing suite that tells our horrible history of de-scription and con-scription precisely through the change in and loss of language. (I encourage all of us to read the volume as a whole and within it—this poem, in particular).

The first and longest section of the poem conflates the factual past and near present with both the real history of an actual woman (Queen Pokou) who established this Boulé tribe in the late 1700s with her successful rebellion against the Ashanti (and the fable that she sacrificed her son to appease a river god to escape and triumphantly cross the waters on the backs of hippopotami), the horrible enslavement of Africans on the Ivory Coast, the crossing over the Atlantic, and the supposed "safe" landing in the New World (and the loss of the ambiguous guiding Great Fish). All of this, interspersed with biblical echoes and with those of "Negro Spirituals" as the call to "come to the water" morphs through the stanzas from the seeming finding of home to the forced removal from home to the utter loss of home in this new "homeland." (We might note, with the rather obvious twist on the biblical miracle of being swallowed by a whale—and surviving—that Nina Simone gave the most well-known version of "Take Me to the Water" [a line Dixon echoes in this poem] with what, for Dixon, is horribly ironic: "Take me to the water to be baptized, because I'm coming back home now" [1970].)

The second section of the poem grotesquely, albeit briefly, recounts the horror of the "passage": our (surviving narrator), though himself enslaved, hears "some black man's cry" and he knows of the "body wrapped in chains." Worse: whereas in the first section this timeless narrator is soothed with the Great Fish's telling him, "Do not be afraid. You have given them a name,"—now he finds/we find that "They have changed their names."

And, so we see, that change in the third section—or description/ conscription as "Baoulé" (through string whips) is forced to change his name from his honorific ethnic tribe to "Bobo." "Bobo Bawlay"—or "good boy," as the white master calls him. As the narrator achingly notes (bearing his real name "on the edge of [his] breath"), "we have all lost our names"—from "Martinique, Cuba. Haitian sun./ New Orleans Market and Virginia Beach./ Little Rock. Selma. Birmingham. East St. Louis.

Chicago. Harlem, New York."(Shall we add to this territory—everywhere? Here? At Notre Dame, where the Potowatami were forcibly removed? Texas? Where I was born? The Tejas long gone? Ellis Island? Angel Island? Dixon's sense of territory—and our own—is crucial here. This is painful to re-member.)

But memory is lost. All roots are lost, as "recorded" in Section Four, where a young and educated and enthusiastic Bobby (a descendent of this family, with absolutely no knowledge of the past) writes to his mother from Africa, where he is a peace corps volunteer, in wonderfully "correct" prose (all linguistic love and lore lost): "Ever hear" of the "Baoulé people"? "Give my regards to the Bawlays. Especially Great-Uncle Bobo and Cousin Jim. That was a swell *bon voyage* party. . . . You'll like the Ivory Coast---- Bobby."

The strategic move from actual African facts and fables, enfolded with the echoes of African-American gospels in the first section, to what is almost severe alliteration and the "required" or "regularized" rhyming of the last four lines of the second section, to the total obliteration of the protagonist's name as he is "registered" in section three, to the curated, ridiculously exuberant (and ignorant) prose of the well-meaning and lost Bobby in the last section tells our whole national story, including how we define in history precisely our territory. As a sometime linguistics professor (in addition to teaching American literature) and, quite ironically, at times, even teaching "The History of the English Language," I find the linguistic (and aesthetic/poetic) changes in the four sections above genuinely re-markable in ways that, again, ironically defy words. The loss, as recorded here, on paper, is palpable. Which is why we need in our own troubled times to recover this poet and his words.

I can best end this introduction to Melvin Dixon by turning to another poet deeply immersed in the politics of her/our time—that is, Adrienne Rich. Included in her 1993 collections of essays, *What Is Found There: Notebooks on Poetry and Politics,* "'History Stops for No One," Rich makes an astute observation that could well summarize Dixon's remarkable endeavors and achievements. After speaking of the "musical language" that African-American poets in particular have created in and contributed to our country, Rich ends the first section of her essay with the following paragraph I cite in full:

Such writers—men and women of color, poets born to a language other than English, lesbian and gay poets, poets writing in the upsurge of the women's poetry movement of the past twenty years—have not started in cultural poverty even though their cultures have been ruptured and misprized. The relationship to more than one culture, nonasssimilating in spirit and therefore living amid contradictions, is a constant act of self-creation. I see the life of North American poetry at the end of the century as a pulsing, racing convergence of tributaries—regional, ethnic, racial, social, sexual—that, rising from lost or long-blocked springs, intersect and infuse each other while reaching back to the strengths of their origins. (A metaphor, perhaps, for a future society of which poetry, in its present suspect social condition, is the precursor.)

I cannot imagine a better tribute to Mel Dixon and his talent than these words. I suspect they will well apply to many other poets' works included in this volume.

BENJAMIN S. GROSSBERG

"NUMBERED NOW WITH THE REST OF THESE": ROBERT BOUCHERON (1952-) AND THE POETRY OF AIDS

Published in 1985, just three years after *The New York Times* noted of "GRID, for gay-related immunodeficiency," that "[t]he cause ... is unknown," Robert Boucheron's *Epitaphs for the Plague Dead* is among the earliest collections of poetry that deals with AIDS.[1]

The book consists of 56 first-person "epitaphs," in which speakers sum up their lives. The poems are not true dramatic monologues; there's little setting or action, and only the occasional gesture toward character voice. In his preface, Boucheron points to his predecessors: *The Greek Anthology*, and Edgar Lee Masters and A.E. Houseman, poets who, he says, gave contemporary life "a classical weight and tone." He tips his hat also toward Tennyson's *In Memoriam*, which he believes unconsciously inspired his form: tetrameter "envelope" stanzas (A/B/B/A) with their air-tight closure, the A rhymes "enveloping" the B. Boucheron's speakers are almost all gay men—thrown in are a few others, a hemophiliac, a baby—and each gets one poem, the longest ten quatrains. The speakers are types, Disco Bunny, Body Builder, Hick, Whiz Kid, and their milieu is easily recognizable to gay men of a certain age: the textures of the '70s and '80s, gay life before protease inhibitors, Obergefell, and rainbow flags hung up in (some) high school hallways. The epitaphs contain a few glimpses of victory, but largely the lives sketched here are hard, if not tragic—unsatisfied, riddled with homophobia (including internalized homophobia), and cut short. But the formal music drives us forward. The collection reads quick.

A 1988 investigation of the literature of AIDS, published in *New England Journal of Public Policy*, discovers about twenty titles, fiction, non-fiction, and poetry.[2] Of these, only two appeared in 1985 or earlier. One is Boucheron's. So, the book was out there, findable. But it never got much attention, and it seems to have been forgotten quickly. Monette,

Doty, Gunn: these are the poets generally associated with the height of the epidemic among gay men in America. Michael Klein's 1992 anthology *Poets for Life*. Reginal Shepherd just a hair later. But though earlier than all of these, Boucheron's work doesn't usually come to mind.

I found my copy of *Epitaphs* at a "tag sale" in a Houston driveway in 1993. I was in my first semester of graduate school. 1993: still bad years, but not the worst. There was an HIV test by then, but it was ungainly, and, in retrospect, had a built-in cruelty. You could take it and find out two weeks later that you were HIV negative three months before—a lag that seemed to mean you could never be sure you were uninfected. There was an HIV treatment by then, too, but that was another kind of cruelty. I recall my first serious boyfriend wrestling with the side effects—severe back pain, headaches—of AZT. But still, definitely not the worst years.

The copy of *Epitaphs* was in a box of old paperback novels. It was a slim, perfect-bound volume, parchment-yellow cardstock cover printed in black with a typesetter's flourish, a vaguely classical looking glyph like a detail from a Roman frieze. The copy was inscribed by Boucheron, "For Joe," and signed. Back then, a book of poetry was a pretty new thing to me, and I'd never seen one about AIDS. But the slimness of the volume and the word "plague" on the cover set my heart pounding. I snatched it up and started flipping through, understanding immediately what it was, even though I hadn't known such a book existed. The proprietor sitting on his front stoop shrugged when I asked how much it was. *You can have it.*

Turns out, I didn't like the poems. In retrospect, maybe there was no way I could have. *Epitaphs* is a modest-looking book, but also elegant in its spare design. At that point in my life, I would have given my teeth for a publication like that, and AIDS was what I was writing about. So perhaps any flaws I could find in the poems—that their music seemed repetitious, their formality rigid—seemed to justify my own ambitions. Petty, I know. That said, I read the collection repeatedly and was deeply affected, even haunted by its portraits. I used a poem from the collection in Ed Hirsh's 1994 spring workshop, when he asked us to write a poem in response to another, and to distribute both in class. My poem was critical of Boucheron's relentless music, and, to my considerable embarrassment, Ed suggested I was being a little uptight. He thought the Boucheron was "pretty good."

Of course, Ed was right. Thirty years later, I see that Boucheron handles the form deftly, often coming up with surprising rhymes and never straining the language. The meter is certainly more regular than contemporary poetics tends to employ (and value), but it's rendered well.

And I think I understand now why the book was so compelling and disturbing to me. It contains an implicit argument that I found deeply troubling—that I felt implicated by, even though I couldn't articulate it. *Epitaphs* gives speakers a handful of quatrains to sum up their lives. Some had ambitions they met; most didn't. Some were happy. But many of the poems end precipitously, even curtly, with the speaker describing how they got infected. The form itself has a classical remove, but in this context, it feels like an existential coldness. Life is reduced to a few turns, a left here, a right there, and then death by AIDS. And the music of that closure is brutal: the silence after an envelope stanza of exact rhyme, landed with exact meter. In Tennyson, the hard containment is so effective because it resists a grief that cannot be contained: 133 cantos, three years of mourning, poem after poem. But here, the closure has the opposite effect. It reinforces an awful finality.

When I think about why this book isn't one of the texts we associate with the pandemic, I consider the books that are, like Monette's *Love Alone: Elegies for Rog*, perhaps the first major collection of poetry related to AIDS. A devastating *cri de coeur* addressed to his lover, Monette's book is raw, eschewing punctuation, barely acknowledging the grammar of formal written English. The music and content echo the rage and pain of those years, and right beneath that rage and pain is intense love. The implicit message is how much Rog matters, how much fight there is to keep him close. The message underlying *Epitaphs* is far colder, if no less true. The poet here is distant, his human feeling largely absent from the surface of the text. Again, a classical kind of reserve—and it reveals a painful truth. HIV, dumb viral particle, has no feeling. Red in tooth and claw.

For me as a 23-year-old gay man, to read *Epitaphs* was to feel how easily my own life, the self I was hoping and trying to create, could be summed up, perhaps *would be* summed up, by the disease—how easily my life could be reduced to a few choices and then ended like these, subsumed and closed. *I went to Houston to study; I tried to be careful; in a passionate moment I lost track of my body; and I died.* You add closing rhyme, you move on to the next life.

The absolute, pitiless simplicity of the end of all we are. The simple plot lines that our lives can (not necessarily *should*) be reduced to. It's not a truth Romanticism has much use for, not a truth that's going to fortify and encourage a population facing an epidemic or that appeals to our American spirit of self-determination. But still for me, rereading now, the book lays bare some of the horror of those years, not just in individual poems, but in its collective power: how many lives passed away so quickly that there weren't enough loved ones around to honor them properly, that strangers with fabric glue and glitter had to make quilt-square memorials based on a sentence or two they read off an index card.

Why isn't *Epitaphs* read much now? There are significant aspects of the book that haven't held up. In some poems, Boucheron writes across race and class in ways that the scrutiny of our moment would find unacceptable. And in a couple of mentions of the book I found in literary histories, another criticism recurs: that the poems are moralizing.[3] I don't find that to be uniformly true, but a few poems do seem to go there. Perhaps another reason the book might not be prominent is that Boucheron didn't go on to publish much more poetry. He has a degree in English from Harvard where he studied with Bishop, and he put out a translation of Catullus in 1987.[4] He has continued to publish stories and essays, and he edits a small magazine, but he pursued a professional

261

career as an architect for almost forty years. So perhaps he hasn't been present in the poetry world in the way he might have needed to be for his work to remain part of the conversation—even part of the more focused conversation of American poetry about AIDS.

But for me, *Epitaphs for the Plague Dead* remains one of the seminal texts of the epidemic, reflecting back some of my id-fears from those years, some of what seemed to be at stake.

The poem below, "Epitaph for a Minor Poet," the one I distributed in Ed Hirsh's 1994 workshop, hits especially close to home. I hear a quiet irony in the speaker naming his award with such pride, when it seems so piddling—a name no one has heard of, "Fanny Cockburn Moody," each component of which seems to contain a hint of mockery, and the oh-so-grand prize of fifty dollars. A little pretention to be laughed at, but also, at least to me, touching, this desire to be somebody. And that makes the final stanza especially jarring. This is the only poem in the collection in which the speaker seems to be aware of the collective project of the book, and that awareness is expressed in the fear—which is not only the province of poets—of losing the name one has worked so hard to make, even in such a small context: "numbered now with the rest of these." Is there a pun on "numbered"? I think of Hamlet telling Ophelia that he is "ill at these numbers" (2.2.120), apologizing for the poem he has composed for her.[5] Boucheron's speaker has been "numbered," summed up in a poem, and not singled out for one—poetry, with which he'd hoped to distinguish himself, has rendered him more or less indistinguishable from all these other lost lives.

Robert Boucheron

Epitaph for a Minor Poet

The Fanny Cockburn Moody Prize
for Confidential Poetry,
worth fifty dollars, went to me
for my ambiguous disguise

of that affair with Reginald.
We were so young and steeped in Greek
mythology, and I was weak—
and then the bastard never called.

My posthumous revenge was decked
in rhyming octosyllables,
like pretty little pinkish pills
that sit awhile, then take effect.

My style was elegant and terse
and lilting as a summer swallow.
My imagery was hard to follow,
so they said, and a bit perverse.

My name appeared alongside those
of more established reputation.
Readers of some discrimination
might spot me sprinting through the rows

of Roman type in quarterlies,
matching pace with life to the letter.
I did well, but deserved much better,
numbered now with the rest of these.

Notes

[1]Altman, Lawrence K. "New Homosexual Disorder Worries Health Officials." *The New York Times*, 5/11/1982, Section C Page 1. Boucheron, Robert. *Epitaphs for the Plague Dead*, (New York: Ursus Press, 1985). The identity of Ursus Press is a bit mysterious. A representative of Ursus Books & Gallery in New York City informed me that they did not publish Boucheron's book. WorldCat suggests that an "Ursus Press" published less than half-dozen titles, including this one, between 1983 and 1997. None of the others are original poetry.

[2]O'Connell, Shaun. "The Big One: Literature Discovers AIDS." *New England Journal of Public Policy*, vol. 4, no. 1, 1988, Article 38.

[3]For example: Woods, Gregory. *A History of Gay Literature: The Male Tradition* (New Haven: Yale University Press, 1999). In the single paragraph devoted to Boucheron, Woods points to the poem title, "Epitaph for an Innocent," about a newborn contracting AIDS from its mother, as implicitly suggesting that the speakers in other poems are *not* innocent in how they contracted the disease (363).

[4]Catullus, Gaius Valeris, and Boucheron, Robert. *Catullus: A New Verse Translation*. (New York: publisher unknown, 1987).

[5]Shakespeare, William. *The Tragedy of Hamlet Prince of Denmark*. Edited by Edward Hubler. (New York: Signet Classics, 1963).

PATRICK PRITCHETT

"THE CRACKS *ARE* THE EDIFICE":
NORMAN FINKELSTEIN'S POETICS OF THE BROKEN TABLETS

"Because I am so much a creature of the Book," writes Norman Finkelstein, "I am able to learn that I am myself. Yet I am only myself insofar as I am part of the book, completing something infinitely greater than myself" (*Radical Poetics* 226). This dialectical process of self and Book marks Finkelstein as a consummate poet of textual spirituality, one for whom completion occurs within the greater context of transmission, transgression, and tradition.

Born in 1954, he is the author, at last count, of 13 books of poetry and 6 volumes of critical studies nor does he show any signs of slowing down after his recent retirement from Xavier University (Ohio), where he taught for forty years. With an entire critical study dedicated to his work, Finkelstein is not so much neglected as scandalously underread. I place him among a small group of poets working on the margins of the neo avant-garde, poets who join a commitment to an innovative spiritual poetics deeply informed by radical postmodern theology. For the most part, poetry scholars, myopically secular, suffer from a marked allergy to a poetics of prophecy and gnosis. With a few exceptions like Robert Duncan, Fanny Howe, John Taggart, and Hank Lazer, such poetry is often met with either an embarrassed silence or a lack of reading competence. Indeed, Lazer observes, "spirit" has become commodified into a "formulaic poetry of Emersonian correspondences ... a repetitive poetry of dumb wonder" (212).

Finkelstein does not traffic in the poetry of sanctimonious affirmation, nor does he abandon lyric investigation in favor of self-serving sermons in sociology. He attends instead to themes of spiritual desolation and renewal, of catastrophe and utopia, of history's ruins and the potential for their redemption. He writes in the gap between the first, broken set of tablets and the second one Moses finally brought down from Sinai.

In her brilliant study of Emmanuel Levinas and Jacques Derrida religious scholar Sarah Hammerschlag maintains that rather than disaster, the broken tablets confer a liberation from tradition, a new beginning out of original calamity. The belatedness of the second set of Tablets must be read as an opportunity to rewrite the past, to form a new consonance between loss and promise. In the wake of poststructuralism, she asserts, "a return to some pure beginning is not possible ... the purifying impulse itself is suspect. There is no pristine past nor can we divest ourselves of all of the sediment that stands between us and ur sources" (xvii). The broken tablets form the inaugural occasion of the messianic, the repair of the world. The 16th Century Kabbalistic Rabbi Isaac Luria's allegory of the Breaking of the Vessels amplifies this tale of primordial catastrophe. In it, God withdrew from creation then created ten vessels to hold his light. The vessels, unable to hold God's light, shattered. Thus, the beginning is a traumatic event. But if the promise of the first covenant is shattered the second set of tablets activates the promise of *tikkun*.

Indeed, as Finkelstein writes in his magnificent poem "A Tomb for Gerhsom Scholem," "the cracks *are* the edifice." They open new possibilities for inhabiting catastrophe. Those constitutive cracks morph into ghosts and the ghosts in turn become "sparks returning, completing a movement / which you thought could never come to rest ... there are folds within folds, / and each fold is a throne, / each throne is a world / each world is a word" (*Ratio of Reason* 59-60). The circularity of this movement incorporates the fallen sparks from the Broken Vessels, which in turns engenders the work of *tikkun*. *Tikkun*, then, consists not so much in patching the cracks (a futile task) but in learning how to live and write from inside them. Scholem himself asserts that Jewish messianism is concerned with "the catastrophic and destructive nature of the redemption on the one hand and the utopianism of the content of realized Messianism on the other. Jewish Messianism is in its origins and by its nature ... a

266

theory of catastrophe" (7).

Finkelstein positions his work in this very breach, situating his poetics in a tradition of rabbinical transmission and the Jewish prophetic mode that is also taken up by poets like Allen Grossman, Armand Schwerner, and Michael Heller. It is richly informed, playfully subversive, lyrically inventive work of the first water.

Drawing on the resources of Judaic mysticism, as well as the oblique, dissonant modalities of the Objectivists, Finkelstein creates a poetry that re-gathers "in its utterance … an act of resistance to silence, even though it is bound, finally, to yield. It is at the moment the poem falls silent, enacting its closure, that a window opens upon a Messianic world" (*Lyrical Interference* 12). His poetry exploits the negative properties of signification as a way to avoid reification and so produce a deeper kind of affirmation, one that can never achieve finality. As he writes in *Track*, the poem can only thrive "so long as the letters arrive to be destroyed" (7). This imperative follows the mandate issued by the breaking of the tablets of the first Decalogue. Derrida comments on this in his essay on Edmond Jabès. The second set of tablets God gave to Moses is not intended to repair the fragments of the first; rather, it preserves and incorporates their break. For Derrida, this break inaugurates speech. "God," he writes, "separated himself from himself in order to let us speak, in order to astonish and interrogate us. He did so not by speaking but by keeping still, by letting silence interrupt his voice, by letting the Tablets be broken" (WD 67).

Finkelstein's classic 1999 serial poem *Track* brings to mind Paul Celan's notion of the poem as always enroute, or on the way. The poem is less a vehicle of revelation than a circuit of iterations. Meaning is disclosed by dispersal and repetition. Beyond that, to track proposes a way forward for poetry after Auschwitz, after disaster—a way to locate a remnant of logos amid the ruins. For the poems in *Track* emanate a ghostliness, a tenuous tryst with presence or the potential of presence to re-emerge.

The ruins were holy
wholly ruins

The fathers came and went
fathers found there

We had come this far
entering the present

Only holy ruins
wholly in the present (*Track* 58)

The movement of holiness into wholeness completes a circuit in which ruin is reclaimed for the fathers, for tradition, so as to empower the ongoing present. The ruins, which are both wholly and holy ruins, inhabit a dual or spliced reality, like the broken tablets. In Finkelstein's hands, the poem becomes an instrument for constellating the shards into a new continuity. The title poem of his 2021 collection *In a Broken Star* conjures a powerful vision of a continuity that arises from fragments:

In a broken star
the words fall into the words

But the machine says
blow across my screen

And the letters rise up
and become a page

A page upon a page
crossing the centuries

The machine says look
and you will understand (1)

The confluence of page and screen, of old and new technologies of inscription and transmission, makes a link across time, creating a consonance, a continuity within interruption ("continuity / as interruption") (*Track* 10). Finkelstein recognizes that poetry, to stay alive, to remain charged with vatic, gnostic potentiality, must continually undo itself. Each poem is indeed a "restless messenger," as one of his early titles has it. This process constitutes the poet's own "utopian moment"—but it is a moment only, before lapsing back into silence.

In his *Daybooks*, George Oppen cryptically wrote: "Because I am not silent, the poems are bad ... because there is something we cannot say, cannot grasp, the poem is an attempt to work it out, to find its form." Finkelstein nods to this when he remarks: "the poem that is almost mute, that rises out of silence, suddenly sings, and as suddenly ceases, reminds us most strongly of our struggle for linguistic plenitude, a struggle that began ... with the Fall" (*Lyrical Interference* 11).For Finkelstein, the incommensurate gap between a desire for a form capable of expressing the fullness of a redeeming logos and the loss of catastrophe is what drives the poem in its search for achieving a silence that is Louis Zukofsky's "rested totality."

So perhaps for "bad" one might read "broken." In this sense every poem is always a failure. Every poem is already broken. Yet that brokenness, the cracks in the edifice, open what Walter Benjamin called the strait gate through which the Messiah might, at any moment, enter. Norman Finkelstein's poems, restless with migration, hover at the edge of such a possibility, resisting the emptiness of homogenous time and the commodification of the poem. Presence is what is always arriving and departing. As Stephané Moses puts it:

The end of belief in a meaning of history did not involve abolishing the idea of hope. On the contrary, it's precisely on the rubble of the paradigm of historical Reason that hope is formed as a historical category. Utopia, which can no longer be thought as a belief in the necessary advent of the ideal at the mythical end of history, reemerges—through the category of Redemption — as the modality of its *possible* advent at each moment of time. (12).

The coming of the Messiah might be announced by the simple measures of a ballad. This is from "The Songs of Pascal Wanderlust":

I wander about
among the nurseries of stars

I wander the fields
where the planets are born

Earth is a cinder
a speck of ash
I and my Other
can no longer dream

We were bound to this world
but are now released

I and my Other
a dream of fire

The Last Dream of Fire
here among the stars (*Broken Star* 71).

Sources

Derrida, Jacques. *Writing and Difference*. Trans. Alan Bass. Chicago: University of Chicago Press, 1978.

Finkelstein, Norman. *In a Broken Star*. Loveland, OH: Dos Madres Press, 2021.

_____. *Lyrical Interference: Essays on Poetics*. New York: Spuyten Duyvil, 2003.

_____. "Secular Jewish Culture and Its Radical Poetic Discontents." *Radical Poetics and Secular Jewish Culture*. Ed. Stephen Paul Miller & Daniel Morris. Tuscaloosa: Alabama University Press, 2010.

_____. *The Ratio of Reason to Magic: New and Selected Poems*. Loveland, OH: Dos Madres Press, 2016.

_____. *Track*. New York: Spuyten Duyvil, 1999.

Hammerschlag, Sarah. *Broken Tablets: Levinas, Derrida, and The Literary Afterlife of Religion*. New York: Columbia University Press, 2016.

Lazer, Hank. *Lyric & Spirit: Selected Essays 1996-2008*. Richmond, CA: Omnidawn Pub., 2008.

Moses, Stephané. *The Angel of History: Rosenzweig, Benjamin, Scholem*. Trans. Barbara Harshaw. Stanford: Stanford University Press, 2009.

Oppen, George. "Selections from *Daybooks*." Ed. Dennis Young. *Iowa Review* 18.3 (1988): 1-17.

Scholem, Gershom. *The Messianic Idea in Judaism and other Essays on Jewish Spirituality*. New York: Schocken Books, 1971.

BARON WORMSER

JOE BOLTON (1961-1990)

When a poet dies young—Joe Bolton died at age twenty-eight, a suicide—we may be tempted to construct the story of the poet around that death. In the case of Joe Bolton that would not be unfair since he was a death-haunted poet. I want to write, "even as a young man," but he died as a young man and age had nothing to do with his being haunted. That was his condition; his feeling for life was mingled with his feeling for death. A so-called regular person might chastise him for such an outlook, but such chastising would be pointless. The poet's appreciation of life was put into his poems. His art was his life and his art was considerable.

Bolton lived his life in what might be called "Poetry Time," a time zone unknown to most people, though sometimes intimated. As a space, it is distinguished by the poet's feel for transience, for change, for impermanence, for moods, for loss. One deliquescent, blue chasm. The round of consuming that takes up our lives, our moving from one purpose to another, our abashed and unabashed credulity, held little charm for him. Thus, the comfort that goes with consuming, that rapt oblivion, was denied to him. I doubt if he minded. He was thrilled, as poets are thrilled, by how feeling is actualized in the physical world: dusk, quiet mornings, palm trees, flamingos, motel rooms, they all spoke to him and through him. So did love-making, especially the feelings afterwards, that sated aimlessness. The enormous tenderness in his poetry stems from his wonder at the gifts of the physical world. He resembles in that regard another poet who died young—John Keats.

His body, however, as it partook of transience was a very equivocal gift, one that literally weighed on him. Indeed, Bolton wrote five weightlifter poems that go through what were for him stages of his particular cross: the body's actuality, "musculature as a way of life"; America, "a glossy page"; dreams about women, "Though I never saw her face / she speaks to me";

272

some sort of rescue, "I want them / To throw the rope to me"; and death, "And I will be the man / No one remembers." If this feels unbearable, it's meant to be. Bolton had the courage of his sadness.

Bolton's biography is unremarkable. He grew up in western Kentucky, a place where many of his poems were set. He went to three graduate writing programs—Houston, Florida, and Arizona—where he wrote the poems that comprise *The Last Nostalgia, Poems 1982—1990*, edited posthumously by Donald Justice who was one of Bolton's teachers. He seems representative of what has become a way of life, using the university as a haven during one's twenties to learn and practice the art of writing. In Bolton's case, however, he wasn't warming up for the second and subsequent acts. The poems happened fully in his twenties and then he was gone.

He wrote during what might be called the Age of Reagan. Bolton had no politics in his poems to speak of but the ambiance savors of the Reagan era—the cities blessed by ever more money, the jets littering the sky, "the topmost towerings / of skyscrapers downtown." Bustling, somnolent, self-satisfied America where Bolton could feel time ebbing more than it was flowing, where despite the endless come-ons, the deep drag of mortality could not be stayed, as Bolton wonders in a third-person mode: "how much / Longer it will be before his body / Fails, or his wife's body." Bodies don't go away until they go away. Meanwhile, the poet, stalked by his memories and forebodings, wandered among the streets of what he termed "The New Cities of the Tropics."

At his best, and in Justice's selection, he often is at his best, Bolton is able to approach suffering without blinking. A prime example is the devastating "Watching Bergman Films with My Father." The poem is in second-person, addressed to his father for whom the movies are "nothing new to you, really," given "your deep understanding of despair." The various ghastly scenarios—insanity, suicide, "the smoke and filth / Choking the lungs of a woman"—are what they are. We need not push them away nor need we insist upon them. The hard import they have is too real to be dismissed or assuaged with conversation, hence "We don't talk / About it or talk about anything." The blunt, conclusive truth cannot be gainsaid: "because we need the world, if it / Doesn't need us."

A poet is someone who asks the perennial question "What is that?" In Bolton's case, his bewilderment and his predisposition to darkness both weigh in, which accounts, in part, for his honesty. As I have noted, he is full of appreciation for the physical world, which you would expect a poet to be—light, for instance, ravishes him. The flux of the physical world, however, plays him false and something in him cannot forgive that falseness. Within the poet lurks a moral child who is outraged at time's usages, to say nothing of the unfeeling habits of socialized life. All the work that goes into pushing away suffering, all the efforts to turn every situation into something somehow therapeutic were lost on Bolton who more or less declared himself to be a warrior of despair, choosing, as he eventually did, a good day to die. Marvelously alert to the world's shifts, he recognized them for contrivances that help us get along, the palaver we pass back and forth.

His stance, thus, was heartbreaking and stubborn. Though connected to academia, he was not one to be seduced by careerist blandishments and attainments. He was literary in the sense that he practiced a literary art and sent his poems to journals where they might be published but he was a poet in the deep, perpetual sense of resolutely following his metaphysical feelings. He was—to use American argot—on his own trip; nothing was going to deter him. Again, that speaks to a bleakness that some may be inclined to write off as headstrong youthfulness—relishing life's physicality while remaining determinedly death-bound. Yet who can refute him? We are death-bound, whether we hasten it or not.

When, however, he lets life be—and he does sometimes—a sort of shine, a resignation emanates from the poems that is very special, a feeling that the world is speaking through him as much as it is speaking to him. This can happen in literary contexts, as in his poem about Daisy Miller that begins with two lines from James and ends with the recognition that "still there was something American in the gyre / Of the moon, though the moon was far from home." The pathos of her situation, her being there in Rome, so very "far from home," and her American identity all resonate. Bolton is her accomplice, privy to life's grim logic, how "the body" is undone "by desire," and yet the body is known by "its beauty." In that regard, the poet will not cede an inch, for such recognition—and again the echo of Keats is palpable—represents a crucial part of being a poet.

In "The Lights at Newport Beach" the shine is literal. Here is the entire poem:

> If there were time for everything
> (And there is): if that phosphorescent light
> Stunning the Pacific meant anything
> (And it does): if all this world of worlds might
> Become more than the museum for something
> We have lost (and it will) . . . but not tonight.
> Tonight, love, Newport Beach is simply on fire,
> The buildings blazing up under the sky,
> The streets running headlong into the sea.
> If we were more than the sum of our desire
> (But we're not): if there were a language I
> Could find to get beyond the opacity
> Of zero . . . But I'm tired of words and all we turn
> Away from. I just want to watch it burn.

Bolton was what one might call an instinctive formalist. He did not believe that some sort of self-conscious virtue went with writing a sonnet. Clearly, he liked the pressure, the bearing down, the sonic pleasures, the opportunities to advance an argument, the devotion to syllables, and the limitations that a form imposed—this much and not more. He was, in a sense, tightly wound. So is the sonnet. Expatiation for its own sake held no attraction. Poetry was all about inwardness—and yet there is the town and the ocean and the sky and the light. That conflict (perhaps too strong a word) impelled him to write poems. Poetry, after all, stems from irreconcilable dilemmas. We write a poem and reach a conclusion and then write another poem. No final poem beckons.

The scintilla of possibility with which Bolton begins the poem, that "if," must have been precious to him. He could be the master of that gambit even when he distrusted it. The reader who knows Bolton knows that after the string of positive parentheses, a negative must occur. And it does: "if we were more than the sum of our desire / (But we're not)." A great deal of weariness in that remark, a great deal of conclusiveness, perhaps more than he was aware of, though a poem is only a series of verbal gestures, as Bolton well knew. In any case, he turns away from words and toward the world. Like a child, he is enthralled by the spectacle. What else is life on earth but our witnessing one spectacle after another? How much meaning we posit for those spectacles is our business. The world is glad to give us ready-made answers, few of which Bolton accepted. He needed to take up the challenge of locating meaning on his own. It was a strenuous endeavor.

In conclusion, I find myself coming again to the amount of sheer beauty in Bolton's work. Not gorgeous but so finely and carefully put together. Only love can do that. In a strange way, Bolton seems like an ancient poet: he knew what doom was. The beauty of poetry was held in a balance of sorts with that doom. When he was writing his poems, he was able to make something out of his torments and his delights. In an age in which so much poetry isn't much more than self-declaration, Bolton reminds us how much resides in the challenges that poetry presents us with, both as writers and as readers and auditors. For a time, he was up to the challenge.

JOE BOLTON

CHILDHOOD

My father holds the twenty-five to his head
  Like a seashell,
Like a transistor radio tuned to a channel
  Nobody else can hear.
He comes bounding down the stairs, almost like a boy
  On Christmas morning
Were it not for the fact that he's weeping
  And saying over and over:

"Do you want me to blow my fucking head off?
  Is that what you want?"
My mother doesn't say yes but doesn't say no.
  She's shaking,
Making a sound not with her mouth but with
  Her whole body,
A chanted, high-pitched wail that contains
  The chaos of the universe,

The rage that *is*, before language was.
  She clenches a clump
Of her hair in each fist, her hair
  Not the color
Of the sun going down so early in the day,
  But the color
Of a child's first clumsy rendering of that sky
  In fingerpaint—

The frail page he brought home, clutched to his chest
  Under a heavy coat,
And which he stood on the cold porch to admire a moment
  Before it ceased to matter.

JOHANNA DRUCKER

WILLIAM GREENWOOD:
INTELLECTUAL PRECISION

Who was the poet William Greenwood, author of *Into the Center of America* (Santa Cruz: Green Horse Press, 1976)? I can find no trace of him after fifty years, though perhaps he will surface as a result of this critical notice. When I met him in my role as typesetter at the West Coast Print Center in the mid-1970s, I think he was pursuing a professional degree—law? education? public policy?—I can't remember. But he appeared, manuscript in hand, wanting to be actively involved in the design of his forthcoming book, a collection of serious poems, framed by intellectual concepts that were somewhat beyond me at the time. I was young, and my literary concerns were shaped as much by conceptual art and language as by the reflections on history and philosophy that informed his practice.

Greenwood's presence was much like his work—careful, meticulous, deliberate, and self-possessed. He lived in a single room where he served me dinner once at the end of our collaboration and did it with a reserve that kept any awkwardness at bay in the close quarters. The event made and left a deep impression. The formality he maintained in our relation had an old-world feel. His actions seemed governed by manners from another time and culture, though he revealed nothing of his family origins or background.

The poems impress me more now than at the time, insensitive as I was to their precision and profundity. Their historicity is vivid. Their language and references have a striking intellectual precision to them. His observations are immediate, direct, and absolutely of their moment, but deeply poetic in expression. This is not journalism, but art attempting to apprehend events in an act of transformative distillation. The first line of the first prose poem, "Tarjeta Postal" begins: "Waking up without you makes me go back to sleep unable to." The next, dated February 1975 in Mexico City, notes that it was written in "the week of the Third International Tribunal Against the Crime of the Military Junta in Chile." We remember. At the time, these events were ongoing. Colonial architecture, military crimes, border issues and delays, the ongoing news and distant events against which vivid details of immediate observation register—these are the elements Greenwood documents. "April 1975, Guatemala City the spring of the Saigon government's collapse."

Tracking his personal story of migration, the poet moves through landscapes, circumstances, modes of transportation, always alert to the nuance of the moment, as in "Centrifugal Force": "The driver's full / -blast radio attacks in the approaching sun, / retreats me through my broken view / to the populations." Or in "A.M. Reconnaissance": "The cause of the head on the sidewalk / is being determined." No maudlin sentiment and no exaggerated sensationalism, and yet, these are not mere statements of facts.

The language of politics and current events shapes these poems. In "Penetración Cultural" we get "the progressive noise of underdevelopment," "reassured by the nonexistent army patrol," or "the same nonnegotiable demands," to describe specific human circumstances. But imagistic language also appears: "the same fat man with the overstuffed money" or a glimpse of "flimsy arms and begging legs." Each phrase is located within the system of its currency, recognizing that words circulate and gain their value in a system of fluid exchange.

Three distinct quotes appear in the book, one from Benjamin Whorf, one from Thomas Paine, and another from a source I cannot identify by its tag, "Back of the Yards." They locate the poems within Greenwood's familiarity with linguistic-anthropological, political, and scientific modes of discourse. The citation from the last of these consists of two sentences. Referencing quantum physics and the subordination of cause and effect to probability, it goes on: "If probability is at the heart of modern physics, then it is also at the heart of social mechanics." I would love to know the longer source from which this is taken. In 1976 this would not have been comprehensible to me the way it is now, when my own work in social physics (e.g. *General Theory of Social Relativity*) is filled with these observations. Elsewhere, fragments of cited text are woven through the poems, keeping present the themes of politics, the rhetoric of the American struggle for Independence, nuclear science, the work of Oppenheimer, the splitting of the atom, and other topics.

But the personal narrative provides the organizing frame for the poems. They began in Latin America as Greenwood came north from El Salvador, Guatemala, Mexico, crossing the border where he was treated without respect. This was *his* story. He was an immigrant. His relation to America had been from its ideological mythology. He had come into its center. Though I imagine he was within a few years of my age, he was private and mature in ways that felt unusual in our California circles. I sometimes wondered if his name had been adopted as part of his journey to America.

Like some active isotope inserted in my memory stream, over time the poems and the impression made by their author have released their time-lapse influence. The book itself is exquisite owing to Greenwood's meticulous attention to detail. The cover was produced letterpress by Wesley Tanner at his shop in Berkeley. A map of the new world from Ortelius's 1574 *Great Atlas* was printed in dark brown ink and above it, the title, carefully spaced, was in deep earthy red. The rich brown paper used for the cover was stiff enough to make deep flap folds. The narrow spine was squared and the title and author's name in a small font size are perfectly positioned in the narrow band. The back cover has a solid coat of that same earth-red titling ink and a quote by Charles Olson, "Like it or not, see it or not, history *is* the *function* of any one of us." I recall Greenwood's intense involvement with the design, his attention to these many elements. Nothing escaped his attention. Fifty years later, the book is still perfect, every feature of its design inscribes the imprint of the poet's aesthetic sensibility.

The combination of personal and cultural history, the language of politics as physics, of the social as a system, of immediate perceptions as mediated and indexical–these are all elements of an articulate and highly attentive sensibility. Greenwood was a man of perception and integrity, his work a model of language culled from and attentive to his historical circumstances. Now, perhaps improbably, the work feels like a crucial reference point for projects of my own like *Deterring Discourse* (1993), *From Now* (2007), *The Fall* (2018), and *Stochastic Poetics* (2012). With their direct engagement with the unfolding experience of historical events, the discourses of politics and news, they now seem to have drawn some influence from William Greenwood's *Into the Center of America*, which I was fortunate to typeset almost fifty years ago.

I can only speculate on why this writer, so precise in his work and so committed to his poetic practice might have disappeared from the literary scene. He may have felt this volume was sufficient, a rite of passage and record of transition into a life that had other priorities and purpose. He may still be writing, occupied with professional and personal concerns that became more pressing. He might have become disillusioned with the intrigues and networking required to establish a profile in a community of writers whose experiences and sensibilities were far from his own, in spite of the deeply intellectual dimensions of his work. Hard to say as no trace of later publication appears when I search. Obscurity comes in many forms, and each has its trajectory and specific ways of erasing a presence. Greenwood was neither self-effacing nor self-promoting but seemed possessed of a personal equilibrium that derived from self-awareness forged through the exigencies of his path towards the goals he was pursuing. At some times in our lives, writing feels so important as a way of making experience into form, creating a trace, a record, document of transformative events. Or, perhaps, this work was a way of embracing the performative dimensions of composition, the act of making precise what might otherwise have remained inchoate. These fundamental purposes of writing—to bring a text into being as a negotiation of self with the world—are demonstrated by the integrity of the act embodied in the work of William Greenwood.

TIME ZONE

WILLIAM GREENWOOD

left at the border empty at dusk, a loose end
no one official in the least
has to answer.

Patience marches in
between my lips like an armed force
settling across my tongue, infiltrating
my infiltrated teeth. No choice
but to have nothing but time.
2nd class time of a foreigner
who speaks the language well so what.

Gratefully lodged in the predawn bus,
upright in the dark
territory of sleep,
losing the battle . . .
As if the snake that comes to suck the roadside shack's
hysterical baby's milk just left,
ribs jump out and bark

CONTRIBUTORS

DENNIS BARONE is the author of *Far-Dale: New and Selected Poems*. He is the poetry editor for the *Wallace Stevens Journal*.

CHARLES BERNSTEIN received the Bollingen Prize for Poetry in 2019. His books of poetry include *All the Whiskey in Heaven: Selected Poems* and among his collection of essays, *Attack of the Difficult Poems*.

CIARAN BERRY is a Professor of English at Trinity College where he directs the program in Creative Writing. He is the author of *States* and other books of poetry.

JULIA BLUMENREICH—a poet and a teacher—retired from the Germantown Academy in 2022. She has received a Milken National Educator Award and a Fellowship from the Pennsylvania Council on the Arts. She is the author of *Artificial Memory, Meeting Tessie, Blue Angel of a Day,* and *The What of Underfoot.*

An expert on Wallace Stevens and Professor Emerita at the University of Notre Dame, JACQUELINE VAUGHT BROGAN is the author of the long poem *Ta(l) king Eyes* and other works.

LAYNIE BROWNE—poet, prose writer, and editor—teaches at the University of Pennsylvania. Among her recent works is the poetry collection *Translation of the Lilies Back into Lists.*

PETER BUSHYEAGER's poetry collections include *Citadel Luncheonette* and *In the Green Oval.* He edited *Wake Me When It's Over: Selected Poems of Bill Kushner.*

DAVID CAPPELLA is a Professor Emeritus in English at Central Connecticut State University. His sonnet sequence loosely based on the life of Giacomo Leopardi, *Gobbo: A Solitaire's Opera*, was published during 2022 in both an English and an English / Italian version. His chapbook *Farther//Father//Further* was published in May by Bottlecap Press.

ABIGAIL CHILD—a filmmaker and poet—received the Rome Prize in 2009-2010. Her work is known for its use of archival materials, including the series: *Is This What You Were Born For?* as well as the reconstructed home movie, *The Future Is Behind You*. She taught at the Museum of Fine Arts, Boston, heading its Fim/Media Department (1999-2016).

MARTHA COLLINS's eleventh book of poetry is *Casualty Reports*. Her tenth, *Because What Else Could I Do*, won the Poetry Society of America's William Carlos Williams Award. She has also published five volumes of co-translated Vietnamese poetry.

JOHANNA DRUCKER is a poet, book artist, visual theorist, and cultural critic. She teaches in the Department of Information Studies at UCLA. Among her many publications is *Inventing the Alphabet: The Origins of Letters from Antiquity to the Present*.

A library assistant at the University of San Francisco, PATRICK JAMES DUNAGAN has written and edited several books. His latest include *City Bird and other poems* (City Lights) and *Reading Writing Reading: essays reviews & notes* (Lithic, forthcoming).

Poet and scholar JULIE R. ENSZER is the author of five poetry collections, most recently *The Pinko Commie Dyke*, and the editor of five works including *Fire-Rimmed Eden: Selected Poems by Lynn Lonidier* (Sinister Wisdom 2023).

JAMES FINNEGAN is well-known in the Connecticut River Valley region for hosting several long-running reading series. His poems have appeared in *Ploughshares*, *The Southern Review*, and other journals.

SUZANNE FRISCHKORN is a poet and essayist. *Whipsaw* is her newest volume of poetry.

An author of many books of poetry and prose, MICHAEL GESSNER taught at Central Arizona College and the University of Arizona. *Nightshades* is among his recent publications.

Professor Emeritus at Temple University, ELI GOLDBLATT is a poet, essayist, and activist-scholar for community-based literacy. Among his publications are *Alone With Each Other: Literacy and Literature Intertwined* and the poetry volume *For Instance*.

BENJAMIN S. GROSSBERG is the author of *My Husband Would: Poems* and *The Spring before Obergefell: A Novel*. He is a Professor of English at the University of Hartford where he directs the program in Creative Writing.

Poet, essayist, and playwright, CARLA HARRYMAN teaches at Eastern Michigan University. *Cloud Cantata*, a blend of poetry and essay, is one of her many works.

ERIC HOFFMAN is the author of *Oppen: A Narrative*, a biography of George Oppen as well as several volumes of his own poetry including *The Transparent Eye*.

BURT KIMMELMAN is a distinguished professor of humanities at New Jersey Institute of Technology. Among his publications are *Visible at Dusk: Selected Essays* and *Steeple at Sunrise: New Poems*.

The author of *Soho: The Rise and Fall of an Artist's Colony* and many other books, RICHARD KOSTELANETZ has had a long and productive career in many forms of art and expression.

JOSEPH LEASE is a professor at California College of the Arts. His most recent book of poetry is *Fire Season*.

JOEL LEWIS has edited books of writings by Walter Lowenfels and Ted Berrigan. His most recent poetry book is *Well You Needn't* (Hanging Loose).

Editor of *Word of Mouth: An Anthology of Gay American Poetry*, TIMOTHY LIU is the author of many poetry books including *Down Low and Lowdown: Timothy Liu's Bedside Bottom-Feeder Blues*.

GIAN LOMBARDO recently retired from Emerson College where he was Senior Publisher-in-Residence. He directs Quale Press and has a special interest in prose poetry.

SHEILA E. MURPHY is a text and visual poet. Her most recent book is *Escritoire*, and recent books include *Golden Milk* and *Permission to Relax*.

Emeritus Professor in English at Penn State University, ALDON LYNN NIELSEN has published thirteen books of poetry, including the new *Hard Gospel*. He has also published six scholarly books, including *The Inside Songs of Amiri Baraka*. His book *Reading Race* was recently banned from the library of the U.S. Naval Academy . . . and then unbanned.

PATRICK PRITCHETT is the author of six books of poetry, including *Sunderland*. He currently lectures in Comparative Literature at Rutgers University.

JED RASULA, author of *What the Thunder Said: How the* Waste Land *Made Modern Poetry* and *This Compost: Ecological Imperatives in American Poetry*, recently retired from the English Department at the University of Georgia.

Professor Emerita in English at Occidental College, MARTHA RONK is a fiction writer and poet. She is the author of 13 books of poetry, most recently *Clay bodies + matter* (Omnidawn).

Art critic and poet BARRY SCHWABSKY recently published *Sleep*, the English language poetry by Amelia Rosselli. Among his many publications are *The Perpetual Guest: Art in the Unfinished Present* and the poetry volume *Water from Another Source*.

Poet and translator MARK STATMAN is Emeritus Professor of Literary Studies, Lang College, The New School. He has published 14 books; his most recent poetry collection is *Volverse/Volver* (Lavender Ink/diálogos, 2025).

LISA STEINMAN, Professor Emerita at Reed College, has written *Invitation to Poetry: The Pleasures of Studying Poetry and Poetics* as well as *Absence & Presence: Poems*.

T THILLEMAN is editor of Spuyten Duyvil books and during the 1990s co-edited *Poetry New York*. He is the author of many collections including a trilogy of poems notes and drawings, *Three Markations to Ward Her Figure* (Mad Hat).

ROSANNA WARREN is the Hanna Holborn Gray Distinguished Service Professor Emerita in the Committee on Social Thought at the University of Chicago. Her books of poetry include *Hindsight* and *So Forth*, and she is also the author of *Max Jacob: A Life in Art and Letters*.

BARON WORMSER has written autobiography, fiction, and poetry. *The History Hotel* is his newest volume of poems. He has been a librarian and a teacher.